ENCYCLOPAEDIA OF
CYBER LAWS AND CRIME

ENCYCLOPAEDIA OF CYBER LAWS AND CRIME

Vol. 2

Dimensions of Cyber Crime

Edited by

S.R. Sharma

ANMOL PUBLICATIONS PVT. LTD.

NEW DELHI - 110 002 (INDIA)

ANMOL PUBLICATIONS PVT. LTD.
4374/4B, Ansari Road, Daryaganj
New Delhi - 110 002
Ph.: 23261597, 23278000
Visit us at: www.anmolpublications.com

Encyclopaedia of Cyber Laws and Crime

First Edition, 2003

ISBN 81-261-1432-0 (Set)

PRINTED IN INDIA

Published by J.L. Kumar for Anmol Publications Pvt. Ltd., New Delhi - 110 002 and Printed at Mehra Offset Press, Delhi.

CONTENTS

PREFACE

In the last years of the twentieth century a phenomenon has been witnessed which is likely to change the shape of human civilization. This is the explosion which has taken place in electronics and as a result of which there has been infinite expansion of knowledge that is commonly described as information explosion. The most astounding development in this area has been the geometric expansion of trade commerce entertainment and information jointly known as the internet or the web. The web accepts no restrictions of the country, race religion or country and has been totally responsible as a decisive factor in taking the world into what is now known as globalisation.

It is generally believed that a website is created every minute and along with its positive aspect it also brings about a new sense of responsibility. The free trade and commerce available through website in what is known as cyber space has also given birth to a mobile population where intent may be basically criminal. Thus we have hachers, virus carriers, sleepers and moles, who may constitute a real threat to the creativity of the web. There is, therefore, the eternal question of intellectual copyright and the policing of vast cyber space to protect and maintain what manhood can truly achieve.

Consequently the TRAI Act 1997 has been enacted by the Indian parliament in the 48th year of Republic of India on 28th March 1997 to provide for the establishment of the Telecom Regulatory Authority of India (TRAI) to regulate the telecommunication services and for matters connected therewith are incidental thereto.

As per Section 11 (2) of the TRAI Act TRAI is empowered to fix/revise tariff for various telecom services provided in India and service providers including the Department service provisions have to implement the tariffs, notified by the TRAI as per provisions of law.

The TRAI has been mandated to fix/revise tariff for various telecom services by virtue of section 11 (2) of TRAI Act.

The Encyclopaedia tries to cover as many laws as possible, promulgated by various countries and unions of countries like the European Union in this area to give a comprehensive and comparative view of CYBER Law.

The editor has no claims to originality and has simply compiled and edited the material collected from various sources. In view of the English language being the medium most of the material has been collected from American, British and Indian sources.

The editor is grateful to the Librarians of the library of the Supreme Court, the Indian Law Institute and the Ministry of Law, Justice and Company Affairs, for their kind assistance in locating the material from various sources.

The editor is specifically grateful to Shri Jawahar Lal Kumar, Managing Director, Anmol Publications Pvt. Ltd., New Delhi for venturing to publish the Encyclopaedia on Cyber Laws.

—Dr. S.R. Sharma

1 FINDING NETWORK OPERATING SYSTEM AND OPERATING SYSTEM WEAKNESSES

Objectives

At the end of this chapter you will be able to:

- Specify ways to make your server more secure
- Use network operating system (NOS) audit tools to keep tabs in server activity
- Describe methods used to secure workstations
- List ways to secure computer hardware physically
- Discuss the relationship between security and disaster recovery
- Understand how directory and file attributes affect security
- Explain security tools present in NetWare 3.X and 4.X
- Discuss ways to protect NetWare servers from viruses
- Describe ways to provide workstation virus security
- Compare and contrast workstation and server-based virus scanning techniques
- Identity where the virus' back door is and how to close the door
- Explain the University of Leiden NOS type of breach and how to prevent it.

- Discuss the Riverbend Group type of breach and how to prevent it from happening to you
- Dissect the weak spots in Banyan Virtual Network Services (VINES) and Microsoft LAN Manager NOS
- Identify attack techniques in operating systems such as time of check to time of use (TOCTTOU), "Superzapping," "browsing," and the "salami attack,"

One of the most common flaws in network security is taking things for granted: The server has never failed. Workstations work. Life goes on.

Right around noontime one day in February, 1993 there was a major attitude adjustment for a lot of people. They were employed in the World Trade Center.

In the days following the bombing, a few people were let into the dark, cold, and soot-encrusted building to retrieve precious computers, disks, tapes—whatever nervous administrators could get out on a handtruck. The television coverage showed PCs, terminals, and every kind of equipment emerging from the dark tower.

How much of this equipment remained usable? The data recovery companies made fortunes trying to recover data from disks that were black with soot. Unsuccessful recoveries cost companies money, information was lost forever, and more than a few administrators lost their jobs.

LAN proponents learned a bitter lesson that day, one their mainframe cousins had learned long ago. The lesson had to do with keeping backups offsite and not allowing one's practices to get sloppy because "nothing ever happens." Contributing to the mistake was the perception that because the server was small and did not cost much, it is nothing special. Wrong. It was a the invisible value of the information *inside* that made it worth protecting. Such data may be irreplaceable or can be rebuilt only at great expense.

It does not take a bomb. It only takes a virus. Perhaps it takes a hacker with a LAN analyzer and a grudge to settle.

Contents of This Chapter

We begin with some recommendations for all systems, regardless of NOS or OS. From there, we become more specific with respect to NetWare, VINES, Apple's System 7, and LAN Manager. Even specific system flaws may have relevance to other NOSs, so it is wise to pay attention to all of the text even if you do not have the particular OS or NOS under discussion.

We also discuss some operating system holes in DOS, Unix, and OS/2. Microsoft's security plans for the Windows NT operating system will also be reviewed. In addition, there have been two significant NOS breaches that have lessons for all NOS users, and we will discuss them both.

Recommendations for All Systems Servers

Disable the server's floppy disk drives. Either unplug them or make them otherwise unusable. This way, hacking programs cannot get into the server nor can a boot sector virus.

- If an adversary brings the server down, he or she cannot boot it as a DOS machine and cannot copy any files.
- NetWare users can enter a console command, REMOVE DOS, to do the same thing.
- Use a screen blanker with a password to lock

the console. In this way, a malicious program loaded into a user's directory cannot be transferred to the server from the console.

Network World, the trade paper, has a bulletin board with a number of security programs on it.[1]NLMLOCK2 is their screen blanking program.

NOS Security Attributes

Use them all. It is amazing how few security features are actually used, even though users have paid for them. A prime example is NetWare's Intruder Alert, which notes repetitive attempts to login. It does no good if disabled. Use NetWare's Security utility or other tools such as Network Security Organiser to discover network weak spots.

Review the audit trail every day. NetWare 3.X does not have audit capability, so use an NLM or Network World's PAUDIT2.Add it to your login script to be sure you do it.

In the server's directory tree, deny users write permission in directories where executable files are stored. *Directory-level* denial is necessary as most viruses can get past the file-level read-only attribute.

Workstations

Network supervisors should log in from a limited-access workstation so that it cannot become infected by virus. Disable (electrically disconnect) drive A on workstations. Boot viruses get to the hard disk from drive A. B drives are not an entry point.

Virus-scanning network interface cards are available from Intel. This is an ideal place to detect and stop a virus.

User login scripts should use the DOS COMP(ARE)

command to compare COMMAND.COM in the workstation to a reference copy in the server. Use the same script to do a local virus scan and limit the connection(s) allowed (if possible).

The DOS MEM(ORY) command shows the workstation's memory. In the script, redirect the information to a file. The next command line should invoke a program to read the file to see if everything is all right. If not, the program should halt the login.

If the workstation can be physically locked, lock it. If it can be protected by password, protect it. Programs such as PROT and PASSWORD are on the Network World Bulletin Board System.

Get Physical

Here are some physical security suggestions:

- Spray computer gear with odd colors to reduce its fence value after theft.
- Cover one screw with nail polish or auto paint so that if someone tries to open the case, the seal will be broken.
- As noted before, lock all servers in a secure room. Limit access and keep keys in a key safe or other secure area.

Security guards should have set procedures for allowing computer gear out of the building. Passes are not enough. They should have a list of who an and cannot take gear out. Some experts recommend photographing anyone removing equipment.

Record equipment numbers in a log, perhaps within the inventory management system. Nonserialised units should be stamped or engraved with your organisation's name or equivalent. Nonremovable lables can also be used, especially inside units where thieves rarely look.

Your insurance agent may be able to get you an IDENTIFAX number. This number is stenciled on everything of value. Hardware can be traced easily by police through the IDENTIFAX registry.

Another topic to discuss with the agent is what proof is required to make a claim and the terms under which computer gear is covered. Receipts and periodic inventories may be necessary to demonstrate ownership and theft if it occurs. Specialised policies exist to protect against damage or theft.

When the Worst Happens

Despite our best efforts, sometimes the worst happens. Note the World Trade Center bombing, or the massive failure at the Hinsdale III, central office that caught fire. For these reasons, the security plan must be inextricably tied to the disaster recovery plan. The center of the disaster recovery plan is backup. Back up everything to a tape that has more capacity than the server drives. Back up only material you really need. Delete duplicate server files.

Network users should be able to back up to the server via menu. Insist that they do so every day. Files not needed by the user can be moved to tape and deleted from the server.

Figure 1.1 illustrates the concept of *online, nearline,* and *offline* storage. Utilities exist that automatically move data downward after it has been unused for a period set by the manager.

The author does not bother to back up .COM or .EXE programs unless they have been substantially customised.

These can always be restored from original disks or duplicate originals. Sometimes its possible to back up only the amended files.

In setting backup parameters, invoke as much error checking as possible. Speed is less important than reliability. Laptop users are not excluded from their backup responsibilities. Laptop users can use external "zero-slot" or PCMCIA network interface adapters to back up their disks to the server.

Test your ability to restore now and then. When the real thing happens, despite your nervousness, you will not fail.

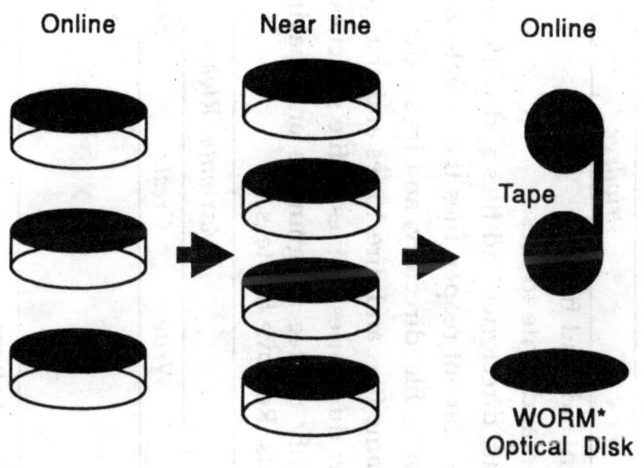

Data migrates from online to offline based on usage.
*Write once: read many (times

Fig 1.1 Online, nearline, and offline storage

Novell Netware

NetWare has excellent security. Security features were built into NetWare from the beginning, not added on. NetWare's special file structure exists for performance

TABLE 1.1

NetWare Rights

Trustee Rights[a]

Right	*Privilege*
Read	Open and read files.
Write	Open and write to files.
Create	Create directories and files and write to files. Users cannot reopen files they create without the read right.
Erase	Delete a file, directory, and its subdirectories and files.
Modify	Rename files and directories and change their attributes.
File scan	View directories or files in file searches.
Access control	Modify trustee assignments and maximum rights masks. Grant or revoke other users' rights. Remove trustees.

Maximum Rights Mask[b]

	Read	*Write*	*Create*	*Erase*	*Modify*	*File scan*	*Access control*
Trustee rights	X	X		X	X	X	X
Directory rights	X	X	X			X	
Effective rights[c]	X	X				X	

a. Trustee rights are rights assigned to users.

b. A maximum rights mask is composed of rights assigned to trustees and directories.

c. Users' file rights depend on the trustee and directory rights combined to form effective rights. These plus the directory and file attributes determine the user's rights in a file.

reasons, but has the additional benefit of not being readable in DOS, Unix, or OS/2 operating systems, even if the user has direct access to the server.

NetWare provides the following:

- Account security
- Password security
- Directory security
- File security
- Internetwork security

User profiles itemise resources to which the user has access, and the rights (Table 1.1) the user has within that resource. The profile can specify the times, dates, and location(s) of access of a specified user.

Directory-level security allows changes to the maximum rights mask (Table 1.2) of a directory. Access attributes can be assigned to directories and files (3.X and up only) to limit access.

Network-level security employs intruder detection and the security monitor.

1. *Intruder detection and lockout* notifies the administer if excessive access attempts are made. The administrator sets how many incorrect attempts will be allowed and any time delay between successive login attempts. The manager has the option of locking the account permanently, or if a specific lockout time is selected, how long that time will be.

2. The *security* utility checks the server bindery (where user records are kept, as Fig. 1.2 shows) for possible breaches. Six breach types are detected, including the following:

TABLE 1.2
Directory and File Attribute*

Attribute	*What it does*
Hidden	Hides files from directory (DIR) scans.
Indexed	Creates an index in memory to improve file access; usually reserved for large files.
Read write (normal)	Lets users modify files. Files are normal unless otherwise flagged. They return to normal when other flags are removed.
Read only	Users may read but not modify files. If not set, files are automatically flagged "read write."
Sharable	Allows several users to access files at the same time.
System	Hides files from DIR scans. Prevents deleting or copying. Usually assigned to operating system files.
Transactional	Tracks the transactions in a file. Ensures that all changes are made to a file, or none are. This is to prevent database corruption.

* Directory and file attributes cancel the effect of trustee assignments and rights permitted by the directory's rights mask.

- No password associated with a username
- Insecure passwords: too short or not unique to the user
- Users who have supervisor equivalence are noted
- Users with rights to the root directory are noted
- A user who borrows someone else's login script
- Excessive rights in the default directories.

Passwords are encrypted both on the hard drive and on the cable.

In NetWare 3.IX, file access rights, encryption services, and secure network console features were all strengthened.

However, there was and is no audit trail capability built into NetWare 3.IX. It must be added as a NetWare Loadable Module or other application.

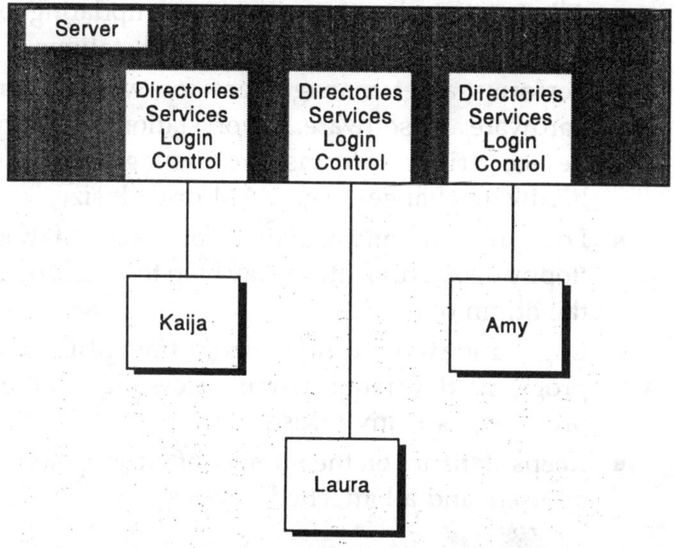

Fig. 1.2 The NetWare Bindery.

Automating the Assignment and Interpretation of Rights

Going through each file by hand and trying to interpret the rights level mentally quickly becomes a mind-bending process. Consistent with our stated goal of trying to automate everything possible to gain better security, a number of vendors offer security managers.

One such vendor is Leprechaun Software International, Ltd.[2] Their Network Security Organiser (NSO) guards against viral infections in NetWare servers. NSO resides in the server. It scans the server as users log in, looking for vulnerable directories. Then it creates a checklist indicating the directories at risk and from which users. Rights can then be modified.

NSO provides the following services:

- Analyses the network's vulnerability to viruses.
- Allows central management and updating of antivirus software in network workstations.
- Performs asset management for workstation hardware and software. A workstation inventory device driver informs the manager of any hardware changes, e.g., RAM or disk size.
- Logs programs and activities from a workstation floppy disk. This feature may help to track down the origin of a virus.
- Logs updated or new programs plus any programs that request write access to another program, as many viruses do.
- Keeps statistics on the number of virus episodes by users and all attached devices.

Workstation Controls

All the controls built into NetWare apply to any kind of workstation, whether DOS, Unix, or OS/2. There is a problem with Macintosh computers. Macintosh machines do not give NetWare 3.11's management utilities specific network addresses as do IBM-compatible computers. This means that the administrator cannot assign, restrict, or exclude access to particular network addresses by Macintosh machines. They are effectively invisible to NetWare 3.11.

This quirk has been responsible for a number of NetWare breaches, especially in the academic community. One breach consisted of a Macintosh program that trapped and recorded passwords, including a supervisor password. The hackers deleted one NetWare account and some files but did no irreparable harm.

This problem is fixed in NetWare 4.X because the

workstation shell includes integrated support of AppleTalk protocols that will pass network addresses to administrators.

NetWare Virus Control

A virus in the public area of a NetWare server will infect many workstations in minutes. By the time virus scanners such as Cheyenne's Inoculan or Intel's LANProtect notice, it is too late.[3]

Since viruses attach themselves to executable files, it is best to use NetWare's trustee rights to give users read-only access. In this way an infected PC cannot infect a server-based program file.

The Back Door

If you log in form an infected PC as the supervisor, you can unwillingly infect every server-based file, regardless of their user's rights. The key is to avoid using the supervisor ID as much as possible. Instead, manage user connections from the console. Create a print queue operator for someone other than the supervisor.

Another technique is to create an ID with workgroup manager status. The workgroup manager can create, delete, and modify accounts without access to the entire server.

Designate a user as workgroup manager from SYSCON using Supervisor Options. In User Information, pick the new workgroup manager's ID. Use the Managed Users and Groups option to make all other users and groups fall under the workgroup manager. Any new accounts created by the manager will give the manager the same rights over them.[4]

Virus-Scanning NLMs

Third-party vendors such as Cheyenne (InocuLAN), Intel PC Enhancement (LANProtect), Central Point (Anti-

Virus for NetWare), and McAfee (NetShield) market NetWare Loadable Modules (NLMs) that scan for viruses when programs are launched (see Fig. 1.3). Since these NLMs run in real time, they delay transfer of the file to the workstation until the scan is complete. This means a delay in getting the file out plus an added burden on the server. Consequently, such NLMs can take a toll on server performance. The more files to be opened, the worse the performance. NetWare SYSCON opens six files. Windows, however, opens 165.

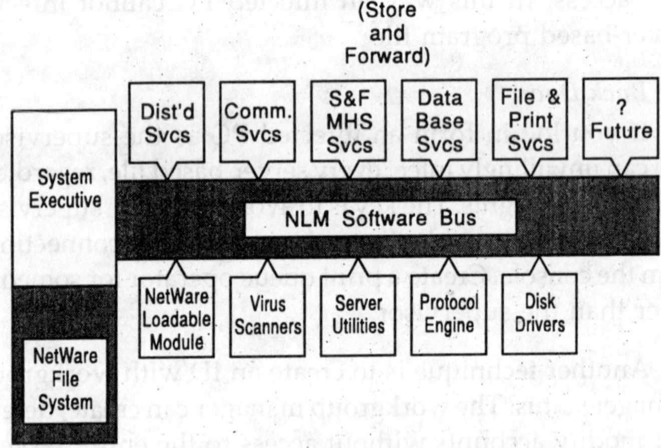

Fig. 1.3 NetWare Loadable Modules

Traffic load effects scan speed because both activities contend for CPU cycles. Heavily loaded CPUs will bog down still further with the added NLM burden. On the other hand, lightly loaded machines may not even notice.

The key is to test. Try opening a Windows application from a workstation with the NLM running and without to see if there is a difference. To improve performance, most NLMs will allow selective scans of volumes and .EXE and .COM files.

The NLM itself should not pose a security risk. If not well behaved, an NLM can interfere with other NLMs, conflict with other server tasks, or even crash a server.

There are no standards for virus-scanning NLMs, so expect a wide variance in capabilities, quality, and performance effects. A full discussion of virus-scanning techniques is found.

Workstation-Based Versus Server-Based Scanning

As a parameter defense, most of these NLMs also come with virus scanning TSR programs for workstations. This is the best of both worlds. Workstation scanning has its advantages and disadvantages as shown in Table 1.3.

TABLE 1.3

Advantages and Disadvantages of Workstation Scanning

Advantages	*Disadvantages*
Low cost	Users must be taught to use the scanners
Versatile and portable: Use in laptops, notebooks, PCs	Workstation scanners must be updated periodically
Can find and sanitise infected machine	Indirect control over user scan implementation

Server-Based Scanning

As Fig. 1.4 shows, server-based scanning can be run as a one-time batch program or in real time. They protect only files on the server. Users are not involved in the scan process. They are useful for the following functions or situations:

- Continuous online scanning
- Many users or a changing user community
- When many foreign machines such as notebooks are routinely attached

- When outside disks are often inserted into workstations
- When LAN application software changes often.

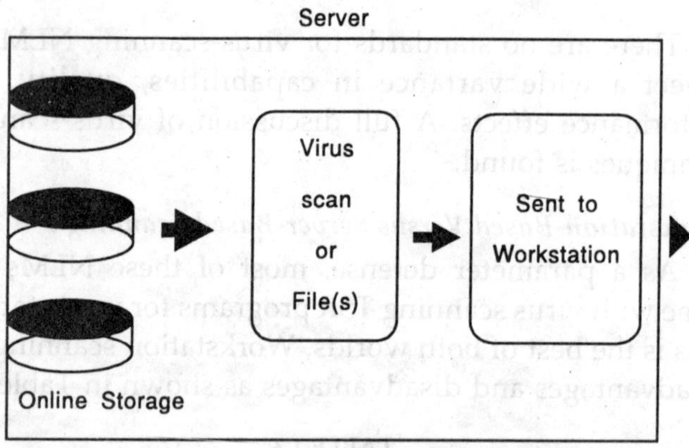

Fig. 1.4 Server-based virus scanning

Additional Security Features in NetWare 4.X

The release of NetWare 4.X improved NetWare's already good security even more. If you are a current NetWare 3.X user, it is important to understand these features because Novell plans to migrate many of them from 4.X to 3.X. This has already happened with respect to System Fault Tolerance III (see Fig. 1.5), which backs up servers in real time.

In the 3.X version of NetWare, it was necessary to administer access to each server (through the bindery) individually. This was difficult and often led to excessively liberal rights. Additions such as Novell's NetWare naming Service and Banyan's Enterprise Network Services consolidated the management of binderies across multiple servers, but did not materially add to NetWare's security.

The new NetWare 4-X adds NetWare Directory Services, including extra access controls that can surround the entire network. As an enterprise NOS, the user logs in once, and uses Rivest-Shamir-Adelman (RSA) public and private-key protection to keep unauthorised users out. NetWare 4.X also adds an audit tool that we will discuss below.

NetWare Directory Services (NDS)

The key to NetWare 4.X-literally-is NDS, as illustrated in Fig.1.6 NDS is a database containing information about all network resources: users, printers, servers, print queues-everything.

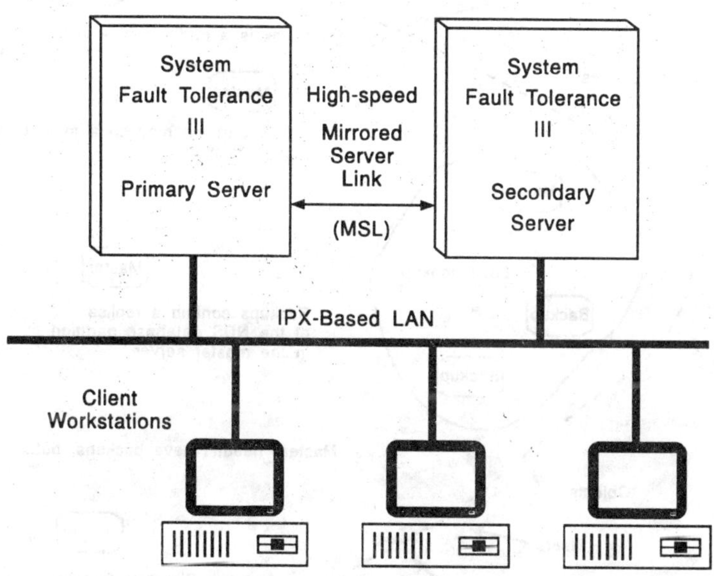

Fig. 1.5 System Fault Tolerance III.

Each resource is called an *object*. Objects are stored in the directory database. In fact, the database is divided into sections called *partitions*. The partitions improve performance because they are intended to be near the objects manage. In this way, NDS does not have to traverse a wide area network to find an object, and the database in which to look is smaller.

The master copy of a partition is kept on one server, while other servers act as backups. This means that there must be at least one more server to back up the partition. Should the master server fail, the backup will recover. If there is no backup, then that section of NDS data-all the objects it—will be inaccessible.

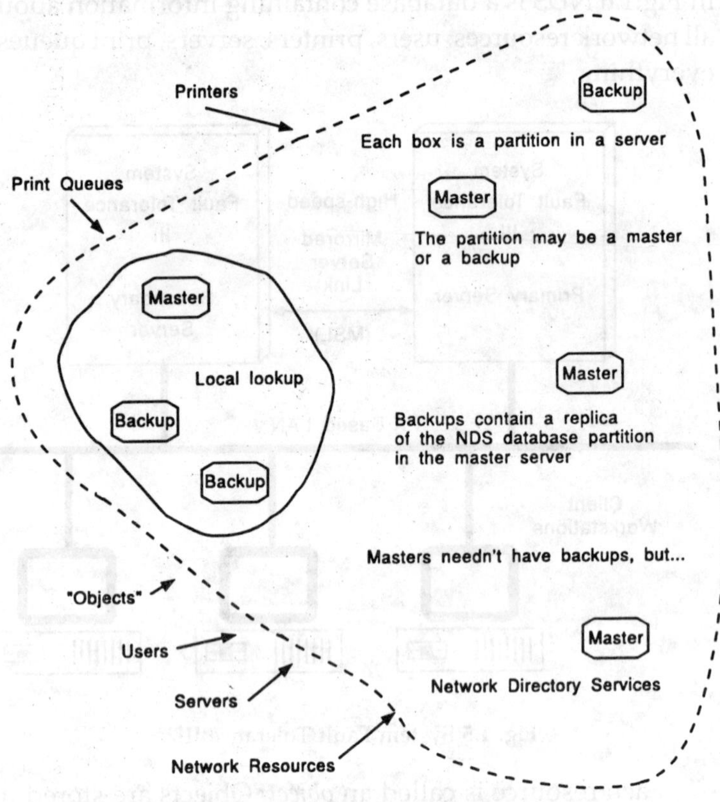

Fig. 1.6 NetWare Directory Services.

The virtue of this system is that the network manager defines an object and all its attributes only once. There is a single account per user and a single set of access rights for each account. Included within this definition are all the rights discussed earlier for *users*. NetWare 4.X also defines what actions a *program* can take

NDS adds ten more access rights for objects plus the five rights we have seen in the NetWare 3.X bindery. While a useful extension, a larger scale—the entire enterprise network—must now be considered from a security standpoint when assigning these expanded rights. The net effect is that in NDS there are now file or directory rights and object rights that include bindery rights plus extensions. Not too different from the parties of SNMP, objects can have a unique property called an access control list that specifies how objects can access each other.

Auditing

As we said earlier, auditing was not part of earlier NetWare versions. Auditing is the metric by which managers measure that proper use of the system consistent with their organisation's mission.

Specific operations may be covered by the audit. A group of network objects called a *container* is one auditable population. The other is server hard-disk volumes. The manager sets one password for each and gives control to the auditor.

The auditor then changes the passwords so tempering cannot occur and sets up the activities to be watched. The passwords are required to get to the acquired data and cannot be changed. Like any other object. auditors must have access rights. No rights means no access.

If the file into which audit data gets filled, auditing can be turned off or the volume dismounted. If dismounted, the data are lost.

Auditing will surely collect an incredible amount of data. As yet, no tools exist to reduce it to a useful form. A second type of currently nonexistent data reduction tool would be useful or performance analysis and for highlighting improper activities.

If the manager gets run over by a truck, audit data become inaccessible unless he or she has foresightedly left them in a sealed envelope and someone knows where to look. The same passwords are needed to remount a volume dismounted due to overflow.

File Compression and Antivirus Scanning Conflicts

NetWare 4.X compresses files that have not been opened for a number of manager-defined days. This creates problems for antivirus NLMs and CRC-based integrity checkers. For one thing, the file must be decompressed first before scanning, adding to the time needed to scan the file, not to mention processing horsepower.

Another snag is that decomposing the file resets the compression utility clock. This means that the virus scanner must run less often than the automatic compression algorithm or no files will be compressed. Scanners will reduce usable disk capacity unless they cause the file to be recompressed after scanning.

File Migration

When the server's free disk space gets too low, NetWare 4.X migrates inactive files to a tape or write once-read many (WORM) drive until space is once again free for them on the main drive. So as not to scare people to death, the file names and sizes remain visible, but the data are really nearline (neither completely online nor totally offline). If a migrated file is called, it is pulled from near line to online.

From a security standpoint, a nearline machine failure means no access until the device is fixed. It is desirable to exclude certain files from nearline storage if they are considered crucial. Of Course, this presumes that backups are performed on the server drive(s). Neither nearline nor offline storage is *backup* storage.

Storage Management Services

Storage Management Services (SMS) was a Novell product long before NetWare 4.D, dating back to 1991. Novell hoped it would become an industry standard, and indeed it has gained the support of Hewlett-Packard and DEC as a generic method of backing up data across a network regardless of vendors, NOSs, media, or platforms used.

SMS is a series of software modules that permits a server to back up and restore not only itself, but other servers, workstations, and especially NetWare 4.X's network directory services. This is the special virtue of SMS, as no other backup system can currently preserve NDS data. SMS can back up server-located files in DOS, file transfer and access management (FTAM), network file system, and server-based OS/s plus OS/2 and DOS data from workstations. It can also do full, incremental, or differential backups.

Unfortunately, SMS needs a lot of server memory and supports only tape drives, not tape changers. However, its implementation is essential if NDS data must be backed up (e.g., there is no replicated server in which to store a copy of the NDS partition).

NetWare Core Protocol Packet Signature

A student at the University of Leiden in the Netherlands wrote a spoofing program for NetWare 3.11 called HACK.EXE in late 1992 that monitors packets flowing between the workstation and the server. By copying the packet's details, It was possible for the program to pretend to be the legitimate workstation.

The server could not tell the difference, and so the spoofer acquired whatever rights that were possessed by the workstation. This even included the network supervisor. (Here is another reason to log in as supervisor only from the server console and avoid using RCONSOLE whenever possible).

To plug this leak, Novell introduced a fix in November, 1992 called NCP Packet Signature (Fig. 1.7). Using RSA public-key technology, Packet Signature attaches an eight-byte identifier to the end of an IPX packet as an authenticator. NCP Packet Signature consists of an NLM on the server, modified client shell software, and user login utilities. A NetWare 3.11 utility, WSUPDATE, lets managers install client software via the network.

NCP Packet Signature became available first for NetWare 3.11 as an NLM (and is built into NetWare 3.12), then was used for NetWare 2.2 and is built into NetWare 4 X. It is also in NetWare for Unix. The fix is available through NetWare resellers, on NetWire (via CompuServe), and NetWare Express or by calling Novell at (800) 638-9273.

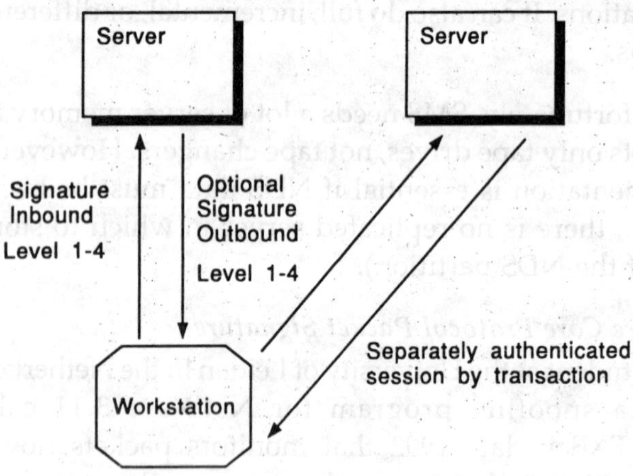

Fig. 1.7 NCP Packet Signature

Signature change by *transaction*, not by *session*, so copying the signature does not permit spoofing. Signature can be used by some or all workstations in a mixed environment and by the server, too if two-way authentication is desired. As an aside, you will enhance security by limiting the number of concurrent sessions allowed a user to a small number, perhaps two. NetWare permits up to eight.

Multiserver networks can each have different packet signature levels. Authentication is by server, not network. Higher-signature-level security is possible by server, so that machines with sensitive data can get more protection than those containing less sensitive information. In all, there are four signature levels.

Servers can be configures to work with both signature and nonsignature workstations, allowing partial migration if desired. Incorrectly signed packets cause an alert message to be sent to the client, the server console, and to the error log. The client-server connection is not broken.

NCP Packet Signature has a few negatives (also see Table 1.4):

TABLE 1.4

When Should One Use Packet Signature?

Do not use if	*Use if*
There are only executable programs on the server.	Workstation user(s) are not very trustworthy.
You know and trust all workstation users on your network.	Physical access to the LAN cable is easy, giving a spoofer an entry point.
Data on the server are not sensitive.	You have publicly accessible workstations or workstations are left unattended.
Loss or corruption will not affect you.	

- Performance degradation is small to midsize networks is small. Larger systems of 250 machines or more will see abut a 10 per cent throughout degradation.
- Packet Signature only applies to NCP sessions using IPX. Protocols such as AppleTalk File Protocol, TCP/IP, and Xerox XNS are *not* protected.
- *Data* are not encrypted. Novell is expected to announce an NLM to encrypt IPX packets this year. Again, non-IPX protocols are not covered.

Security of NLMs

It has long been known that application NLMs can corrupt data because they can intrude on memory reserved for the server. Improperly written, the NLM can crash the server.

NetWare 3.1X and all NLMs for it run at privilege level ring 0, the least protected level. A misbehaving NLM can write over memory not its own and cause a crash and possible data loss. In NetWare 4.X this problem is fixed. NLMs run in ring 3 (OS-protected domain), the most protected ring. NLMs venturing out of their domain are caught and terminated. While there is a small performance loss with this method, it is well worth it.

The Riverbend Group Breach

In March 1993, a Novell instructor with the Riverbend Group of McLean, Va. accidentally set a supervisor password during a training session. He was then faced with finding a way around it in order to regain system control.

His solution was ingenious. He first dismounted the SYS. volume at the server, which contains all the core NetWare operating information. He then renamed it something else and brought it back up. The system thought it was a new volume and asked for a new password. The instructor then entered a password and regained full supervisory access to the network and server. The entire process took under a minute.

Lessons to be Learned

This would not have been possible had:

- The server been locked up
- A console password been in use
- The keyboard been locked
- The "attacker" been less knowledgeable

Bypassing Novell Login Scripts

Most Novell networks and some other LANs use login scripts to automate the login process. Just before login, at what is called the *attach point,* Novell security can be breached. This is done by typing IPX, NET and ATTACH. If entered at the right time, many Novell scripts and security programs will not run. However, the user will attach to the server. There is no easy defense for this oddity, save for "security through obscurity."

Novell Summary

The user community gives NetWare high marks for security (see Table 1.5). Novell has shown that it addresses security holes quickly and aggressively, as they did with the Leiden breach. Novell also has plans to certify NetWare under the National Computer Security Center Trusted System program at the C2 level, considered industrial-grade security. Novell has further shown its security commitment by making it such an integral part of NetWare 4.X. However, these security features are useless if they are not implemented.

For a listing of Novell security utilities, see the end of the chapter.

TABLE 1.5

Novell Network Security Recommendations

- ❑ Use only the must current versions of system, client, and patch software.
- ❑ Check periodically for viruses
- ❑ Use the Security utility to detect vulnerable server access points.
- ❑ Lock servers in a secure room.
- ❑ Issue the SECURE CONSOLE command from the NetWare console. Then NLMs can only be loaded from SYS : SYSTEM.
- ❑ Activate the lock file server console from the monitor main menu when the NetWare console is not being used.
- ❑ Always use a password different from the supervisor password for RCONSOLE.
- ❑ Limit the number of users possessing rights. Use a workgroup manager instead.
- ❑ Avoid logging in as supervisor whenever possible.
- ❑ Avoid assigning security equivalence that give one user the same access rights as another user. If you must, revoke it as soon as possible.
- ❑ Use access control features to limit not only users 'but virus' access to data and applications (directory level.)
- ❑ Enable intruder detection and lockout.
- ❑ Ask users to log out whenever they leave their workstations, or install a product like NetOFF that logs them out after inactivity.
- ❑ Lock up, disable, or otherwise secure unattended workstations.
- ❑ Require passwords for all accounts of at least five (Novel) characters. At least six mixed characters are recommended.
- ❑ Make users change their passwords at least every 90 days.
- ❑ Require unique passwords, as we have discussed.
- ❑ Limit the number of grace logins (login attempts).
- ❑ Limit the number of concurrent connections in NetWare 2.X or 3.X NetWare's maximum is eight concurrent workstation to server connections.
- ❑ Enforce network login time restrictions and station restrictions.
- ❑ Train users and administrators how to use NetWare security features.

Banyan Virtual Network Services (VINES)

VINES was intended from its outset in 1984 to be an enterprise-wide NOS. Until NetWare 4.X, it had virtually no competition at the enterprise level.

Rather than describe all the security features of VINES, many of which parallel those of NetWare, we will focus on the unique strengths and a few weaknesses of VINES.

Authentication Services

Like NetWare 4.X's Network Directory Services, VINES has its own set of directory services called StreetTalk (see Fig 1.8). StreetTalk exists in VINES servers. When a server

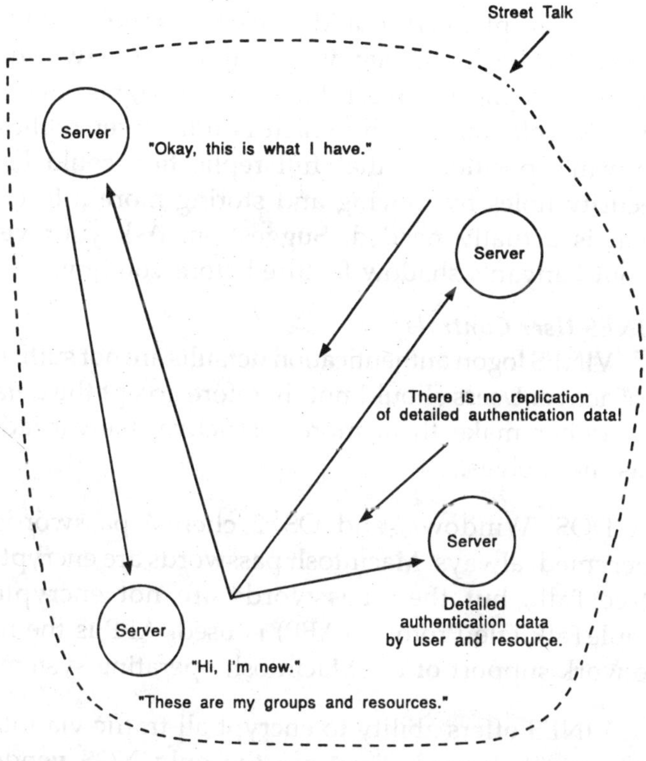

Fig. 1.8 VINES Street Talk directory services.

joins the network, its StreetTalk tells everyone else about the groups and resources within it. The other servers tell it their groups and resources. But detailed authentification information for each user and resource exists only in the server who owns that user or resource.

Should the server fail, there is no replication of these authenticators at all, so these resources and users would not be available, nor would users have access. Recall that in NetWare 4.X, if there is more than one server, it (or they) will back up NDS partition as hot spares. However, there is no way to back up the NDS *database* except to Novell's SMS backup system.

Banyan planned to add StreetTalk fault tolerance by the end of 1994. The plan was to allow up to two shadow servers to replicate StreetTalk user access rights only, rather than Novell's approach, which is full server replication. Banyan's position is that full replication could lead to security holes by moving and storing more information than is actually needed. Suggestion: Ask your vendor about Banyan's shadow feature before you buy.

VINES User Controls

VINES logon authentication defaults are not sufficiently restrictive. Users should not therefore accept the defaults, but rather make them more restrictive. Banyan advises this themselves.

DOS, Windows, and OS/2 clients' passwords are encrypted, always. Macintosh passwords are encrypted in StreetTalk, but their passwords are not encrypted if AppleTalk File Protocol (AFP) is used. AFP is the native network support of the Macintosh operating system.

VINES offers ability to encrypt all traffic via internal software if desired. They are the only NOS vendor to presently offer this capability.

Disk Space Usage

It is standard practice to allocate maximum disk space by user in a large network. If not done, a "disk hog" can take up disk space required by the system itself, slowing service to users. NetWare offers this feature, but presently VINES does not.

Rights

VINES rights, like NetWare rights, are sophisticated, flexible, and complicated. The antivirus principles that apply to NetWare rights apply equally to VINES. Similarly, the file and directory attributes are just as complex and require experience and planning to use them as a security-building tool.

Unlike NetWare, VINES has few utilities to help out in this area. This is because Banyan was until recently a semiclosed environment and because VINES has under 10 per cent of the NOS market to Novell's 64 per cent.

Interserver Security

VINES excels in its ability to limit the type of access that can occur between networked servers. This feature is unique to VINES. The preferred implementation method is to secure each machine fully and the set the proper access level for each interconnected server.

Auditing

Like NetWare 4.X, VINES has auditing capability to detect logon attempts, security violations, and like. Also NetWare, there are no data reduction tools to make sense out of all the data it produces.

"Dongles"

VINES uses plug-in hardware keys called "dongles" or "birds" that enable use of its software in servers. Plugged into the first parallel port. VINES software interrogates it to see which services are allowed. The parallel port can still be used to attach a printer.

New services require another dongle to be cascaded behind the first. Once an upgrade is complete, the dongle(s) may be disconnected and returned to Banyan for credit.

These devices are obsolescent. They can fail or be lost, damaged, or stolen. They add unneeded complexity and create another vulnerability. Other vendors enforce licensing rights through their software. There is no reason for VINES to be different.

VINES's Future

It is clear that StreetTalk needs fault tolerance. It is unacceptable to have resources and users offline until a server gets fixed. Banyan is working on StreetTalk's shadow backup, and it may well be available now.

Banyan had planned to submit VINES to the National Computer Security Center to gain a C2 government security rating. Banyan later put the project on hold pending enhancements that would affect the project. If C2 security is important to you, ask your vendor regarding its status; Banyan did say that they remained committed to gaining C2 security for VINES.

NetWare 4.X offers System Fault Tolerance III, which means online duplexed servers. Banyan offers to such capability at present. Banyan does offer RAID level 1 duplexed disks, but none higher as yet. All levels of RAID (1 to 5) can be accommodated in NetWare 3.X or 4.X.

The Banyan development environment had been relatively closed to third-party developers. This has been a matter of Banyan attitude and the fact that they have a seventh of the market compared to Novell.

The result for users is that the wealth of NLMs for security, virus detection, and everything else is largely missing in VINES. That is changing, but third-party support remains well behind NetWare.

Microsoft LAN Manager

LAN Manager is a holdover product. Based on OS/2, it is highly unlikely that the company will expend further effort on it than necessary to maintain present customers. Microsoft is pressing LAN Manager customer to upgrade to Windows NT Advanced Server.

The New LAN Manager is Windows NT (Advanced) Server (NTAS), although it still requires LAN Manager's presentation format. Based on Microsoft's Windows NT. (Advanced) Server is the latest in a new series of NOSs.

For the moment, though, about 10 per cent of NOSs are using LAN Manager. In the same spirit as VINES, let us look at LAN Manager's security strengths and weaknesses.

Domain-Based Architectures

LAN Manager is based on *domains* (Fig.1.9), groups of servers where one login will suffice. Domains are an older NOS concept that was implemented in products like LAN Server (which is closely related to LAN Manager) and DEC Path Works, whose origins LAN Manager shares.

A domain is not a global directory. One might think that domains implement the need-to-know principle by dividing the network into parts. In reality, it is easy to list resources in other domains, and get to them. The bottom line is that domains are cumbersome to work with and add little to security.

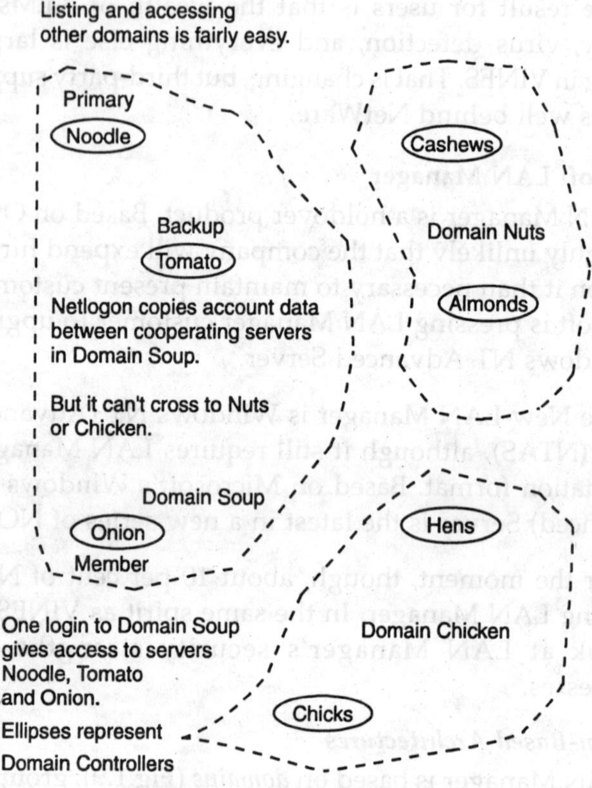

Fig. 1.9 LAN Manager domains.

Management of the domains is easier if a program called *Netlogon* is running. Netlogon copies user account data between cooperating servers in a domain. If the primary domain controller fails, logons can be validated by backup controllers. Lower-level member controllers hold user account data but cannot validate logons.

The problem is that even Netlogon allows no logical connection between domains. This means that each domain must be managed individually, Consequently, management is easier if users are limited to just one domain.

Share-Level Security

The less sophisticated of two models that LAN Manager contains share-level security defines a sharename for a resource, and then a password to get to the sharename. Access permissions define what can be done with the resource specified by the sharename. By using different passwords with different access permissions, several layers of access can be created for the same sharename. The result is that many users wind up having the same password (always a bad idea). While it might be all right for purely generic resources, using LAN Manager seems an expensive way to do it.

User-Level Security

This is the alternative to share level and has much finer resolution. Here, specific resources are allowed for each user.

Encryption

In order to encrypt passwords on MS-DOS client workstations, an optional service called Encrypt must be installed and running. Otherwise new passwords selected at the workstation will not be encrypted.

If LAN administration is done remotely, away from the server, Microsoft recommends that it be done from a Windows or OS/2 workstation. The reason is that on other platforms (except as noted), passwords travel from workstation to server *unencrypted.*

LAN Manager comes with two default named accounts, ADMIN and GUEST.GUEST does not need a password and is intended for those simply using printers and such. Regardless, it should be protected by password anyway.

Securing Resources

A program called *Netrun* accesses the resource needed

to execute a program on the server. Although Netrun can be restricted. It might be possible to run an unsafe program from a safe one. Also, general applications can be extended using macros to do entirely new and uncontrolled functions beyond system controls.

While most server programs cannot be run using Netrun, OS/2 command line applications using STDOUT will work. When all is said and done, the opportunity for a breach is jut a little too great.

Permissions

Execute permission allows clients to execute applications and nothing else in a server directory. However, it can only be compelled for clients using MS-DOS 5.0 or OS/2. For pre-MS-DOS 5.0 versions, Windows, and Macintosh, the selected application will not be executable and the looser read permission must be used (read allows copying, so it is weaker).

Users get permissions for a resource from all groups to which they belong. If a user has read and write permission in one group and read and create in another, that user gets all three. However, individual permissions can be set to override group assignment. When many large groups of users are defined as in large servers, this becomes a difficult problem to manage.

If the standard file allocation table is used for disk partitions, new subdirectories have no permissions assigned to them. On the other hand, partitions using the OS/2 High Performance File System (HPFS) inherit the permissions of the parent directory. Microsoft recommends HPFS.

Audit

LAN Manager has a respectable audit function,but

like VINES and NetWare 4.X, has no reduction tool to turn *data* into useful *information.*

Summary

LAN Manager has gained some good reviews and is implemented in some very large firms. It is nicely integrated with other Microsoft products: Windows for Workgroups, MS-DOS, and Window;S; even LAN Manager for Santa Cruz Operation (SCO) systems. The SCO supports LAN Manager under Unix. If you have LAN Manager in your IS environment, make use of all the security tools it offers. As Microsoft draws support away from LAN Manager, users will be forced to consider Windows NTAS more seriously.

DOS

Various hacker tools have been written that can penetrate almost any DOS-based system. Oddly, the most often used methods of penetrating NetWare LANs are not NetWare specific. This circumstance is a variation of "Maginot Line thinking" where Novell built stout controls that hacker s beat by simply taking a different approach.

Be alert to three programs that hackers can use:

- NETCRACK is a program that finds user passwords on NetWare LANs.
- THIEF and GETIT are two programs that capturc NetWare passwords and IDs before they are encrypted.
- KEY COPY copes every key stroke entered by a user on their PC.

Unchanged passwords recorded as keystrokes by hackers gain them entry before NetWare controls are invoked.

The defense to these programs is a token password as would be generated by a system like SecurID. Then recorded keystrokes become useless.

Unix and OS/2

Some versions for Unix AND OS/2 will return a superuser prompt if the input buffer is grossly overloaded by a very long message. Test your system to see if this can be done.

Unix is a fine operating system but it was never designed for great security. Only one version of Unix, System 4.2, has earned an NSA B2 classification.

The problem with Unix is that it is mainly a peer-to-peer system. As much, access privileges are determined on a station-by-station basis. It is easy to get a copy of the file containing the account names and (encrypted) passwords. Once in a cracker's hands, they can break the passwords at leisure.

CERT suggests the following:

- Check your accounting, C2, and system logs. Unusual entries or activity signal trouble. Nothing unusual may also signal trouble if the cracker has tempered with the logs.
- Hidden files are sometimes created by hackers as places to store their ill-gotten gains. Odd, cryptic names are often a giveaway, such as dot-dot space or dot-dot-control-z (or some other letter.)
- Run this command to find files that set the other ID to root or some other privileged account: find/user root-perm-4000-print.
- Trojan Horses in Unix take the form of Unix commands that actually contain something else.

These might include popular TCP/IP commands such as *Telnet, ftp,* or *finger.* Unix commands such as *su* (substitute user) or *login* are popular for this purpose. Make sure the file lengths are the same as the lengths you recall as the real thing.

- Look at the path. Unusual or unfamiliar subdirectories, especially at the beginning, imply trouble.
- Check the *cron* and *at* control files. They should run only programs you recognise. Files referenced by *cron* or *at* should not be writable by everyone.
- Similarly, keep an eye on the */etc/passed* file. Accounts without passwords, new accounts, and user IDs bear special watching.

Windows NT

Microsoft intends to certify Windows NT at the federal C2 level first and later at the higher B2 level. If you need this level of security, request the status of the certification effort from your vendor. Such certification can take years.

Apple System 7

System 7 file sharing lets any Macintosh computer be a file server. If a user turns on file sharing to do a transfer, turns on guest access, and later forgets to turn it off, his or her machine is open to everyone. Solutions to this problem include:

- Remove the sharing setup control panel from each Macintosh. While secure, this solution feels like throwing out the baby with the bathwater.
- Better still, teach your users to set up a share folder instead with guest access. AG Group's [(510) 937-7900] Nok Nok ($50) software advises you whenever anyone connects to your machine

to do personal file sharing. Another product, ultraSecure ($239) from usrEZ [(714) 756-5140] does the same thing but has more features.

- Inventory your system with Network Security Guard ($259) from MR Mac Software. It will find out which servers are running what software; which have guest access and which ones have easily-broken passwords.

Later versions of System 7, specifically 7.5 and System 7 Pro have more security options. One is the Apple Open Collaboration Environment (AOCE). AOCE includes a keychain holding several user IDs and passwords. All are encrypted until unlocked by one password from the user.

The problem is that once unlokced, individual passwords are sent around the network in plaintext by many network servers. Tapping into these passwords in a snap. The main benefit of AOCE is that it keeps people from writing passwords down or placing them in accessible documents such as Preferences.

AppleShare

There is not much security in AppleShare. Repeated attempts at entry will not be cut off as with NetWare's intruder Detection and Lockout. Nor does AppleShare allow a manager to specify who can connect to what resource at what location during a given time of day, or during a given day for that matter.

One partial solution is to use *Nok Nok A/S* is odd logging and restrict the time that active, idle, and guest users can connect to the server. Nok Nok A/S identifies guest users by their machine names, and will alert you when someone logs on to AppleShare (if you are near the server and can see or hear it);

For better protection, switch to AppleTalk Filing Protocol as a file-sharing system. Its cost is greater, but its security is on a par with NetWare for Macintosh, VINES Option for Macintosh, and DEC PathWorks. The administrative workload is a significant hidden cost that goes along with a more sophisticated NOS.

PowerBooks and Macs can be stolen like any other machine. For a list of Macintosh desktop security software, see the end of the chapter.

General OS Security Notes

Electronic Mail

It is easy to forge electronic mail messages. This is why products such as Lotus Notes offer digital signing or encryption. If a message seems out of character, it could well be a fake.

Time of Check to Time of Use (TOCTTOU)

Between the time an operating system checks security and the time it begins a process, security information may be stored in memory and therefore subject to modification by an attacker. This is called a TOCTTOU attach.

Superzapping

Sometimes a computer will freeze or lock up, and a *superzapping* routine will be used to thaw it out. These routines can sometimes bypass normal security controls.

Browsing

Often, memory given to a new user will to have been erased by the last user or by a process designed to wipe the memory clear before the next user logs in. The new user can browse the first user's memory for useful information they should not have.

This same principle applies to erased files. The actual

data are not erased, only the name. Tools like Norton Disk Doctor can read and recover this data. Some operating systems are designed to randomise erased file and memory space. Utilities can also be bought that do this.

A successful security breach occurred when an adversary read "scratch" (supposedly empty) tapes that contained useful seismic data. This went on for months before it was caught.

The Salami Attach

A few cents here... a few cents there..no one will ever notice. That is the essence of a salami attack. By stealing roundoff of an interest payment, for instance, a thief can steal thousands or millions over several hundred customers. This is more of an applications program than an OS breach, but it is worth mentioning.

Review

- We underestimate the value of information by mistaking it for the value of the system that contains it.
- For all machines, disabling floppy drives adds to security.
- Review your insurance coverage so you know what is and what is not covered, and how to present a credible claim.
- The security plan is backed up by the disaster recovery plan.
- Novell NetWare has very good security, *if it is used* (as with other NOSs).
- In all NOSs, restricting rights and permissions adds security and can prevent the spread of a virus.
- Server-based virus scanning and workstation-

based scanning each have their merits. There is nothing wrong with using both.

- Novell's security recommendations apply nearly equally to all NOSs.
- Banyan VINES is also a secure NOS, with some notable weak spots in authentication backup and disk space allocation.
- Microsoft LAN Manager has a number of weaknesses, several having to do with unencrypted passwords. It is unlikely that these will be fixed as Mocrosoft has moved toward its next generation NOS, Windows NT Advanced Server.
- Common to all NOSs, the audit process generates reams of data but very little usable information. Data reduction tools do not as yet exist.
- Several DOS-based programs exist to copy passwords. Use a token password system to get around these programs.
- NetWare security and login scripts can be bypassed by a certain sequence of commands prior to the server attach point.
- Unerased media, be it memory, disk space, or tape, can create an inadvertant security breach. This is called *browsing*.
- Some operating systems can be breached using TOCTTOU or superzapping.

APPENDIX

NETWARE AND MACINTOSH SECURITY

NetWare Scurity Software Utilities

Cheyenne Software, Inc.
Roslyn N.Y.
(800) CHEY-INC
Netback (also called Cheyenne Utilities)

Intrusion Detection, Inc.
New York, NY
(212) 360-6104
Kane Security Analyst, analyses NetWare weak spots

LAN Support Group
Houston, Tex.
(800) 749-8439
NetSqueeze + Encyption offers data compression and optional encryption

ON Technology
Cambridge, Mass
(617), 374-1400
AudiTrak, also a NetWare auditor

Frye Computer Systems
(800) 234-FRYE
Frye Utilities for NetWare

Software Inc.
Portland, Or.
(503) 294 6025
Smart Pass (NLM), a password manager, available from this supplier and others.

Brightwork Development
(800) 866-6585
Brightworks/McAfee Tool Suite

Symantec
(408) 253-9600
Norton Network Administration Suite

Macintosh Desktop Security Software

These products are made by Kent Marsh:

FolderboltPro is for single-user Macintoshes. It locks individual folders via password such that they can be set for read or write only, or no access at all.

NightWatch II is activated by events, such as shutdown or sleep. It then requires a password to do anything new.

CrypptoMatic encrypts files using ANSI DES. Decryption calls for a password.

Magna *Empower Remote* and usrEZ's *ultraSecure* include all of the above and then some. All the above offer both DES and non-DES encryption for faster speed. Note that this is your only real protection for critical information; breaking an encryption algorithm is harder than unlocking a disk.

NOTES

1. The Network World BBS telephone number is (508) 620-1160 from 300 to 2,400 bits/s. Set 8 bits, no parity, and one stop bit (8NI). For speeds up to 9,600 bits/s, call (508) 620-1178 (also 8N1).
2. Leprechaun Software is at (404) 971-8900; fax (404) 971-8828.
3. Edward Liebing, "How to Use NetWare's File Attributes to Provide Security," *LAN Times*, December 7, 1992.
4. "Network Supervisor or Typhoid Mary?," Corporate Computing, May, 1993.

SOURCES OF LEAKS IN LANs AND WANS

Objectives

At the end of this chapter you will be able to:

- List the most common threats to LANs and WANs
- Discuss forms of interception in wired and wireless systems
- Itemise the finer points of dial-in security procedures
- Describe techniques for improving packet switching network security
- Explain how leased lines can be compromised
- Show how routes can add security
- Indicate how routers can add security
- Identify which router protocols can be risky
- Show how gateways can be used to breach a network
- Outline secure backup procedures
- Understand how removable media can effectively connect two isolated networks
- List ways to anchor computer equipment physically
- Place the entire computer security topic where it belongs: in the people perspective

Introduction

Between the years 1988 and 1991, the number of reported security breaches on the Internet, the world's largest data network, increased from 6 to 405, a 67-fold increase in four years.

Captain Midnight made his debut on the HBO channel of cable TV when he invaded their satellite TV uplink in 1986. Home Box Office subscribers across the country found themselves paying to hear his harebrained political opinions.

The FBI caught 400 illicit wiretappers last year. There was no word on how many there *really* were.

Financial institutions are special targets. When asked why he robbed banks, Willie Sutton said, " That's where the money is."

Threats to networks come in five general forms:

- *Interception* of information.
- *Alteration* as with replaying data packets, masquerading as someone else, intercepting signoffs, or sending false messages.
- *Jamming,* primarily a problem with radio-based systems.
- *Denial of service* as could be caused by a virus or sabotage.
- *Loss of network integrity,* as with a major outage due to a cable cut or the Signalling System 7 failure experienced by AT&T that caused a massive voice network outage.

Interception: Cable Taps and LAN and WAN Monitors

Physical taps may be detectable using sensors of various kinds, but inductive pickups with no physical connection will be harder to catch. LAN and WAN monitors should be locked up. Unfortunately, any PC can become a network analyser with the proper software. One version called *IPX Permissive* is often found on hacker bulletin boards. It can read Novell LAN packets and reporgram a workstation to any desired address. Some inventory programs can detect the presence of programs like IPX Permissive.

An analyser may not even be needed. Some LAN network interface cards (NICs) and workstations allow their addresses to be modified so that they will accept frame they see, not just the ones destined to the NIC's address.

Radio-Frequency Systems

Microwave links, satellite uplinks and downlinks, cellular phones, and wireless LAN's are all vulnerable to interception. Frequencies are published, data framing formats are standard and public, and equipment is inexpensive and readily available. As a stratagem, forget security through obscurity.

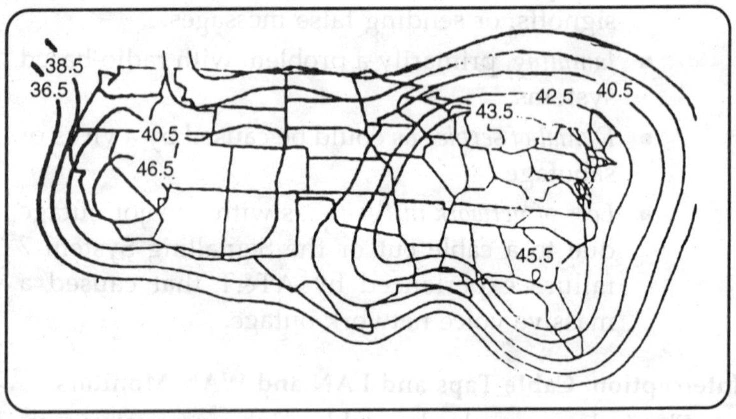

Fig. 2.1 A satellite footprint indicating signal strength by area.

The National Security Agency (NSA) reportedly has listening stations near major carrier earth stations. The former Soviet embassy has line-of-sight visibility to all of Washington, D.C., and a forest of antennas on its roof.

As shown in Fig 2.1, satellite downlinks have a "footprint" that illuminates a large portion of the earth. Receiving these signals is easy, and today the land is dotted with mushroomlike antennas doing just that.

Captain Midnight appeared uninvited on HBI by overriding HBO's satellite uplink signal. Premium cable TV downlinks from satellites are scrambled now to prevent theft of service.

More and more companies are using very small aperture terminal (VSAT) satellite transmitters and receivers, especially in the retail trade. The security of these links is vital to them.

Satellite attackers steal service by sending a very narrow-band signal up to the satellite that is then repeated through the satellite's *transponder* on the downlink. While not disturbing the main channel, the attackers are able to create a secondary channel link. The illicit link also robs the main signal of a small amount of transponder energy.

Satellite in geosynchronous orbit are threatened by more than 300 pieces of space junk *visible enough to see on radar*. In fact, satellites have had to be moved to avoid potential collisions.

Cellular phones are unencrypted and opened, as Prince Charles learned to his embarrassment. While analog receivers were supposed to go off the market in early 1994, it remains easy for a technician to modify a receiver to receive cellular transmission. Even tuning a UHF TV receiver to the high end of the band can sometimes catch cellular transmissions.

Cellular fax and the new Personal Communications Systems are just as vulnerable. (AT & T now offers Surity Transportable Cellular Telephone 9300 using Clipper-based encryption. The price is $1,695.)

Wireless LANs have varying degrees of vulnerability. Fixed-frequency systems such as Motorolas' Altair are stationary targets. Spread-spectrum systems are harder to monitor because the frequency changes constantly. However, a receiver bought from the same vendor will work, and will be passive or active as the hacker decides. All wireless LAN vendors offer optional encryption. Buy it.

Dial-in Security

Here are a few more tricks to enhance dial security.

Modems that answer calls should delay presenting carrier tones for at least ten seconds. in this way, attack dialers will see no carrier and more on.

Do not use a banner for sign-on that identifies your organisation or where you are located. Just show a message that advises the system is for authorised users only and that improper usage will be noted and intruders prosecuted to the fullest extent of the law.

Glaring

Test your dial-back system to see if it recognises dial tone. When a caller dials in and enters the right authenticator, *the dial-in line should hand up.* A moment later, the dial-back machine should go off-hook, *recognise the dial tone,* and call the user back.

Some dialers mindlessly dial back *whether they are see dial tone or not.* If the cracker stays on the line, dial tones will be ignored and the dial-back system will *think* it has reached the right caller. Crackers look for this kind of logical fault: they call it "glaring" (as in glaring unblinkingly at the port protector).

Encrypt important files. Some experts feel it is better to just encrypt everything. WAN analysers can do everything LAN analysers can do:encryption is your only protection against such attacks.

Disconnect unneeded connections to the outside world. You should know exactly how many modems are in your own as your users' hands. *A Network World* BBS program called LOGINCHK will detect a modem in a user's workstation when they log into the LAN.

Limit where a dial-in user can go once into your system. Make functions they do not need inaccessible. Obeying the need-to-know principle, do not give users *carte blanche.* Some modems used for dial-out can automatically answer as well. Automatic answering should be disabled if not needed.

Modems signals at 2,400 bits/s and below can be recorded. At the beginning of a transmission, these signals may well include an embedded password. Then they need only be played back by a masquerader to gain access. Token passwords are the only defensc.

Packet Switches

Many of the successful attacks on computer systems were through dial-up modems and packet switches. The infamous "Dalton Gang" from the Dalton School in New York's Manhattan broke into two networks, one in the United States and another in Canada in 1980. The leader of the gang was all of 13 years old, and in the eighth grade.

In Illinois, the Argonne National Laboratory was penetrated via a packet network. Attackers used default passwords on installation tapes that had not been removed.

You will recall the anonymous firm that had addresses in its virtual private network installed by the vendor for maintenance and test purposes. The customer was not informed. Ultimately, a security audit revealed their presence.

In an effort to add to the security of their packet networks, BT North America and Infonet Services Corporation have added security offerings to their services. BT's Security Products Portfolio includes the following:

- User authentication is accomplished by PIN number and dynamic password.
- Data transmitted by BTs X.25 packet-switching services is encrypted internally by BT (see Fig. 2.2).
- Users receive daily, weekly, or monthly reports that track security violations and analyse traffic patterns.
- BT offers consulting services to assess users' voice and data networks.

The Portfolio works with any application running on BT's X.25 network, including X.25, TCP/IP, and frame relay. The cost is about $6 monthly per user.

Another X.25 vendor, Infonet, offers a similar security service via its InfoLAN TCP/IP product. AT&T and Spirit currently offer only data encryption security service. CompuServe offers encrypted frame relay, a relative of ITU-TSS X.25.

These features are attractive to users because they

avoid forcing users to buy equipment or divert staff energies to these security functions.

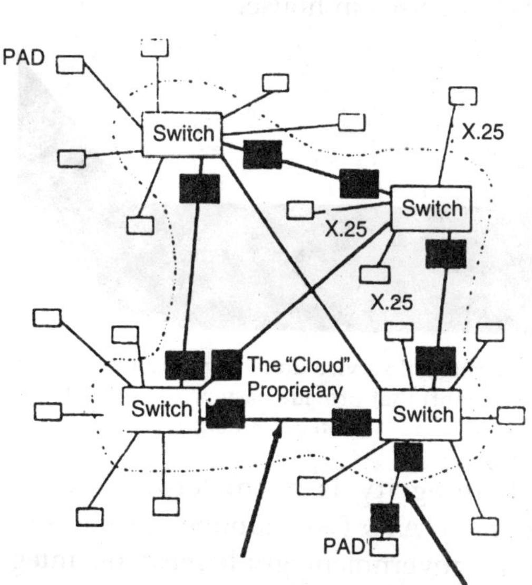

Fig. 2.2 A packet-switching network. (A PAD is a packet assembler and disassembler).

Leased Lines

Because they are static, leased lines are among the easiest to tap. Almost invariably, they are marked nicely and neatly by the telephone company. Find a circuit number beginning with FDDC or FDDN and all you need is a modem and a recording device to steal information.

Demarcation points should be in a locked room, telco 66 blocks and RJ-21x junctions blocks likewise. Encode circuit labels so that people cannot tell what they are. With their myriad of wires going everywhere, distribution frames are the perfect place to tap data. Lock them up.

T-1 or T-3 circuits have channel service units (CSUs)

with convenient plug-in ports (see Fig. 2.3) for monitors. CSUs carry many channels of data, and their data formats are easily dissected. CSUs should be locked up along with any T-1 or T-3 analyses in house.

Fig. 2.3 Many channel service units have front panel test ports (right) that provide easy access. (*Courtesy Larsecom Corp.*)

Network integrity is a concern. Until the 1984 diversification of AT&T, telephone lines were routed accordingly to government guideliness on integrity, in part due to survivability concerns in case of war. Today, outrages are tracked by the Federal Communications Commission (FCC) and the Exchange Carriers Association. Outages of 30,000 lines or more must be reported to the FCC.

Bridges, Routers, and Gateways

All these machines should be locked up (see Fig. 2.4)

Bridges

Bridges can filter addresses that pass from one side to the other, but they cannot see what the attached information is. It could be a virus. If there is a maintenance port, should be protected by a port protection device of the type. Even a simple asynchronous port meant for use directly with a VT-style terminal should be disabled when not in use, or it should be protected by password.

Bridges decrease system availability by passing along network problems from one segment to another. A broadcast storm one segment will instantly cripple another. Routers, being more aware of protocol, can detect and mitigate a storm, and so isolate the problem.

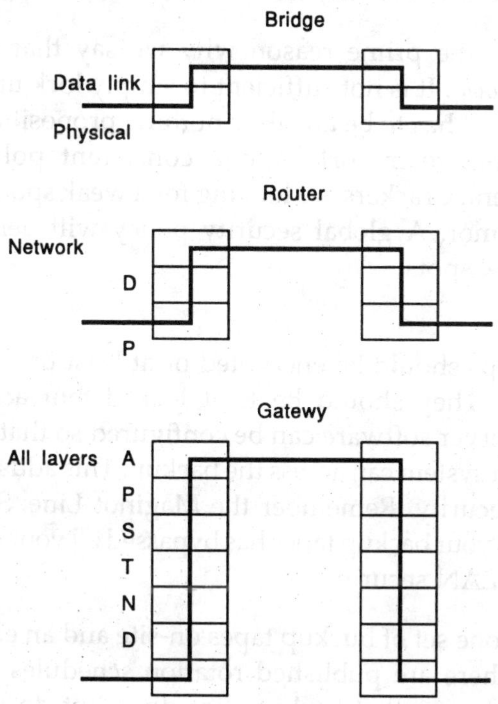

Fig. 2.4 Bridges, routers, and gateways.

Bridges can unlock a secure network if the bridge links it to an unsecured net. For instance, a caller dials in a to a LAN and breaks the fairly simple password. Any bridges connected to the LAN will allow the intruder to top from segment to to segment without restriction unless address filters are installed on the bridge to disallow source and/or destination addresses from passing through the part or all of the network. In effect the intruder has bypassed whatever security barriers are in place on the adjacent LANs with respect to dial-in security. Unless neighboring LANs are encrypted or authenticated or bridge filters are enabled, the intruder will have free rein, no matter how good the dial-in security is.

This is the prime reason why we say that security must be *global.* It is not sufficient to simply lock up part of the system; it has to be an all-or-nothing proposition, with cooperation, teamwork, and a consistent policy and commitment. Crackers are looking for a weak spot, a chink in the armor. A global security policy will deny them those weak spots.

Backups

Backups should be encrypted or at least protected by password. They should be kept locked, but accessible. Archive server software can be configured so that only an automated system can access the backup. This adds another layer of security. Remember the Maginot Line: Someone who reads your backup tapes has bypassed all your carefully designed LAN security.

Keep one set of buckup tapes on-site and an earlier set off-site. There are published rotation schedules you can follow to assure that backups are done but do not bury you in tapes. Backups edge into the category of disaster recovery, and we have noted that security and disaster recovery are intertwined.[1]

Removable Media

Many times access controls are placed on the hard disk. In ODS, these can be bypassed by placing a bootable disk in d rive A: and booting from there. Then programs like Norton Disk Doctor can capture, read, and modify disk data, amend access privileges, or change security login routines.

Diskettes that are cleared of files still contain the old data unless magnetically erased, reformatted, or randomised. Disks containing sensitive information should be encrypted using DES. Then backups of these disks will automatically be secure.

Deliberately partitioned networks can be breached by a simple diskette carried from one machine to another. An insecure network can thus contaminate one with substantial security protection.

PCs, Macintoshes, and Notebooks

Machines should be physically secured if they are important. Various vendors make straps and wire cables that secure a PC to a desktop. Notebook machines can be secured with locks when in docking adapters. Do not embed password scripts in portable machines that can be stolen.

Transborder Data Flow

As an example of the extreme, international networks use many of the above facilities. General Electric Information Services' network spans 75 cities in 30 countries. They use both DES and ANSI encryption *and* proprietary message and user authentication tools. Such a system requires sophisticated key management, advanced cryptosystems, and constant vigilance by everyone involved. It also costs lots of money.

Keeping Perspective

Once again, we do not wish to fall victim to "Maginot Line thinking." The majority of risks come from *inside* the organisation. Eyeball leaks are the best example.

As a people issue, *employee education* is the best weapon. Most people want to protect company data and they are the losers if it is compromised. Help them by keeping them aware of the need for security, so that it runs as a background program in their minds, all the time.

As one ex pert put it, "Most data thieves don't use superadvanced technologies. Instead, they sneak in through the back door." Help your people clamp those doors shut.

Review

- Network threats are basically interception, alteration, jamming, denial of service, or loss of integrity.
- LANs may be intercepted through network monitors or analysers.
- Radio-frequency systems broadcast RF waves all over, making them easy to tap.
- Dial-in systems should be as low key as possible. Delay carrier tones. Give no information in the banner except a warning.
- Packet-switching network ubiquity has given hackers a rich hacking medium.
- There is some security in packet networks since individual packets can take different paths. This makes it hard for a hacker to copy an entire message.
- Leased lines, being "nailed-up," are fixed targets for tappers.
- Bridges are relatively insecure networked *firewalls.*
- Routers are better *firewalls* to keep intruders out.
- Remove unnecessary protocols from routers.
- Gateways can be hacker targets if the hacker is knowledgeable.
- Removable media can contaminate even a secure network.
- Media should be erased to keep others from recovering files.

- In the end, the majority of leaks are internal. Using they are unintentional, but there are those that are malicious.
- Employee education remains the best security tool you have.

NOTE

1. Regis J. (Bud) Bates, *Disaster Recovery Planning: Networks, Telecommunications, and Data Communications,* McGrzw-Hill, New York, 1991; Disaster Recovery for LANs: *A Planning and Action Guide,* McGraw-Hill, New York, 1993.

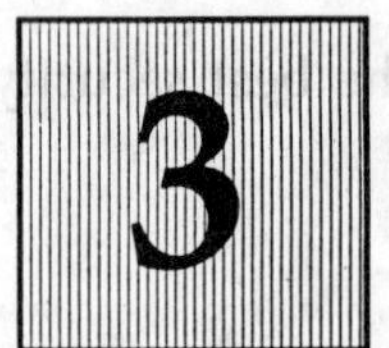

CREATING A NETWORK SECURITY POLICY

Objectives

At the end of this chapter you will be able to:

- Explain why network security plans fail and how to avoid failure
- Formulate an effective network security plan
- Identify the information needed in a quick look and its sources
- Compose an effective security questionnaire
- Outline elements of a security task force charter
- List areas to be scrutinised
- Design a workable implementation plan
- Know when security through obscurity is an appropriate policy
- Recount the inviolate rule of security

Network Security Policy

Network assets worth protecting demand a professional, organised response. That is why a network security policy is mandatory. It shows that the issue has been thought out and committed to paper. It avoids potential claims of arbitrary enforcement when the imposition of disciplinary action becomes necessary. It tells you what to do when an incident occurs. In short, a network security policy shows management that you have done your homework.

A security policy is a reference document, but it is not static. It is subject to amendment as systems and circumstances change. It should be reviewed at least annually, and more often than that if your environment changes rapidly.

From the outset, it is essential to acknowledge that executives, managers, and individual users all have security responsibilities. These responsibilities are summarised in the Tables 3.1 to 3.3

TABLE 3.1

Executive Responsibilities*

- Set the security of the organisation (nothing short of global security is sufficient).
- Allocate staff, funding, and positive incentives.
- State the value of information to your organisation.
- State your organisation's commitment to its protection.
- Make it clear that this responsibility is everyone's job.
- The above said, assign responsibility to specific individuals.
- Require computer security and awareness training.
- Hold employees personally accountable for the resources in their care.
- Monitor and assess security through external and internal audits.
- State penalties for nonadherence.
- Goal include:

  Risk reduction to an acceptable level.

  Assure operational continuity.

  Comply with applicable and regulatory requirements.

  Assure the integrity and confidentiality of information in your hands.
- As the every dimension of leadership, *you* will set the example.

* This is a brief abstract of NISTs FIPS Publication No. 500-169

Acceptable Use Policy

It is not reasonable or fair to hold people accountable for nebulous or unstated security rules. An acceptable use policy makes clear what standards will be enforced. At a minimum, an acceptable use policy should include:

- Password management, protection, and change rules
- Strictures prohibiting the illegal duplication of Software
- Antivirus policy with specific do's and do nots
- Encouragement to use screen savers and automatic log out features
- Rules regarding the use of organisational computing resources for personal use (you may wish to be a little liberal in this regard; this is an excellent way for people to learn).

TABLE 3.2

Management Responsibilities*

- Assess the consequences of a security breach in the areas for which you are responsible. This includes outright network failure due to a virus or other cause, corruption, or theft of information under your care. Risks include:
  Inability or impairment to perform necessary tasks.
  Waste, misuse, or theft of funds or resources.
  Internal and external loss of credibility.
- Be cost effective: find the right balance of acceptable risk versus dollars spent on security.
- Assess operational continuity: How long can each system you have be down before the consequences become unacceptable?
- Maintain accuracy of the data in the system.
- Maintain the necessary degree of confidentiality.
- Comply with any laws or regulatory agency directives.
- Set an acceptable use policy.

* This is a brief abstract of NIST a FIPS Publications No. 500-171.

TABLE 3.3

User Responsibilities*

- You are individually responsible for protecting the data and information in your hands. *Security is everyone's responsibility.*
- Recognise what data are sensitive. If you donot know or are not sure, *ask.*
- Even though you cannot tough it, information is an asset, sometimes a priceless asset.
- Use the resources at your disposal only for the benefit of the organisation that provided them. Do personal work on your own system. Do not use computing resources for anything illegal.
- Abide by the acceptable use policy provided by your organisation.
- Understand that *you* are accountable for what *you* do on the system.
- If you observe anything unusual, *tell your supervisor.*
- Some specifics:

  Do not share or disclose your password.

  Choose a password that would be hard to guess.

  Log off before you leave your terminal.

  Lock up sensitive information kept on disk or paper.

  Do not give others the opportunity to look over your shoulder if you are working on something sensitive.

  If someone in your area looks like they do not belong there, *speak up.* Ask them their business in your area.

  Protect equipment from theft or damage due to water, electrical surges, and the like; kept it away from cigarette smoke, food, and drinks. Know where the fire extinguishers are.

  Do backups religiously.

  Do not do things that would permit a virus to spread.

*This is a brief abstract of NIST's FIPS Publication No. 500-171.

- Penalties for violations; an annual review item; other human resources concerns.

Why Network Security Plans Fail?

If it is to be effective, a network security policy cannot be implemented by decree. Since it affects every user of the system, its reach goes far beyond the information system department's walls. A policy, no matter how sound, that is not established by a consensus of those to be governed by it is a sure way to fail. Some of these reasons for failure are shown in Table 3.4.

TABLE 3.4

Why Network Security Policies Fail

1. The policy is implemented in a vacuum or by decree.
2. It is not coordinated with other policies and the disaster recovery plan.
3. The plan or part thereof is illegal.
4. The focus is misplaced on technology and not on people.
5. The policy is not promoted or made sufficiently visible.
6. "It cannot happen here."
7. A lack of penalities makes the policy hollow and toothless.
8. A predestined sense of failure exists, e.g., "It is impossible to get our people to do this."
9. There is a failure or an inability to see the need for security policy.
10. Users may fear that they will be locked out of useful resources.
11. A lack of focus exists, exemplified by an excessively broad or too narrow a scope (e.g., people, systems, applications).
12. Lukewarm management support is given. A survey by Ernst and Young LLP found that 42 per cent of senior management in U.S. companies considered information security to be "somewhat" or "not" important. Fully 15 per cent devoted no full-time resources to security, even though more than half the respondents reported some kind of information loss. For those citing "mission-critical" applications on their LANs half said the attendant security was "unsatisfactory."

Cummins Engine Company in Columbus, Ohio has an Information Security Council consisting of volunteers from the computer, telecommunications, legal, auditing, marketing and human resources divisions. Such teamwork helped tighten mainframe security, solve an unauthorised software duplication problem, and set up an Internet application firewall. The firewall effort required telecommunications, networking, and software people to work together. In other words, it took teamwork.

At Northwest Airlines Corp., the information security division learns from the human resources department when layoffs and voluntary departures occur. Conversely, the human resources department needs assurance that this advance information will be kept confidential. All understand that disgruntled ex-employees can be a real security threat.

Northwest, also has a policy regarding the handling of files and electronic mail. Shall the mail be rerouted, returned, or inactivated? Who will inventory the files and see what must be preserved and what deleted?

As you can see, establishing and maintaining a network security policy is an interdepartmental process. It calls upon the network manager to work with other departments toward a communal goal.

As above, network security plans will not work in a vacuum. They must be integrated with overall information systems and telecommunications security policies and the disaster recovery plan. (Please do not say you do not have one.) They must be consistent with all company policies including those originating in the human resources department.

Policies must also be legal. In some states it is illegal to use a lie detector to hire an employee and illegal to monitor their telephone conversations, as many help desk and telemarketing managers do where allowed.

Security is always a people issue, not a technology issue. Properly addressed, employees will not only abide by security policy but enforce it on coworkers who stray. Improperly addressed, employees will collude with one another to get around rules they think silly, cumbersome, or arbitrary.

A dusty policy book sitting on a half does not do much to improve security. As a people issue, it must be resident in the fore-brain of every network user. This means that a network security awareness campaign must be an ongoing part of network policy.

The federal government is a superb example. You cannot go anywhere in a federal without seeing on bulletin boards promoting security. Security is firmly implanted in every employee's forebrain.

Some users think security breaches cannot happen to them. They, too, need some attitude adjustment. Computer viruses are not too common, but they do happen. If you are struck by a virus for example, publicise the experience as a way to promote sound antivirus policy. To the same extent, publicise security breaches reported in the news or trade magazines.

Policy violations have to carry a penalty or they will be ignored. The policy should state the penalty for a first infraction, such as a warning, leading up to a negative review and even dismissal. For example, restitution would be required from a person who transports a virus into the network and causes a loss.

Some managers believe the task of establishing and maintaining security is impossible because of today's dynamic distributed computing environment over which they have little control. As decision making migrates to the PC level and employees acquire notebook machines, data are on the move. Not only are data moving targets, the risk of exposure increases as our organisations become less hierarchical. Here is a classic case of misfocus, on technology and not on people. It is people who operate all these systems, wherever they are.

A few managers do not see the need for a security plan. They have difficulty in conceiving the risks. That is why it necessary to publicise losses due to security breaches. Simply because the odds favor it happening to someone else does not mean that it cannot happen to them. In that case the odds jump to 100 per cent. Upper management will want answers if there is damage to the business because of such a laissex-faire attitude.

Users bridle at a security plan that locks them out of areas where they formerly had open access. It is our job to see that security does not improperly impede employees going about their daily tasks. It is also our task to see that they do not go places where they have no need to be. We must find and maintain that balance. It is important to explain to employees that the less access they have the less exposure they take on in case of a security breach.

Policies also fail due to a lack of focus. Support for security is an apple-pie issue: it is impossible to be against security. Blanket policies inevitably fail. Tailored policies succeed and this is why we conduct an initial assessment.

Building an Effective Security Plan

The converse to the above is embodied in Table 3.5 and Fig 3.1. It is possible to build effective security plan, and the balance of this chapter is intended to illustrate how to create one.

Scope

Network security is one element of computer security and an element of overall organisational security. Early on in the process, beginning with the "quick look," decide on the scope of the inquiries to be made.

While it may be easier to deal with a limited scope, the result may be incomplete and inconsistent with the balance of the security structure. The scope of the inquiry and contemplated changes must be broad enough to fit comfortably into the larger picture, but not so broad that progress becomes impossible.

TABLE 3.5

How to Build an Effective Security Plan

- Admit that you have information requiring protection.
- Executives, managers, and users all have their role in security.
- Develop specific plans to protect your information.
- Begin at the outer edges of the information or telecommunications structure.
- Establish standards once.
- Develop consistent standards for all departments.
- Consistency will limit costs and improve productivity.
- If it is protected on the mainframe, it must be protected in a PC.
- All machines must be secured.
- Perform some kind of risk assessment, whether formal or informal.
- Maintain a global, enterprise-wide security philosophy. Global security is more effective, cheaper, and less visible to users.

The Quick Look

A quick look by a small working group is the best start toward a workable, effective network security plan. It is always wise to look before one leaps.

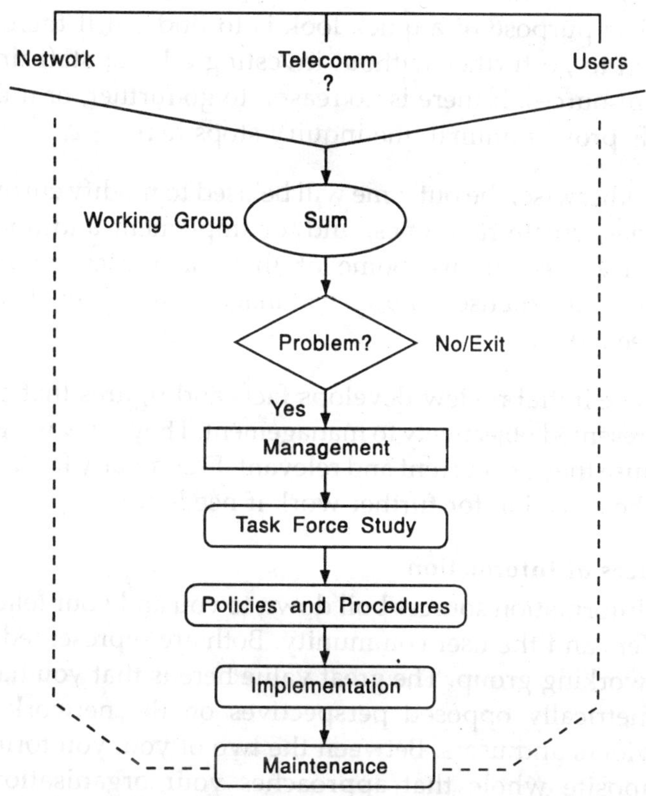

Fig. 3.1 Developing the network security plan.

An initial study avoids the trap of implementing preconceived notions as to where security is good or bad. More often than we would care to admit, those preconceived notions turn out to be off or even dead wrong. Approach the inquiry with an open mind. Let it take you where it will.

Perhaps a network security incident triggers the probe, or maybe it is just something everyone knows needs to be done. Perhaps it is in the list of projects for the year Lacking these catalysts, perhaps you need to take the initiative.

The purpose of a quick look is to find out if there is reason to go further without investing a lot of staff time and resources. If there is no reason to go further, or if the needs prove minimal, the inquiry stops here.

Otherwise, the outcome will be used to modify current policies, create new ones, and/or implement additional security precautions. Some of those activities involve significant expense, so upper management approval will be needed.

The initial review develops facts and figures that can be presented objectively to management. They carry weight because they are current and relevant. Preliminary findings set the direction for further work if needed.

Sources of Information

Information sources boil down to you and your fellow staffers and the user community. Both are represented in the working group. The great value here is that you have diametrically opposed perspectives on the network as providers and users. Between the two of you, you form a composite whole that approaches your organisation's perspective.

The User Community

People who live with the system, day in and out, get to know it pretty well. Often they know it better that the providers. (Ask any help desk analyst).

A questionnaire or survey of the user community is very useful. Assembling a questionnaire is a bit of an art form. In addition to the example in Fig. 3.2, here are some suggestions:

- State that you are conducting a network security survey and ask for their help.

The Network unit of the MIS Department is conducting a review of our security procedure in an effet to identify areas for improvement. At the same time, we are trying to find solutions that will steamline security procedures and so not interfere with your daily activities.

Would you please take a moment to answer these few questions? Thanks.

I use the following system(s):

LAN e-mail Mainframe Mini Other (specify):

WAN Windows PC or clone Macintosh

The three most important system tools that help me do my job are

1. ________________________

2. ________________________

3. ________________________

I think we are vulnerable to:

A computer virus Theft Other.__________

A hacker A major disaster

We need protective measures (specify): __________

Have you discovered a "back door" into a system that we should fix?

If so, what is it? ____________________

Do you feel the existing security is

Too restrictive Too loose Just right

Have you experienced a security problem such as a hacker or a virus? If so, what was it? ______________

If you could implement just *one* security mechanism, what would it be?

____

Your name (optional)________________

Please return to Mail Stop B-114 or a mail: survey @ unico.com

Thanks for your input. All responses will be individually evaluated.

Fig. 3.2 A sample security questionnaire example.

- Do not ask for names unless respondents wish to supply them voluntarily.
- Automate the survey: put it on a login screen and save the results into a file. It will make the survey visible, make reducing the data easier, and the cost for the entire survey will be minimal.
- If you survey on paper, send the survey to *department managers* for distribution and completion. Receiving a directive from the loss puts a special spin on the survey.
- Ask people which system (s) they use, but do not be so specific that you can identify the individual.
- Ask the user if they have noticed ways to gain system entry through unexpected paths, privileges in excess of those really needed, unusual events that might imply tampering, viruslike symptoms, laxness in controlling physical access, vulnerable systems, and servers or applications that are insecure yet whose absence could damage the organisations.

Ask *focused questions,* neither too specific and narrow nor so broad that users do not know form their answers should take. It is also important not to convey a sense of the kind of answer you would like. "Is system security satisfactory?" is a poor questions both because the user reads it in the context of the requester, and because a yes-or-no answer is possible. Use even-numbered, not odd, graduated responses. These force the user to take a position.

Check-off items on the survey are fine, but ask for measured, thoughtful responses. Indicate that the survey results will be used in a security evaluation: The time they take to answer will not be wasted. Ordinarily, publishing the result of a survey is the best way to get good response.

Yet a security survey may show weaknesses that you would rather not publicise. Instead, thank everyone for their input, indicate the response sale, and assure them that their input was used.

If it is possible to conduct personal interviews, do so. In the interest of time, it may be best to focus on managers' views but all strata of the organisation should be sampled.

Some enterprises go so far as to conduct many in-depth interviews and even focus groups. If your can afford the time and expense, that is fine. The responses will be that much better in quality.

The MIS and Telecommunications Community

Network and computer professionals must also be polled, but the smaller number of individuals involved should make it possible to obtain their major-views in one or two meetings. An agenda should be prepared to keep the discussion on track. MIS and telecommuications staff may beet separately to discuss unique issues and jointly where information and telecommunications priorities coincide or clash.

Methodology

The general form of inquiry should be the same as that applied in the last chapter: identifying assets, threats, vulnerabilities, protective measures, and responses if all else fails. This consistently applied framework allows information created in the last chapter to be mapped into a larger evaluation.

Form a Working Group

A working group consisting of information and telecommunications systems and the user community should reduce the information recieved into tabular form from the surveys and include brief summaries of other vulnerabilities noted. The working group should reach one of three conclusions:

- Nothing more than minor changes are needed.
- Changes are required but they do not call for an organisation-wide effort.
- A full-scale review plus substantial changes are required.

In the last case, a formal presentation is required to management in the format discussed.

The Network Security Task Force

If approved by management, a task force including every element of the organisation should be assembled. Subcommittees may be needed if the organisation is very large, with a representative from each of them on the task force committee itself. The subcommittees could be organised by department or by the system type to be studied (e.g., telecommunications; LANs; WANs). For focus, it may be useful to have a charter, for which a sample is shown in Table 3.6.

The task force approach can dramatic results. When the General Accounting Office issued a scathing report concerning the Resolution Trust Corporation's (RTC) security weaknesses, the report gave RTC staff the ammunition it needed to centralise access management by having each LAN user sign an access control form before gaining access. The form also determined whether the user would have wide area access as well, affixing acountability.

Deactivated IDs are found by periodically comparing the mainframe access control list to the LAN ID and master payroll list. A chronic virus problem was solved when a LAN administrator was found to be logging in from an infected PC. RTC now uses antivirus software weekly to check individual disk drives. All of this was made possible once the problems were identified and management gave its support.

TABLE 3.6

A Sample Task Force Charter

Develop appropriate controlled access to hardware, data, and applications deemed sensitive.
Within the above context, achieve end-user transparency such that user productivity is wither unaffected or improved by steamlining security procedures.
Provide flexible, modular, and adaptable security features that will not become obsolete as the organisation changes.
Develop enterprise-wide security solutions, not piecemeal ones.
Minimise the need for administrative and training overhead.
Incorporate virus prevention, detection, and recovery mechanisms.
Build in audit trail capability.
Make full use of existing security tools.
Identify where baseline and extended protection measures are needed.
Establish minimum security features that must be included in new software, hardware or computers purchased by us.

Even as the task force meets, you may note a subtle change as security awareness penetrates to the core of the organisation, rather than residing on the fringes. Group members begin to internalise the goals of security and by example, it begins to diffuse throughout every department even before a new policy is set.

Areas to be Scrutinised

The target areas for the task force or working group should include those itemised in Table 3.7. Each area is discussed individually in the following paragraphs.

Physical security. Is your building like Grand Central Station? Do people wander around whom you have never seen before? Perhaps a badge system is appropriate.

Yet badges are no solution if people do not consider security their personal responsibility. The author has visited many facilities where obtaining a badge was necessary before entry. Once inside, he could then wander around, looking officious all the while, badge in pocket (not displayed). Suitably dressed and businesslike, in 20 years he has yet to be stopped and asked. "Who are you?"

We have already noted that vulnerable points such as servers and hubs should be in restricted areas. Where do you violate this rule? Similarly, cables should not run rampant. Unused ports should be disconnected. Unused cables should be removed.

TABLE 3.7

Areas to be Scrutinised

- Physical security
- Access control
- Secure the medium
- Personnel policies
- Audits
- External media policy
- Backups
- Security agreements
- Training
- Administrative policies

Access control. We have said that group user IDs can be shared, but, individual passwords should not. Make the uniqueness of passwords a policy. Then help people carry it out by helping them pick passwords from a human-readable phonetic list. Do not let them pick excessively easy passwords or ones that have been used already. Establish a policy that sharing or writing down passwords is a security policy violation, with penalities for first and successive offenses.

Foster stale password turnover by having the system remind users that their password is getting old (90 days or more). Some systems warn the user a few times and then force the user to do so before they can continue. Others simply do not allow them in any more without contacting the system administrator. Henceforth, they will be a little more mindful (for a while) when the system first politely asks them to change their password.

As noted passwords should always be encrypted. Some systems such as NetWare 3.1X offer the option of *not* everything passwords. Remember to automatically log users out after a period of inactivity. Someone else could use their workstation.

Multiple systems create a multitude of user IDs and passwords. In such cases, it may be better to use a front-end security server to allow a single login. NetWare 4.X and Vines' StreetTalk typify directory services that maintain security as well as ease of use.

Secure the medium. Encrypt or authenticate as required. No form of wireless transmission is secure without encryption. Even the leased data circuits you rent from a common carrier may pass through microwave links somewhere along their route. It is essential to have an alternate plan in place should a backhoe dig up one of your backbone network circuits. One element of such a plan is to have two entry-exit points for the building's communications. Another is to split traffic carried between several carriers. One affected customer in the Hindscale,

III. central office disaster had backup telephone lines stationed in the false ceiling of the cafeteria. When a fire occurred, his company's staff moved to the cafeteria and resumed business. Another had a number of cellular telephones on hand for just such an emergency.

Personnel policies. Some organisations subject employees in sensitive positions to psychological screening and/or polygraph examination before and/or after hire. This may seem extreme, but database or system administrators can break your company if they are dishonest or have serious personality flaws. It is easier not to hire someone than to terminate them after a serious flaw has been discovered. A disconcerting statistic from the U.S. Department of Health and Human Services study showed that *20 per cent of the people who committed computer crimes had prior criminal records.*

Employee terminations must be handled with care. When an employee is terminated, they should be escorted out the door promptly with no further computer access allowed.

This calls for a sense of timing. An employee whose career path is about to be changed should not make the discovery that they suddenly cannot login any more before they are terminated. While acceptable from a security standpoint, the only way to let an employee go more crudely is to fire them by facsimile.

Divide responsibilities. It makes the dishonest person's task harder, but not impossible. Don Parker, a well-known security analyst, estimates that about half the cases he has investigated have involved collusion. So dividing responsibility is no panacea. Honest employees do not mind and even prefer such division as evidence of their integrity and a reduction in their personal exposure.

Publicising terminations, disciplinary actions, or prosecutions due to security violations is a psychological deterrent. It is a hardball tactic indeed, but it works. The understandable tendency to hush up an embrassing security breach only encourages hackers. Silence encourages apathy and neglect by the user community. The notion that "It cannot be a problem if it cannot be seen" is obsolete.

Audits. Much as we dislike snooping an our own people, auditing has shown itself to be a highly useful and worthwhile security technique. Be sure to publicise the fact that auditing of login activity, phone and credit card use, and so on is ongoing.

Simple awareness by supervisors and managers means a lot. A fine employee whose performance suddenly slips for no perceptible reason should trigger a warning. Aldrich Ames, the confessed spy, gave off many obvious warning signs that should have signaled his supervisors of a problem such as living beyond his means. They were either not noticed or worse ignored, until it was too late.

Something out of the ordinary routine may not mean a security laps. However, it is an unfortunate fact that most computer crimes have been discovered accidentally. An anonymous hotline or mailbox may be useful for tips, just as the Federal Aviation Administration has a "snitch line" for members of the aviation community to report problems of any kind anonymously. Many urban police departments have a similar facility.

Auditing software can produce reports by exception, send them via eletronic mail or even trip a pager. The reports may prove to be crucial evidence in court. To be able to tie events in chronological order, system clocks should be set to official time (e.g. the CBS radio network chine on the hour) and reset periodically. Many net work security managers recommend that the audit logs be reviewed daily. Though tedious, it does give the manager a clear picture of what is normal and sensitises them to abnormalities when they occur.

External media. Disks, diskettes, and tapes should all be scanned for viruses before use. Shareware and excutable program down-loads from bulletin boards should be prohibited into networked machines.

Using these programs and diskettes brought into work from home is not necessarily a crime. An excessively rigid policy baring their use precludes the use of valuable software (i.e., the *Network World* BBS utilities mentioned in Chapter 8). A too-tough policy will be ingnored or spited. Simply scan incoming material thoroughly before its use is allowed. Similar rules apply to notebooks connected to a LAN temporarily. A notebook's hard drive should be scanned before connection.

As a corollary, it may be desirable to disallow by policy the transfer of information on diskette from one network to another as a way of preventing a handheld network leak. It is important to let people know why this policy is effected in order to avoid the appearance of being arbitrary.

Backups. Backups should be performed more often if the data change more often. Several backups into the past should be kept. If a file is damaged or lost, one can go far enough back into the past to recover it. It may be necessary to go back several generations to find a backup set that is reliable.

There are many forms of backup rotation plans. Typically the rotation plan includes an older off-sets backup and more recent on-site backups. But sure to keep all backups accessible but under lock and key.

Security agreements. Every employee should receive a summary copy of his company's security policy. Employees should be required to sign a statement indicating that they will comply with the policy. It should be renewed annually, perhaps at the time of the employee's performance review. Special agreements may be needed depending on the activity in which the employee will be engaged.

Training. Training makes people aware of the security rules and helps them understand the rules and their purpose. Proper training leads to acceptance of security rules and is also a deterrent to improper behaviour. "Proper" means that the training curriculum is matched to the audience. The curricula will change depending on the system(s) used by a group and their levels in the organisation. Production workers need one kind of training, accountants need another.

Administrative tools. Organisational policy should require people to take vacation every year. One habit pattern of abusers is that they dislike, sometimes, intensely, the suggestion that they take their vacation.

The reasons are twofold. One is that someone taking over their tasks will see what they have done. Another is that they will lose ill-gotten income during their absence. Some individuals who do not take vacations lead undimensional lives and this is sometimes read properly as a sign of instability. Insisting that such people take their vacation moves them toward being at least two-dimensional and so toward greater stability.

The Product: Policies and Procedures

Philosophies beget policies that take real form as procedures. If a person uses an eight-letter password as a mandated procedure, then they are implementing a policy whose philosophy is that long passwords are safer.

Procedures eliminate ambiguity, provide direction, and are measurable as to accomplishment or not.

The task force may classify information resources as to criticality and mandate backups, redundancy, or encryption as a matter of policy for systems at a given level. Such a policy encourages that appropriate security measures will be applied even after the task force disbands.

Wherever possible, make use of existing policies. There is little point in reinventing the wheel. Policy changes also require a change in behaviour. Users find this unsettling and disruptive. Keep it simple.

Implementing Policies and Procedures

The hardest part of a network security policy is the execution. This is not so much the addition of encryption to a WAN, but much more a matter of changing peoples' behavior.

Old habits die hard. Replacing them with new habits takes time, skill, and patience. Often, a year will pass before the new policies really take hold. It takes persistence by the network manager and indeed all of management. This includes the folks at the top. Start your implementation with them in a half-day or so briefing. An announcement of the new policy by the boss is a way of making the new policy official and visible.

Since the help desk has so much user contact, they should be briefed next. Spend a day or even two (not consecutive) days telling them about the security provisions you have made in operating systems. NOSs, audit tools, and antivirus software, with an emphasis on how it will affect their operating environment.

Changes in procedures and policies should be discussed

to let them know that there has been a shift. The help desk people set the example for users, so they must understand the policies and procedures thoroughly. A full copy of the network security plan should be in the help desk area, as well as a summary for quick reference. Users should also receive a half-day briefing as to policies and how their systems and work procedures will be affected. It is appropriate and convenient to have all employee sign their security agreements at the end of their respective sessions.

"Security Through Obscurity"

Does it still have a place? The quasiexotic nature of what we do as communications people does indeed provide a measure of security. Some adversaries are deterred by the ever-growing complexity of the communications environment, but not all. A small, intelligent number of hackers have developed techniques as exotic as our own systems. In addition, they have a strong profit motive, where as we are trying to keep what we have earned. We are in a defensive posture while they are on the offensive.

It is no longer adequate to assume that your dial-in ports are safe because they are lost among millions of telephone numbers. Attack dialers obsoleted the needle-in-the-haystack approach. Nor is it sufficient to presume that your IPX/SPX or TCP/IP LAN protocol will save you. Analysers can chop packets into byte-size slices any way the hacker wants them.

Reliance on being a needle in a haystack as a threat deterrent grows less reliable every day. If you insist that you are too small an organisation for hackers to bother with, then you have let the vandals through the outer perimeter.

The inviolate NLYGD Rule.

NEVER LET YOUR GUARD DOWN

Security Awareness

After all the planning work above, there is more. As noted earlier, security must be embedded in the forebrain. One achievers this by implementing an ongoing security awareness program. It takes the form of articles in company and help desk newsletters, posters, stickers on terminals, and newspaper articles about recent virus attacks, computer frauds, and hacker attacks being circulated.

The objective is always the same: to keep security in the forebrain. The message, too, is the same: It *can* happen.

> "So much of security is mine set." GREG SCOTT, *Computing Services Manager, Oregon State University Corvallis, Oreg.*

Review

- Network security plans fail mainly because people forget they are dealing with a people and not a technology issue.
- An effective network security plan comes to pass because it has management's backing, and because all involved have a say in its formulation. The perception of being arbitrary, high-handed, or insensitive must be avoided at all costs.
- A quick look includes the views of users and network staff.
- Effective security questionnaires are brief, specific, and unbiased.
- A security task force charter gives members direction and a means to achieve their mission.
- There are at least ten areas of scrutiny; they are technical, personnel-related, and administrative in nature.

- A network security plan is half the task.
- Implementation is the other, and harder, half.
- The reason for the difficulty with implementation is that changing peoples' habits takes time.
- High and higher technology provides some obscurity, but the earlier forms are no longer effective.
- *Never, never let your guard down.*

MANAGING NDS SECURITY

Certification Objectives

1. Introduction to NDS Security
2. Controlling Directory Access with Object Trustee and NDS Rights Assignments
3. NDS Default Rights
4. NDS Rights Inheritances
5. Blocking inherited Rights
6. Determining an Object's Effective Rights
7. Guidelines for Implementing NDS Security
8. Troubleshooting NDS Security

To manage a NetWare 5 network effectively, you must have a thorough understanding of Novell Directory Services (NDS). By virtue of their integration, NDS and NetWare 5 are nearly synonymous.

On the surface, NDS appears to be simply a directory of the NetWare network resources and users. Much like an inventory, the NDS directory seems to be a mere listing of what is on the network. However, as we'll see, that is just a surface evaluation. In fact, NDS provides a comprehensive set of administrative tools that can manage a global enterprise network as easily as a single network with a few client workstations. NDS provides a single seat of administrations, regardless of the number of users, workstations, or servers. Additionally, NDS will secure the resources on the network.

CERTIFICATION OBJECTIVE

Introduction to NDS Security

NDS provides security to an enterprise network by creating a hierarchical tree structure for all network resources. Since all network resources reside in a single structure, they can also be managed from a single seat of administration. The NetWare Administrator program is the primary means for the single seat of administration for NetWare 5. An administrator who has access to the entire NDS tree can execute the NetWare Administrator program from any network client and manage any network resource, even if that resource is located halfway around the world.

Three types of objects exist in the NDS tree structure:

- *[Root]* The root of the NDS tree, contains either Country or Organisation container objects and very limited types of leaf objects
- *Container objects.* Objects that can contain either container objects or leaf objects
- *Leaf objects.* Objects that represent a network resource

The NDS container objects organise the leaf objects into manageable units. Designs for NDS trees can be based on location, business unit, or other functional criteria, which demonstrates the flexibility of the NDS architecture.

NDS security is established for each leaf object within the NDS tree. Security can be applied at a container object level, which then influence the security of the child contained within the parent container, thus simplifying the management of security.

CERTIFICATION OBJECTIVE 4.2

Controlling Directory Access with Object Trustee and NDS Rights Assignments

Security in the NDS tree is established for an object by granting *rights* to objects in the tree. When an object has been granted rights to another object, it is considered a *trustee* of the object. An object must be a trustee in order to access other network resources. Objects can also be trustees of themselves. Objects and property rights do not necessarily have to be granted to other objects. For example, each user is a User object within the NDS tree and each printer is a Printer object in the NDS tree. For a user to print to a printer, the user object must be granted appropriate rights to the Printing objects. By the same token, an object must be granted the appropriate rights to itself in order to make changes to its own status.

The NetWare Administrator is the tool used to administer the NDS tree from any workstation within the enterprise network. One major advantage of the hierarchical structure is the capability to create container administrator. Distributing administrators in this way creates a hierarchical administration structure, which is comparable to the way enterprises organise their network managers.

Container administrators are User objects that have been granted Supervisor rights to a container, but not any other container objects within the tree. Figure 4.1 illustrates this process. Using an Organisational Role object for the container administrators allows multiple container administrators to have the same rights and facilities alternating administrators. For example, when creating a container administrator with Supervisor rights granted to the Organisational Role, the Organisational Role will have Supervisor rights to the file system of any servers within that container. In order to create a container administrator using on Organisational Role object, follow Exercise 4.1.

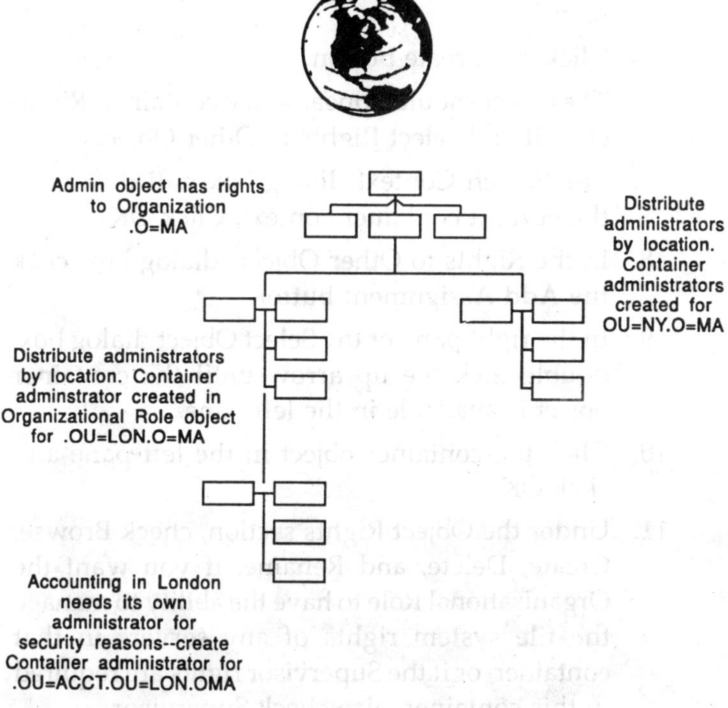

Fig. 4.1 Container Administration

Exercise 4.1

Creating a Container Administrator

1. In the NetWare Administrator, browse to the container that will be administered. The Organisational Role object should be created in the container where it will have administrative rights.
2. Choose the Object menu and select Create.

3. Select Organisational Role from the Object Creation dialog box.
4. Give the Organisational Role an appropriate name.
5. Click the Create button.
6. The object should appear in the container. Right-click it and select Rights to Other Objects.
7. The Search Context dialog box will default to the current container context. Click OK.
8. In the Rights to Other Objects dialog box, click the Add Assignment button.
9. In the right pane of the Select Object dialog box, double-click the up arrow until the container object is available in the left pane.
10. Click the container object in the left pane and click OK.
11. Under the Object Rights section, check Browse, Create, Delete, and Rename. If you want the Organisational Role to have the ability to manage the file system rights of any servers in that container, or if the Supervisor rights are required in this container, also check Supervisor.
12. Click OK to save the new object rights.
13. Double click the Organisational Role object to view its details.
14. Click the button with three dots next to the Occupant box. Using this button will allow the addition of multiple occupants to the Organisational Role object.
15. Click Add.
16. Select the User objects in the left pane of the next dialog, which will occupy the Organisational

Role object. It may be necessary to navigate the tree in the right-pane window if the User objects do not exist in the same container context. Click OK. Repeat until all occupants are added.

17. The User objects will appear in the Occupant dialog box. Click OK.
18. Click OK to save the occupant changes to the Organisational Role object.

Exam Watch

The administrator can change object rights by selecting either Rights to Other Objects or Trustees of this Object. The Rights to Other Objects will show the NDS rights that the current object has granted to other objects in the tree. The Trustees of this Object will display the objects that have been granted rights to the currently selected object in the tree.

Object Rights

In Exercise 4.1, the container administrator was grunted objects rights to all objects within a container. Object rights are shown in Table 4.1.

The object rights are the basic rights needed to change objectives within the tree. When a User object is granted rights within the NDS tree, the user who logs in with that User object ID will have those same rights to the other objects in the tree. The Browse rights are the most important, since they allow the basic access of seeing the objects in the tree. If a user does not have the Browse rights to objects, they will not be able to view the resource or any of its details. In fact, the Browse rights are required for a user to even know whether a resource is on the network.

TABLE 4.1

Object Rights

Right	*Abbreviation*	*Function*
Supervisor	S	All object rights are included in the Supervisor rights. In addition, the rights to the file system of any servers in the context where this rights is applied are included. The Supervisor rights imply all property rights to that object.
Browse	B	Browse objects in the NDS tree.
Create	C	Create new child objects. Applicable only to container objects (leaf objects cannot have objects created in them).
Delete	D	Delete objects such as User objects in the NDS tree. Requires Write property rights for all properties.
Rename	R	Rename objects in the NDS tree.
Inheritable	I	Describes whether a right can be inherited by lower-level objects in the NDS tree. This right is enabled only for [Root] and container objects.

Property Rights

Each NDS object has specific attributes or *properties*, which are listed in Table 4.2. An example of a User object property is the Login Script property, which represents the user login script. Before an object can view or modify a property, it must have rights to that property. For example, a user object must be granted Write property rights to the User object's own Login Script property in order for that user to be able to create, modify, and use their own user login script.

Exam Watch

By default, NDS objects are not automatically granted full rights to their own properties.

TABLE 4.2

Property Rights

Right	*Abbreviation*	*Function*
Supervisor	S	Entails all other property rights to that property.
Compare	C	Allows comparison of the property value to a given value in order to return a true or false.
Read	R	Allows viewing of the property value. The Read rights incorporate the Compare rights.
Write	W	Allows modification, addition, or deletion of any property value.
Add Self	A	When granted this right the trustees object can add or remove itself as a value of the applicable property. The Write rights are implied by this right.

As illustrated in Figure 4.2, a trustee can be granted property rights to all properties or to selected properties. Using a selected property method for granting rights can fine-tune security. Note that in some cases a trustee can inherit all property rights from a parent object and be granted explicit rights to select properties.

CERTIFICATION OBJECTIVE 4.3

NDS Default Rights

When NDS installs the first time, it provides object and property rights that are generally sufficient for the network resource access required by users. Although the default NDS rights are available to users when they log in, these right are not necessarily rights granted explicitly to User object. Instead, some of the rights are granted to other objects to allow user access to the network.

The default rights for NDS may be extended when an NDS-aware application is installed. The NDS-aware application may add a default object or property right for its application to work appropriately. More often, that new default right is applicable to a new property or object within the NDS scheme. For example, when Z.E.N. works is installed, the Workstation Manager adds several properties to container objects. One of these properties is the WM: Registered Workstation property. The container object is then granted the default property rights of Write, Compare, and Read to the WM: Registered Workstation property. This enables the importing of Workstation object into the NDS tree. These rights are not part of NDS prior to Z.E.N. works installation.

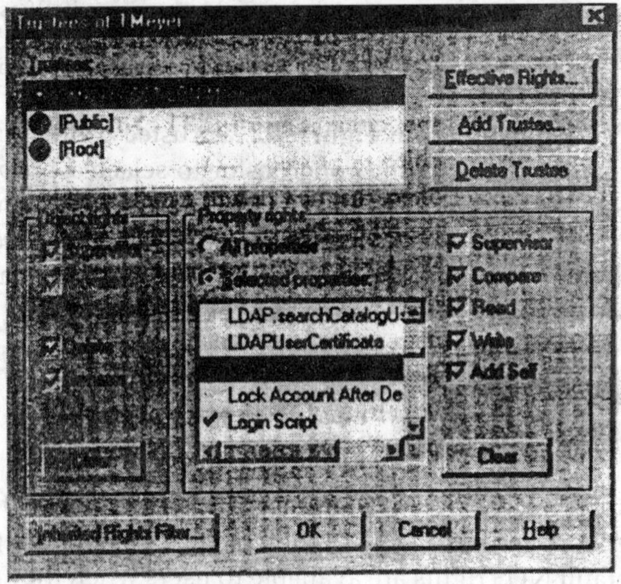

Fig. 4.2 Object and property rights

[Public] Trustee

The [Public] trustee is not an object within the NDS

tree. It is a special trustee rights holder that is applicable to all users, whether or not they have logged in to the network. By default, then, each User object is security equivalent to [Public]. Any rights granted to [Public] are valid rights for everyone. Since [Public] is not an object within the NDS tree, but a trustee rights holder, the only way to grant to revoke rights to [Public[is to right-click the object and select Trustees of this Object. Then, after selecting Add Trustee, the [Public] trustee will appear as one of the available trustee options. Both object rights and property rights can be granted to [Public] in this way.

Default Object Rights

The [Public] trustee is granted Brows Object rights to the [Root] of the NDS tree. This right enables users to see objects in the tree before and after logging in. Users are thus able to browse for their context before they log in.

The NDS tree [Root] is granted the Browse and Inheritable object rights to all NDPS [printer, and non-NDPS Printer, Print Queue, and Print Server objects. This enables enterprise-wide printing.

When a User object is created, it is granted the Browse Object rights to itself. This allows the User object to "see" itself in the NDS tree.

Default Property Rights

By defaulter, the [Public] trustee is granted Read rights to each User object's Default Server property and Read rights to each NetWare Server objects' Network Address property. The combination of these two rights allows the login process to locate the default server name, and, secondarily, to find that server on the network through its Network Address property.

[Root] is granted Read property rights to each User object's Group Membership property and Read property rights to each User object's Network Address property. [Root] is also granted Read property rights to each Group object's Members property. These property rights enable members of groups to be located on the network.

Container objects are granted Read property rights to their own Login Script property. This is required for User objects to inherit that right at login and be able to read and execute the container login script. Container objects are also granted Read property rights to the Print Job Configuration property. Since some print job configurations are created for a container, inheritance allows User objects to use the print job configuration.

New User objects are granted the following property rights that enable the object to read its own properties and modify the user login script and user print job configuration:

- Read property rights to all of the User object's own property.
- Read and Write property rights to the User object's own login script.
- Read and Write property rights to the User object's own Print Job Configuration property.

CERTIFICATION OBJECTIVE

NDS Rights Inheritance

Inheritance is the facility by which NDS passes rights (object rights, property rights, and/or file system rights) from one object to another. Rights flow down the NDS tree from as high as the NDS tree [Root] through container objects to leaf objects. Figure 4.3 displays object rights inheritance, which could apply to any NDS object.

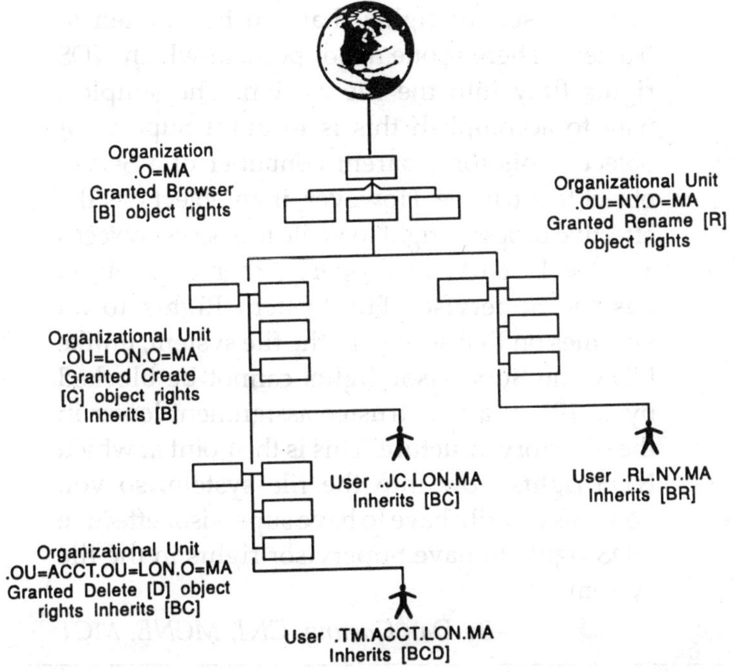

Fig. 4.3 Inherited object rights.

An *explicit right* is a trustee assignment that has been granted to an object directly. An *inherited right* is a trustee assignment that was granted to an upper-level object and is received by the lower-level object through the NDS flow-down relationship. Property rights can be inherited the same as object rights. Figure 4.4 demonstrates a property right inheritance using a Login Script property as an example.

FROM THE CLASSROOM

When NDS Rights Flow into the File System

NDS security and NetWare file system security are administered separately. They even have different sets of rights that can be granted to trustees. There is one major point at which NDS rights flow into the file system. The simplest way to accomplish this is to grant Supervisor object rights for a parent container of a Server object to a trustee. However, if an object has the effective property right to Write to a Server object's Trustee List (ACL) property, then that object has the Supervisor File System Rights to all volumes on that server. In the file system, unlike NDS, the Supervisor rights cannot be blocked by an IRF or a new trustee assignment lower in the directory structure. This is the point at which NDS rights flow into the file system, so you don't necessarily have to have supervisor effective NDS rights to have Supervisor rights in the file system.

—By Dan Cheung, CNI, MCNE, MCT

Security Equivalence

It is easy to confuse *security equivalence* with inheritance, but they are not the same. Although both are methods of passing rights from one object to another, security equivalence applies when an object is made equivalent to another object's explicit trustee assignments, but not to that object's inherited rights. Inheritance flows down the tree such that inherited rights can continue to be inherited by even further lower-level objects.

User objects are security equivalent to the Group objects of which they are members. Any NDS object can be granted explicit security equivalence to any other NDS object, leaf, or container through the Security Equal To property page of the object that will receive new rights form other objects. There is an implicit security equivalence between a leaf object and its direct parent container object.

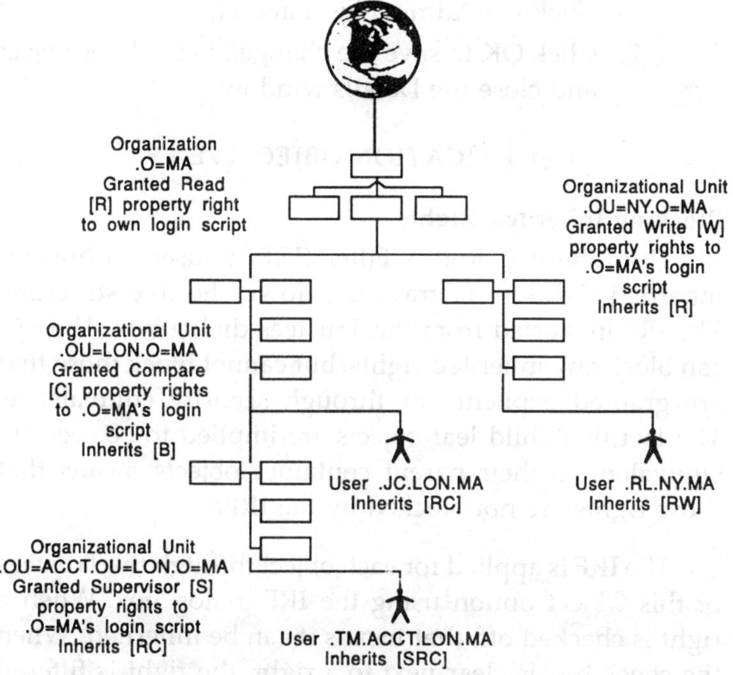

Fig. 4.4 Property rights inheritance

Exercise 4.2

Making a User Security Equivalent to the Admin Object

1. In the NetWare Administrator, navigate the tree until you locate the User object.
2. Double-click the User object to display its details. Alternatively, highlight the User object, choose the Object menu, and select Details or right-click the User object and select Details from the pop-up menu.
3. Click the Security Equal to property page.
4. Click the Add button.
5. Navigate through the tree until the Admin object is displayed in the left-pane window.

6. Click the Admin object and click OK.
7. Click OK to save the changes to the User object and close the Details window.

CERTIFICATION OBJECTIVE 4.5

Blocking Inherited Rights

The Inherited Rights Filter (IRF) is used to prevent inherited rights from traveling down the tree structure. The IRF in started from the Trustees dialog box. The IRF can block any inherited rights, but cannot block those that are granted explicitly or through security equivalence. The fact that child leaf objects are implied to be security equivalent to their parent container objects means that those rights are not blocked by the IRF.

The IRF is applied for each object through the Trustees of this Object option using the IRF dialog box. When a right is checked off, that means it can be inherited. When the check box is clear next to a right, the right is filtered out and cannot be inherited.

Both object rights and property rights can be filtered. The rights that this affect are those that are inherited from upper level containers. When a rights is explicitly granted, even though the IRF blocks that right, the object still has that right. For example, when setting up a container administrator, you may want to filter out upper-level administrators. The container administrator would make sure to have explicit supervisor rights to the container and then set up an IRF for the container with the Supervisor rights check box cleared. Although the IRF does not allow the Supervisor right, the container administrator has an explicit trustee assignment and maintains Supervisor capabilities.

QUESTIONS AND ANSWERS

Janet is the network administrator for an aeronautical design firm. The research and development business unit of the firm works on some projects that are considered top secret within the company. Janet has been informed that all resources within the R and D organisational unit are to be hidden form all other users. How can Janet achieve this but still be able to manage it herself?

The R and D organisational unit will require Browse object rights and Supervisor object rights (since it implies the Browse right) to be filtered for all objects in the tree. Before filtering the Browse right, Janet will need to explicitly grant her own User object the Browse and Supervisor rights to that container unit.

CERTIFICATION OBJECTIVE 4.6

Determining an Object's Effective Rights

Effective rights are those rights that are in effect for any NDS object. Effective rights can be inherited, filtered out, explicitly granted, or applied through security equivalence.

Effective rights are the combination of all the rights available to an object. Determining the effective rights is a matter of adding and subtracting the appropriate rights. The following steps should give you the effective rights for an object:

1. Determine the inherited rights.
2. Subtract the rights that are filtered out by the IRF.
3. Add the rights explicitly granted to the object.
4. Add the rights granted through security equivalence; that is, parent container object rights, group rights of which the object is a member,

and explicit rights of objects to which this object is, Security Equal To.

Exam Watch

Effective rights = (inherited rights — IRF) + explicit trustee assignments + Security equivalence rights.

In Figure 4.9 each user has been granted identical rights at the organisation level. In figuring what object rights the users have within their own contexts, the IRF will apply. The NY context IRF allows [SB] to flow down. That means that user RL's inherited rights are [SB]. Add RL's explicit [SB] and security equivalence [CDR] rights to obtain the effective rights of [SBCDR] within RL's own context. User object JC will have the inherited [SBCDR] rights filtered by the IRF [B]. Add the security equivalence rights of [CDR] and no explicit rights for the effective rights of [BCDR]. For User object TM, all rights except Brows are filtered out though the .LON.MA IRF. Then the [B] rights are also allowed to be inherited through the .ACCT.LON.MA IRF. Through security equivalence, the TM user receives both [B]and [C]. The final effective rights for TM in that context are [BC].

QUESTIONS AND ANSWERS

Marian is a network administrative who has been tasked with ensuring that the printers on F3 are not able to be seen by any users except the on that floor. However, both Marian and the president on Floor 2 need supervisor access to the printer. The NDS tree has two organisational units beneath the SEC organisation: EastBldg and WestBldg. Beneath EastBldg, there are three organisation units: Floor 1, Floor 2, and Floor 3. Beneath WestBldg, there are three organisational units: Basement, Floor 1, and Floor 2. How can Marian set this up?

Marian granted the Floor 3. EastBldg.SEC container object explicit Browse rights to the Printer objects. Since all users within the container object are implied security equivalent, they were able to access he printers. Marian also created a group that contained her own User object and the president's User object, and granted explicit Browse and Supervisor rights to the printers. Finally, marian created an IRF on each Printer object that filtered out the Browse object rights.

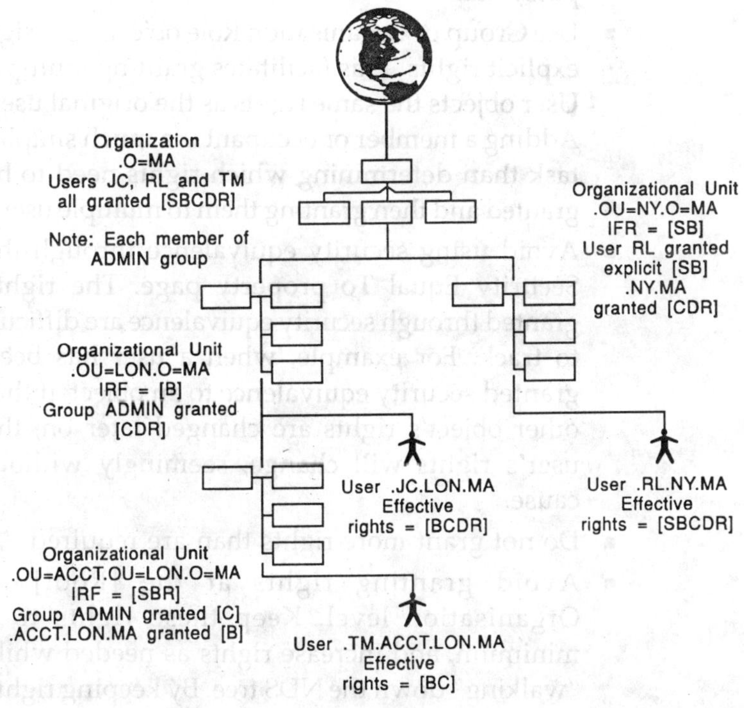

Fig. 4.5 IRF and effective rights.

CERTIFICATION OBJECT 4.7

Guidelines for Implementing NDS Security

NDS security is the key to keeping enterprise network resources protected. When implementing NDS security, it is best to follow some basic guidelines:

- Do not depend on the default Admin object for the administrative login. Instead, create multiple administrator objects with names that are not necessarily indicative of their administrative capabilities. After creating the administrators, disable the Admin abject so that hackers, or the merely curious, do not attempt to find its password.
- Use Group or Organisation Role objects to assign explicit rights. This facilitates granting multiple User objects the same rights as the original user. Adding a member or occupant is a much simpler task than determining which rights need to be granted and then granting them to multiple users.
- Avoid using security equivalence through the Security Equal To property page. The rights granted through security equivalence are difficult to track. For example, when a user has been granted security equivalence to an object, if that other object's rights are changed later on, the user's rights will change, seemingly without cause.
- Do not grant more rights than are required.
- Avoid granting rights at the [Root] or Organisation level. Keep these rights to a minimum, and increase rights as needed while "walking" down the NDS tree. By keeping rights to a minimum at the upper levels of the tree, it is easier to control inheritance without IRFs.

- Avoid using IRFs, except where absolutely necessary. When there are security problems, many times in troubleshooting the problem the IRF is forgotten, and the problem goes unsolved or managed by granting too many rights when it was not required.
- Beware of assigning rights to the [Public] Trustee. Any rights assigned to the [Public] Trustee are available to users who have not yet logged into the network.

CERTIFICATION OBJECTIVE 4.8

Troubleshooting NDS Security

On the Job

If NDS security has been planned prior to implementation, it is much less likely to require troubleshooting.

There is a basic four-step model to troubleshooting NDS security:

1. Gather information
2. Develop a plan of attack
3. Execute the plan
4. Document the solution or return to Step 1 and start over.

The first step is to gather information about the security problem. What is the user attempting to do? Does the user have too much access? Does the user have too little access? Is the security of another object the problem?

The history of the problem is valuable in troubleshooting. Did this problem always exist, or did the security work before and now has changed? When did the problem start occurring? Have any changes to network security been made around this time?

If the security worked before and has suddenly changed, the plan of attack should concentrate on the changes that were made during the same time period. If the problem has always existed, the plan of attack would most likely be to start with a layout of the effective rights for both objects and properties as they apply to the target NDS objects.

If there were prior security changes, the plan execution would most likely reverse the security changes and test the results. If the problem has always existed, the plan would be to determine:

- Which effective rights are required
- Which effective rights are actually there
- Which rights must be added or removed

Then the plan would be to change the rights so that the correct effective rights are in effect, and then to verify that they are the correct rights.

Finally, the verified solution should be documented to avoid the same issue from recurring.

CERTIFICATION SUMMARY

Novell Directory Service (NDS) is the key to network security. NDS is set up as a hierarchical tree consisting of container and leaf objects. The container objects organise the leaf objects into the hierarchy, and each object has properties.

NDS security is implemented by assigning trustee rights to the NDS objects or the properties of those objects. The object rights are Supervisor [S], Browse [B], Create [C], Delete [D], Rename [R], and Inherited [I]. Object rights apply to actions that can be done to the object themselves, not to the values within those objects. The only exception to this rule is that the Supervisor right will allow actions to be taken on the object's properties.

Property rights are Supervisor [S], Compare [C], Read [R], Write [W], and Add Self [A]. The supervisor right includes all other rights. Property rights are required for an NDS object to view or modify the values of an object's property.

When NDS installs the first time, it includes some default security assignments that are designed to allow users the flexibility and access required to use the network. These rights are applicable to a special trustee, the [Public] Trustee. The [Public] Trustee is not an object, but a trustee assignment that is automatically granted to all users, whether or not they have logged in to the network.

NDS object and property rights can flow down the NDS tree and be *inherited* by objects. Although similar, security equivalence is the application of rights through making one object equal to the explicit trustee assignments hat have been granted to another object.

Inherited rights can be blocked through the use of an Inherited Rights Filter (IRF). However, the IRF does not block rights that have been granted through security equivalence.

Effective rights are the trustee assignments in effect when an object is being accessed by another object. The effective rights are calculated by adding the inherited rights, subtracting the IRF blocked rights, and adding the explicit trustee assignments and the rights granted through security equivalence.

There is a four-step process for troubleshooting NDS security problems:

1. Gather the information.
2. Develop a plan of attack.
3. Execute the plan.
4. Document the results or return to Step 1.

Two-Minute Drill

- NDS provides security to an enterprise network by creating a hierarchical tree structure for all network resources to reside in. All network resources reside in a single structure and can be managed form a single seat of administration. The NetWare Administrator programme is the primary means for the single seat of administration or NetWare 5. An administrator who has access to the entire NDS tree can execute the NetWare Administrator programme from any network client and manage any network resource.
- Three types of object exist in the NDS tree structure: [Root], container objects, and leaf objects. The NDS Container objects organise the leaf object into manageable units. Designs for NDS trees can be based on location, business unit, or other functional criteria.
- NDS security is established for each leaf object within the NDS tree. Security can be applied at a container object level, which then influences the security of the child objects contained within the parent container.
- Security in the NDS tree is established for an object by granting rights to objects in the tree. When an object has been granted rights to another object, it is considered a trustee of the object. An object must be a trustee in order to access other network resources. Objects can also be trustees

of themselves. Object and property rights do not necessarily have to be granted to other objects.

- Container administrators are User objects that have been granted Supervisor rights to a container object and all the objects within that container, but not to any other container objects within the tree.
- The object rights are the basic rights needed to change objects within the tree. When a User object is granted rights within the NDS tree, the user who logs in with that User object ID will have those same rights to the other objects in the tree. The Browse rights are the most important, since it allows the basic access of seeing the objects in the tree.
- Each NDS object has specific attributes or properties. An example of a User object property is the Login Script property, which represents the user login script.
- A trustee can be granted property rights to all properties or to selected properties. Using a selected property method for granting rights can fine-tune security. In some cases, a trustee can inherit all property rights from a parent object and be granted explicit rights to selected properties.
- When NDS installs the first time, it provides object and property rights that are generally sufficient for the network resource access required by users. Although the default NDS rights are available to users when they log in, these rights are not necessarily rights granted explicitly to User objects. Instead, some of the rights are granted to other objects to allow user access to the network. The default rights for NDS may be

extended when and NDS-aware application is installed.

- The [Public] trustee is not an object within the NDS tree. It is a special trustee rights holder that is applicable to all users, whether or not they have logged in to the network yet. By default, then, each User object is security equivalent to [Public]. Any rights granted to [Public] are valid rights for everyone.
- The [Public] trustee is granted Browse Object rights to the [Root] of the NDS tree. This right enables users to see objects in the tree before and after logging in. Users are thus able to browse for their context before they log in.
- By default, the [Public] trustee is granted Read rights to each User object's Default Server property and Read rights to each NetWare Server object's network address property. The combination of these two rights allows the login process to locate the default server name and find that server on the network through its Network Address property.
- Inheritance is the facility by which NDS passes rights (object rights, property rights, and/or file system rights) from one object to another. Right flows down the NDS tree form as high as the NDS tree [Root] through container objects to leaf objects.
- An explicit right is a trustee assignment that has been granted to an object directly. An *Inherited right* is a trustee assignment that was granted to an upper level object and is received by the lower-level object through the NDS flow-down relationship. Property rights can be inherited the same as object rights.

- It is easy to confuse security equivalence with inheritance. Security equivalence applies when an object is made equivalent to another object's explicit trustee assignments, but not to that object's inherited rights.
- User objects are security equivalent to the Group object of which they are members. Any NDS object can be granted explicit security equivalence to any other NDS object, leaf, or container through the Security Equal To property page of the object that will receive new rights form other objects. There is an implied security equivalence between a leaf object and its direct parent container object.
- The Inherited Rights Filter (IRF) is used to prevent inherited rights from traveling down the tree structure. The IRF is started from the Trustes dialog box. The IRF can block any inherited rights, but cannot block those that are granted explicitly or through security equivalence.
- Effective rights are those rights that are in effect for any NDS object. Effective rights can be inherited, filtered out, explicitly granted, or applied through security equivalence. Effective rights are the combination of all the rights available to an object. Determining the effective rights is a matter of adding and subtracting the appropriate rights.
- NDS security is the key to keeping enterprise network resources protected. When implementing NDS security, it is best to follow some basic guidelines: Do not depend on the default Admin, object for the administration login. Use Group or Organisational Role objects to assign explicit rights. Avoid using security equivalence through the Security Equal To property page. Do not

grant more rights than are required. Avoid using IRDs, except where absolutely necessary. Beware of assigning rights to the [Public] Trustee.

- There is a basic four-step model to troubleshooting NDS security:
  1. Gather information.
  2. Develop a plan of attack.
  3. Execute the plan.
  4. Document the solution or return to Step 1 and start over.

Self Test

The Self-Test questions will help you measure your understanding of the material presented in this chapter. Read all the choices carefully, as there may be more than one correct answer. Select all correct answers for each question.

1. How does NDS establish security?
   A. Through rights for container objects
   B. Through trustee assignments for User objects
   C. Through rights granted for each NDS object
   D. Through file system rights

2. What is the term for an object that has bene granted rights to another object?
   A. Security equivalence
   B. Trustee
   C. Inherited Rights Filter
   D. Effective rights

3. Which of the following objects facilitates applying rights to multiple users?
   A. Organisational Role
   B. User object

C. Workstation policy
D. User policy

4. Which of the following is not an object right?
   A. Supervisor [S]
   B. Create [C]
   C. Browse [B]
   D. Read [R]

5. Which of the following is not a property right?
   A. Create [C]
   B. Read [R]
   C. Write [W]
   D. Supervisor [S]

6. George wants to allow every user, whether logged in or not, to be able to print to the graphics printer. Aside from enabling anyone to be able to place print jobs in the queue, how can he accomplish this?
   A. NDS will not support this.
   B. George can grant the [S] object right of the printer to the [Root].
   C. George can grant the [B] object right of the Printer objects to [Public].
   D. George can grant the [SBCDR] object rights of the Printer objects to the group "Everyone."

7. What is the default object right granted to [Public] for the tree [Root].
   A. Supervisor [S]
   B. Browse [B]
   C. Create [C]
   D. Delete [D]

8. What are the default rights for a User object to its own Login Script property?
   A. Read [R] and Compare [C}
   B. Supervisor [S] and Read [R]
   C. Write [W] and Add Self [A]
   D. Read [R] and Write [W]

9. What is the method through which rights flow down the NDS tree?
   A. Security equivalence
   B. Inheritance
   C. Trustee assignments
   D. Inherited Rights Filter

10. What is the method through which an object is granted the same right as another object's explicit trustee assignments?
    A. Security equivalence
    B. Inheritance
    C. Trustee assignments
    D. Inherited Rights Filter

11. What is use to block inherited rights?
    A. Explicit security equivalence
    B. Implied security equivalence
    C. Trustee assignments
    D. Inherited Rights Filter

12. What are the actual rights that an NDS object has when it is accessing another object?
    A. Trustee assignments
    B. Inherited rights
    C. Effective rights
    D. Security equivalence rights

13. When determining the effective rights, which are subtracted?
    A. Inherited rights
    B. Trustee assignments
    C. Implicit security equivalence
    D. IRF

14. Aaron is a network administrator who has changed the rights for a User object. The next morning, three other users call Aaron to complain that there were problems with network access. Aaron called the user whose rights he changed and finds that there are no problems. What may have happened? Select the best option.
    A. Someone else changed those three users' rights.
    B. A group that all three users belonged to was deleted.
    C. The users depended on the security equivalence to the changed user.
    D. A change was made to the Organisation container object.

15. Which of the following is not a troubleshooting step?
    A. Create a test security scenario.
    B. Gather information.
    C. Document the solution.
    D. Execute a plan of attack.

NETWORK SERVICES

CERTIFICATION OBJECTIVES

1. Networking Technologies
2. Network Services
3. Network Management

In this chapter you will learn a great deal about networking as a whole, not only in logic, but in physical nature as well. The Networking Technologies exam is one of the most challenging because the topics covered don't lend themselves to a "hands-on" approach. For the Network Administration exam you can pull down field or lab experience, but the Networking Technologies questions challenge you to know what makes a network function, both at a software and hardware level. Furthermore, much of the material must be memorised, as anyone who has taken this exam will tell you.

CERTIFICATION OBJECTIVE 5.1

Networking Technologies

The basic task of networking is the sharing of information between two entities. When two people talk to each other and share information, they are networking. In the computerworld the sharing of information and services is also known as networking. Services are included in this definition because, for example, printing and Internet access are services that can be provided by a computer to another computer on a network.

Before computer networks were available to share information and services, people had to use disks and switch boxes. The term "sneaker net" used to be a very popular one describing the sharing of files by copying to a floppy disk and "running" it to another computer. The thing to remember about networking in a computer environment is that you must have at least two things (usually computers) that want to share information. You then need a medium for them to communicate over. This medium can be a network cable, or possibly even a wireless connection. There are different types of networking that fall into different networking models, which we will look at now.

Computer Networking Models

The technologies of networking are broken down into three areas:

1. Centralised computing
2. Distributed computing
3. Collaborative computing

There are also two areas to look at with networking services; client/server and client/network. We will look at each of these briefly. The exam may not ask directly about these areas, but this knowledge will help you better understand exactly what makes a network tick.

A mainframe computer is the heart of *centralised computing*. In a centralised computing environment, you have a series of terminals attached to a mainframe computer that handles all the service and computing work. The terminals are nothing more than input/output devices. In a computer today, the CPU what handles all of the processing.

Distributed computing is what you see more today. The processing tasks are shared between the workstation and the server. The workstation has its own processing capabilities and the server also has processing capabilities.

Collaborative computing is when two or more computers share in processing the same task, which can help in load balancing. The type of computing is more common when there are servers doing different parts of the same applications.

The services area has two categories. The first is the client/server approach, which is the most common network service platform in use today. The *client/server* network consists of workstations that are computers and servers that are computers. The distributed computing model conforms to this kind of network service environment. The way that applications are handled can be distinct in different environments. In some cases the application will run completely on the workstation, and the data is saved on the server. An example of this is a word processing program where the data is saved in the user's directory on the server. Another way applications can be handles is with a front end on the workstation and a back end on the server. An example of this is a database program that has a client piece that runs on the workstation. The back end on the server does much of the database processing.

In a *client/network* approach, the workstation logs into a set of services, not a particular server. This is what Novell Directory Services is and how NetWare can work for you.

Network Sizes

There are three different computer network sizes:

1. Local Area Network (LAN)
2. Metropolitan Area Network (MAN)
3. Wide Area Network (WAN)

Novell only hits on two of the three. The MAN is rarely used anymore. LAN and WAN are terms you have probably heard before. A LAN typically does not exceed 10 kilometers. A LAN is usually for a small company, building, or location. LAN speeds are measured in megabits per second.

A WAN is a group of LANs. WANs can span a city, country, or even the world. WAN speeds are measured in kilobits per second. WANs are broken down into enterprise and global. An *enterprise network* is what connects LANs of a single organisation. A *global network* is similar to the Internet in that it connects various LANs of the same organisation at different locations.

Network Components

Every network requires things to do considered a network:

1. Two or more entities with information to share
2. A common communications to share
3. Rules for communicating

The way these things come together is in network services, transmission media, and protocols. When two or more individuals share something, they use *network services.* In order for communication to happen you need a *transmission medium* such as a cable, satellite, or infrared connection. Communicating across a medium is one step in communication. If the receiving party cannot understand you, then there is no communication. This is where protocols come into play. *Protocols* are the rules that enable communication to happen.

CERTIFICATION OBJECTIVE 5.2

Network Services

Network services are a combination of hardware and software that is shared by networked computers. Within the computer industry there are service requestors and service providers. *Service providers* are a combination of hardware and software that provide services or fulfill a particular role. For the CNE, remember that servers are service providers. They provide only services. The *service requestor* requests from service providers. For the CNE, remember that workstations/clients are service requestors.

The other piece to network services is the peer relationship between computers. Sometimes you will see an environment where a computer fills both roles of service provider and service requestor. These enable *peer-to-peer networking* the computers request services from peer servers and provide services to other peers requesting services Windows 95 is an example of an operating system that has built-in peer-to-peer networking capabilities.

Now that we know that there are service providers, service requestors, and peers we can break network services into two distinct categories:

1. Server centric
2. Peer-to-peer networking

Server-centric networks are more common, and NetWare is an example of the type of software that enables a computer to provide network services. There are strict guidelines as to what a computer does in a server centric environment. Each computer fills the role of either a service requestor or service provider. In a server-centric environment one computer cannot fill both roles. In a *peer-to-peer* environment a computer can be either a requestor, a provider, or both.

File Services

File services provide the ability to move, back up, synchronise, and handle general everyday file storage and management. One of the main functions of file services is file transfer. File transfer is any service that handles saving, retrieving, and moving of files for network clients. Another function of file services is file storage and data migration. There are different types of storage that you may see on the exam:

- **Online storage** Storage devices containing data that is immediately available to the computer, such as hard drives.
- **Nearline storage** Can be a CD-ROM jukebox or a carousel, which isn't immediately available but does not require the user to do anything special to access it.
- **Offline storage** Removable tape cartridges fall into this category. This requires a user to insert the tape to get to the data.

The main thing that you need to know for the exam regarding file services is when to implement them. You must decide when to use the various type of storage in your network. I cannot explain in detail here when to use them because of all of the different possibilities when it comes to network services. I will give you the information for you to make your own inferences.

There is also also *file update synchronization,* which allows us to have multiple copies of file, and the operating system will synchronize our files to the most current. There is one drawback here though. If both files change, we currently cannot merge the changes from both, only the newer of the two. The most basic feature in a network requires the use of file services. For the exam, know that these functions are in order to do most file management functions.

Print Services

Print services allow us to print, fax, and copy across the network. These services provide an important function of networking. For example, sharing, printers on a network helps reduce costs because not everyone needs their own printer.

The functions associated with print services revolve around allowing multiple users to access a printer, along with queuing those requests. With the distributed print services, management of printing and configuration is integrated into NDS. True communication between the workstation and the printer via the network allows distributed print services to work. Centralised administration and almost automatic serup and configuration of the printer drivers on the workstation are key benefits of distributed print services.

Exam Watch

Make sure you understand when network print services should be implemented. There are so many different scenarios that it is hard to tell you exact ways to do things. From the information you'll be given in the questions, came up with your own inference as to when to implement print services. If you need to share a printer, fax capabilities, or copying functions, then print services will be used.

Message Services

Message services bring e-mail to mind, but it actually

includes much more. Not only does messaging give you e-mail, but it also gives us the ability to transfer graphics, audio, video, and binary information. This allows for integrated voice and e-mail and workgroup applications. One thing to consider when choosing to implement messaging services is your LAN or WAN speed. Video and audio can consume a lot of bandwidth, while simple e-mail and voice mail usually do not consume a lot of bandwidth. If e-mail, audio, or video will be transmitted across the network, you need to have messaging services in place.

Application Services

Application services run applications for clients. Sounds simple, doesn't it? You may wonder why we don't see file services doing this piece. File services handle the transfer of data. Application services transfer the processing power from the client to a server to run the application. Processing power can also be shared, as it can in file services.

This service has a couple of functions. Server specialisation is a big one. One server may handle your voice mail system or your telephone switch. This service also allows for scalability and growth because applications today may be on their own separate server. If this is the case and your application is suffering due to high demands, you could simply upgrade the server or get a new, higher performing server to give the application more processing power. This way, will servers do not need to be upgraded simultaneously, thus saving money and resources. If you find that you will need to run applications from your servers or do basic application execution across the network, then application services will be used.

Database Services

This is another area where specilaisation is important.

Database services provide a server with the ability to process and handle the database back end for clients. Most databases are client/server, which means that the processing is divided up between the server and the client.

There are two aspects of database services to be concerned with for the exam: distributed data and replication. *Distributed data* is a way to break the database into smaller units while making it look one large database. This makes for cooperative processing between various computers. *Replication* enables multiple copies of a database. This can be more efficient, since the database can be maintained and accessed locally. The challenge with using replication is synchronizing all the copies into one so that data is kept current. One other advantage to this is the fault tolerance provided by having multiple copies. In environments with large SQL database applications, for example, database services are used.

CERTIFICATION OBJECTIVE 5.3

Network Management

Being a good administrator includes managing the network. The network management scheme can be broken down into five areas, which were on the original 200 Series and may be on the new 565 exam. We will look at each briefly.

Configuration Management

Configuration management is the tracking and controlling of inventories, software distribution, service agreements, service requests, and procurement files. The main goal of network management is to track and keep records on past, current, and future network configuration. Good documentation is vital to servicing and maintaining your network.

Fault Management

Fault management involves everything an administrator does to prevent, diagnose, test, and repair network failures. The main goal is to isolate faults in the network quickly to keep it functioning. Good fault management will not guarantee a network without problems but it will help identify problems before they become unmanageable or catastrophic.

Security Management

Every network needs *security management* to protect it from physical harm and unauthorised use of valuable data. This covers securing the operating system and the hardware as well. Locating your servers in an area that everyone has access to gives them a chance to get their hands on the server physically, potentially causing intentional or accidental harm. Securing the operating system and file system prevents unauthorised people from accessing information.

Accounting Management

Accounting management is concerned with the tracking and evaluating of network costs and how they affect your current and future business. Knowing the trade-off between performance and cost for improved performance are important to maintaining a successful and up-to-date network.

Performance Management

As an administrator keeping an eye on how the network performs is vital to success. *Performance management* and fault management go hand-in-hand. Identifying bottlenecks, performing trend analysis, and making future performance predictions are the major components to performance management.

Certification Summary

As stated in beginning of this chapter, this exam is not a given easy pass, even though you might think it would be straightforward. Preparing for this exam is nothing more than pure memorisation.

In this chapter we looked briefly at the basic axiom of networking: sharing information. To have a network with computers you need three things: two or computers who want to share something, a medium to transmit the communication, and rules to govern the communication. These boil down to network services, transmission medium, and protocols.

We also looked at the different networking models: centralised computing, distributed computing, and collaborative computing.

There are different network sizes: LAN and WAN. A LAN is local to a building or campus, while a WAN can span a country or the world. We also looked at server-centric environment a computer is either a service requestor or service provider. In a peer-to-peer environment computers can fill both roles simultaneously.

One other area that you may see on the exam is the different types of services in networking. File services manage files; moving, backing up, and synchronizing them. Print services allow network users to print, fax, and copy across the network. Messaging services give us not only e-mail, but voice mail and the ability to transfer graphics, audio, and video. Application services allow users to run the applications from the network. Database services manage the front-end and back-end processing of database applications. We looked briefly at distributed data and replication.

Network Management was on the original 200 exam, and we briefly looked at the different areas; configuration management, fault management security management, account management, and security management.

Two-Minute Drill

- ❑ The basic task of networking is the sharing of information between two entities.
- ❑ The technologies of networking are broken down into three areas; centralised computing, distributed computing, and collaborative computing.
- ❑ A mainframe computer is the heart of *centralised computing*. In a centralised computing environment, you have a series of terminals attached to a mainframe computer that handles all the service and computing work.
- ❑ In *distributed computing,* the processing tasks are shared between the workstation and the server. The workstation has its own processing capabilities, and the server also has processing capabilities.
- ❑ *Collaborative computing* is when two or more computers share in processing the same task, which can help in load balancing. This type of computing is more common when there are servers doing different parts of the same applications.
- ❑ There are three different computer network sizes: Local Area Network (LAN), Metropolitan Area Network (MAN), and Wide Area Network (WAN).
- ❑ Every network requires certain things to be considered a network: two or more entities with

information to share; a common communications pathway; and rules for communicating.

- There are three types of storage: online storage, nearline storage, and offline storage.
- *Distributed data* is a way to break the database into smaller units while making it look like one large database. This makes for cooperative processing between various computers.
- *Replication* enables multiple copies of database. This can be more efficient, since the database can be maintained and accessed locally.
- *Configuration management* is the tracking and controlling of inventories, software distribution, service agreements, service requests, and procurement files.
- *Fault management* involves everything an administrator does to prevent, diagnose, test, and repair network failures.

Self Test

The Self-Test questions will help you measure your understanding of the material presented in this chapter. Read all the choices carefully, as there may be more than one correct answer. Select all correct answers for each questions.

1. What three things are needed for a network? (Choose all that apply.)
   A. Two more computers that need to share something
   B. A communication medium
   C. Rules for communication
   D. A rules medium
2. Which of the following is not a computer networking mode?

A. Collaborative
B. Synchronized
C. Centralised
D. Distributed

3. Which type of computer networking model has a mainframe computer at the heart of the network?
   A. Collaborative
   B. Centralised
   C. Synchronised
   D. Distributed

4. Which network does not usually exceed 10 kilometers in size?
   A. LAM
   B. WAN
   C. MAN
   D. PAN

5. What gives us the rules needed to communicate successfully on a network?
   A. Two or more computers that need to share something
   B. The transmission medium
   C. The protocols
   D. The network packets

6. What are the two distinct categories of network services? (Choose all that apply.)
   A. Server mainframe
   B. Server centric
   C. Peer-to-peer
   D. Client/server

7. What are the three types of storage in file services? (Choose all that apply.)

A. Online storage
B. Offline storage
C. Internal storage
D. Nearline storage

8. Which type of storage with file services would include a CD-ROM jukebox?
A. Online storage
B. Offline storage
C. Internal storage
D. Nearline storage

9. Which service gives us the ability to fax or copy documents across the network?
A. File services
B. Print services
C. Message services
D. Backup services

10. Which service enables video and audio to be transferred across the network?
A. File services
B. Print services
C. Message services
D. Mackup services

TRANSMISSION MEDIA AND CONNECTIONS

As we looked at previously, the three things necessary to make a network. One of these was a transmission medium for the clients to communicate across. No communication will happen across a network unless a communications medium carries the signals.

If there is one thing that you will troubleshoot a lot, it is your transmission media. There are different types of transmission media and this is what we will look at here. We will discuss cost factors as well as cable media types and types of wireless media. We will decide the different types of hardware that may be involved in how your network is connected to itself and possibly to the outside world.

CERTIFICATION OBJECTIVE

Media Types

When selecting media for a computer network there are a few factors to keep in mind:

- Cost
- Ease of installation
- Capacity
- Attenuation
- Immunity from interference

Cost

The cost of the media is an important consideration when confronted with other possible choices. When comparing different transmission media, it is useful to make a chart listing each of the choices, side by side. Certain implementations may cost more, or less, depending on the layout of the facility, the number of workstations, and other factors. You can make some assumptions regarding the cost per foot, for example, of the medium itself. This will give an estimated cost and help you decide which medium you will use.

Installation

Ease of installing the cable is another important factor to consider. Often a third-party company will do the installation for you, but you still have to consider the difficulty in installing media types. The more difficult something is to install, the more likely the cable provider is to charge you more.

Capacity

The *capacity* refers to what a transmission medium can support for data transfer. Referred to frequently as *throughput,* the capacity varies from cable type to cable type or wireless type to wireless type. Bandwidth is measured in hertz or cycles per second that a medium can physically accommodate. This is one area that can be a bottleneck in your network if you're not careful in choosing the transmission medium.

Attenuation

Different types of transmission media can transport information for only a certain distance before they start encountering problems, such as signals becoming weak, a distortion in the information the farther it travels, and generally losing their clarity. This is known as *attenuation.*

When a signal attenuates, it loses strength or becomes unreadable by the receiver.

Electromagnetic Interference

With any electrical equipment there is a chance for interference from other electrical items, including the atmosphere and the weather. *Electromagnetic interference* occurs when the signal in the transmission media is interfered with by other electronic signals, which ends up distorting the signal to the point that receiver cannot successfully interpret the information.

CERTIFICATION OBJECTIVE

Cable Media

Now that we've looked at the considerations that must be made when selecting a transmission medium, we will look at the different types of cable media. Cable media use electronic signals or light conducted across copper or glass to communicate from one end to the other. There are three main types. The first is called *twisted-pair cable,* which is a series of individual copper cables encased in plastic. There is also *coaxial cable,* which is similar to what we use today for television and VCR connections. The last and the most expensive is *fiber-optic cable,* which is made up of glass or plastic fibers.

Twisted-Pair Cable

Twisted-pair is the most common type of cable us d today in computer networking. Used heavily in LAN systems, twisted-pair cable uses a series of individually wrapped copper wires encased in a plastic sheathing. Each cable is individually encased in plastic and then the overall outer shell is plastic as well. Each cable inside is twisted together with another. Most cable today comes with eight cables or wires, making four pairs. The cable is twisted to cut down on crosstalk.*Crosstalk* is when two wires in close proximity inadvertently share information due to interfering with each other. Figure 6.1 shows a simple example of twisted-pair cable.

Twisted pair cabling is made up of 22-or 26.gauge copper wire. There are two types of twisted-pair cable:

- Shielded twisted-pair (STP)
- Unshielded twisted-pair (UTP)

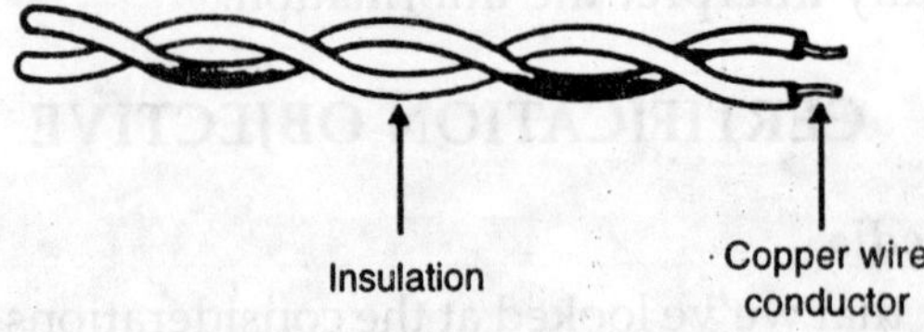

Fig. 6.1 Twisted-Pair Cabling

Unshielded is the more common of the two types of twisted-pair. Unshielded twisted-pair is a series of pairs of wires twisted together with their own distinct plastic insulation, and then the group of wires are encased in a plastic sheathing that holds all the other wires together as shown in Figure 6.2.

There are five types of twisted-pair cabling as ranked by the Electrical Industries Association:

- *Category 1(CAT 1)* Low speed data and voice; less than 4 Mbps
- *Category 2 (CAT 2)* Low speed data and voice; less than 4 Mbps
- *Category 3 (CAT 3)* Data; 10-16 Mbps (100 possible)
- *Category 4 (CAT 4)* Data: less than or equal to 20 Mbps
- *Category 5 (CAT 5)* Data: High speed 100 Mbps

Typically, twisted-pair cable consists of RJ-45 or RJ-11 ends. RJ-11 ends, are what you see for most telephones. RJ-45 is similar but wider than the RJ-11 connector. RJ-45 has an 8-pin connection and RJ-11 has a 4-pin connection.

When considering the factors we described earlier in this chapter, we see the following:

- Cost Less expensive than other forms of transmission media.
- Installation Installation is easy and necessary equipment is relatively inexpensive.
- Capacity UTP can support from 1 Megabit per second to 1 Gigabit per second at distances of 100 Meters. Most common are 10 Mps and 100 Mbps.
- Attenuation UTP attenuates more quickly than other type due to the copper conductor. For this reason, distance is limited.
- Interference The copper conductor is very susceptible to interference from outside signals.

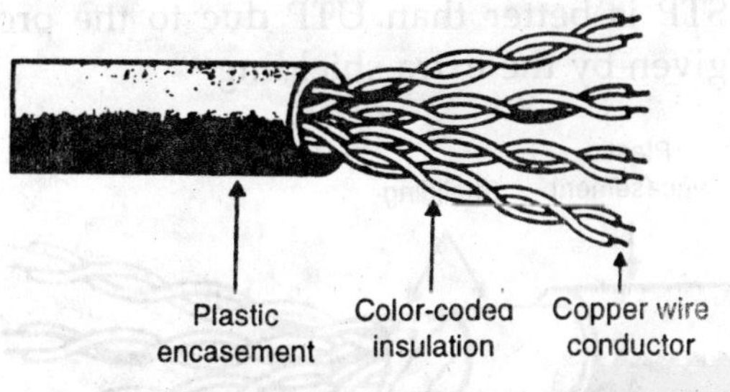

Fig. 6.2 Unshielded twisted-pair cable

Shielded twisted-pair cable is similar in features to UTP. The main difference is the extra shielding that STP has. Figure 6.3 illustrates this difference.

Shielded twisted-pair cable has enhanced protection with a foil wrap and extra shielding outside the individual twists inside the cable. The consideration for STP are as follows;

- **Cost More.** More expensive than UTP but less expensive than other forms of transmission media like coax and fiber.
- **Installation.** Similar to UTP but there are a few other considerations. Certain STP implementations will use special connectors. STP also requires an electrical ground like that of coax.
- **Capacity**. STP can support from 500 Megabits per second at distances of 100 meters. The most common is 16 Mbps. This is not widely implemented at over 155 Mbps.
- **Attenuation.** STP attenuates more quickly than other types due to the copper conductor. For this reason, distance is limited.
- **Interference.** The copper conductor is very susceptible to interference from outside signals. STP is better than UTP due to the protection given by the extra shielding.

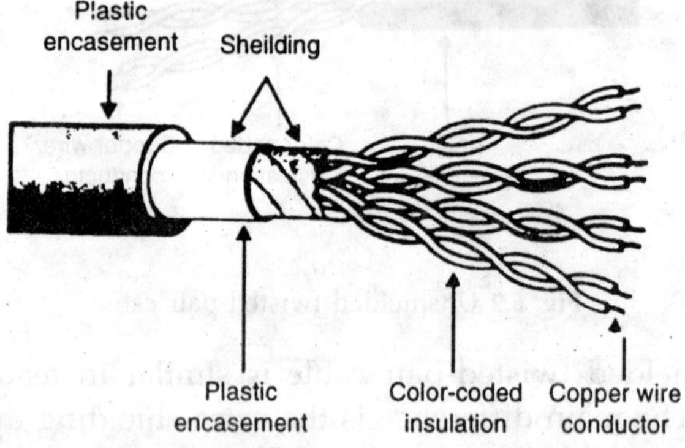

Fig. 6.3 Shielded twisted-pair cable

Coaxial Cable

Coaxial cable is made up of two conductors that share a common axis. This is where the name comes from. Figure 6.4 shows an example of coaxial cable.

The inside of the cable is made up of a solid or stranded copper wire typically surrounded by foam. Next is an outer wire mesh tube that further protects the signal travelling along the inner wire. The outside is a tougher plastic encasement that protects all the inner components.

There are different types of coax that are used in computer networking. The main difference is the ohm ratings and size standard:

- 50 OHM RG-8/RG-11 (Thick Ethernet)
- 50 OHM RG-58 (Thin Ethernet)
- 75 OHM RG-59 (Cable Television)
- 93 OHM RG-62 (ARCNet)

When connecting coaxial cables the most common type of connection is a T-connector. Another type of connection that is used is the "vampire" tap.

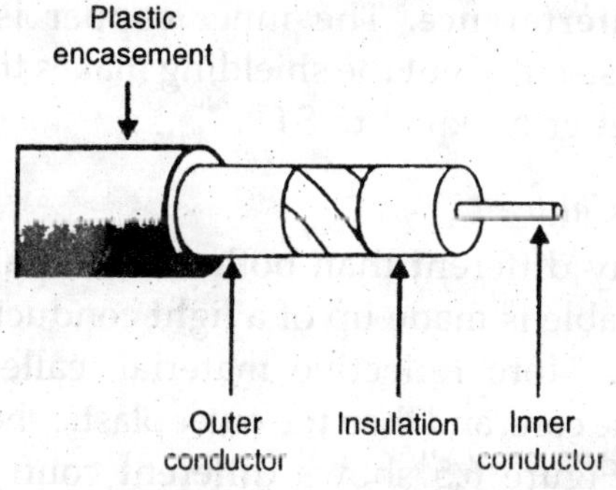

Fig. 6.4. Coaxial cable

T-connectors are more generally used, since thick coax is no longer common. Remember in either ca se, the cable has to be grounded on one end only and terminated on both ends. If the cable isn't grounded and terminated, you will not be able to successfully communicate across the medium. Coax has the following considerations.

- **Cost.** Increases as the cables get bigger in diameter and depends on the construction of the internal conductor. This coax is relatively inexpensive (less than STP and CAT 5 UTP). Thick coax can be more expensive than STP or UTP.
- **Installation.** The initial installation of coax is easy. Most of the coax cabling situations use one long cable (referred to as a drop) that connects each computer to the network.
- **Capacity.** Current limitations allow for transmission speeds somewhere between twisted-pair and fiber-optic cables. The most common speed is 10 Mbps.
- **Attenuation.** The attenuation of coax is less than either form of twisted pair. Nowadays distance in the thousands of meters is possible.
- **Interference.** The inner copper is limited in resistance but the shielding makes the resistance better or equal to STP.

Fiber-Optic Cable

Distinctly different than both twisted-pair and coax, fiber-optic cable is made up of a light conducting glass or plastic core. More reflective material, called cladding, surrounds the core, and then the outer plastic sheath protects the inside. Figure 6.5 shows different configurations of fiber-optic cable.

Common types of fiber-optic cable include the following:

- 8.3 micron core/125 micron cladding single-mode
- 62.5 micron core/125 micron cladding multimode
- 50 micron core/125 micron cladding multimode
- 100 micron core/140 micron cladding multimode

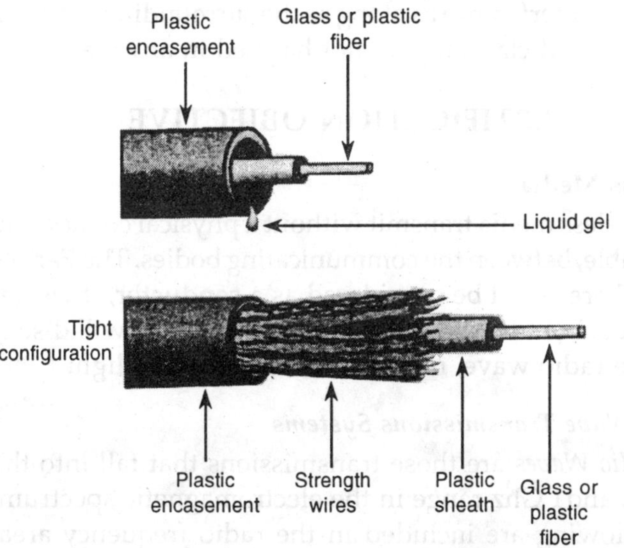

Fig. 6.5 Fiber-optic cable

When deciding on a transmission medium consider the following:

- **Cost.** Fiber cable used to be much more expensive than coax or twisted-pair but the costs are coming down. The major cost is doing the installation.
- **Installation.** Installation is much more challenging than with coax or twisted-pair.
- **Capacity.** The optical nature of fiber allows for high bandwidth over great distances. The current capacity is 100 Mbps to 2 Gbps at distances of 2 to 25 kilometers.

- **Attenuation.** Attenuation is much less in fiber-optic cables versus any copper conductor cables. Attenuation for fiber-optic cable is measured in kilometers.
- **Interference.** Due to the fact that signal is a light transmission, there is no chance for interference as along as the surrounding covering and cladding are not harmed in any way.

CERTIFICATION OBJECTIVE

Wireless Media

Wireless media transmit without a physical connection, like a cable, between the communicating bodies. The Earth's atmosphere could be considered as a conductor, if we get technical about it. The three common types we will discus here are radio wave, microwave, and infrared light.

Radio Wave Transmissions Systems

Radio Waves are those transmissions that fall into the 10 KHz and1 Ghz range in the electromagnetic spectrum. The following are included in the radio frequency area; short wave radio. VHF television and FM radio, and UHF television and radio.

Attenuation can be the result of atmospheric conditions with radio wave transmission. Foggy, rainy, or cloudy weather can greatly affect how well the information can be transmitted. There are three classes of radio wave transmissions:

1. Low-power single frequency
2. High-power single frequency
3. Spread spectrum

The *low-power* radio wave is a single frequency that is used in a short distance over an open area. The *high-power* radio is also a single frequency transmission that can cover greater distances and even go through dense materials. *Spread spectrum* uses multiple frequencies simultaneously.

Microwave Transmission Systems

Microwave transmission systems exist in the form of terrestrial and satellite. *Terrestrial systems* are earth-based and use directional parabolic antennas.

The terrestrial-based transmission is direct or line of sight, which means it requires an unobstructed path. *Satellite microwave systems* communicate from a directional parabolic antenna to a geosynchronous satellite in Earth's orbit.

Infrared Transmission Systems

Another type of wireless media is *infrared,* which uses light emitting diodes or injection laser diodes to transmit signals. The receiving piece is a photodiode. The signal can be line of sight or it can be received after being bounced off walls. This type of medium is most useful in small, open environments. The signal cannot penetrate walls or other opaque surfaces.

CERTIFICATION OBJECTIVE

Public and Private Network Services

One other common a area that is often overlooked is the public or private networks available for connecting people all over the world. You may not see this on the exam, but it is worth mentioning. The reason I say that is the Internet is a combination of public and private networks. The most commonly known network is the *public switched telephone network* (PSTN). A dial-up account uses the PSTN to communicate with various routers and service providers all over the country. T1 and T3 lines and other forms of connectivity with telephone companies make up the backbone of what we call the Internet.

CERTIFICATION OBJECTIVE

Transmission Media Connections

In order to use the mediums available, whether it is cable or wireless, we need a way to connect the computer to the medium. This is where the transmission media connection comes into play.

Network Connectivity Devices

There are various types of network connectivity devices. From the ends that go on a cable to the network interface board that is installed in your computer you have a series of different types of network connectivity devices that you use every day. The ones we will look at here are transmission media connectors, network interface boards, repeaters, hubs, bridges, and multiplexes. The first three are what we use to connect a computer to a media segment. The other four are for connecting various media segments to form a larger network.

Transmission Media Connectors

There are different kinds of transmission media connectors that we can use to connect to a cable segment on the network. Figure 6.6 shows some common media connectors.

The transmission media connector is what plugs into the connection on the back of the computer. The RJ-45 connector is commonly used with twisted-pair. The BNC connector is commonly used with coaxial cable. The DB-25 and DB-15 connectors are commonly used for printers and serial connections, respectively.

Network Interface Boards

Network Interface Boards are the logic boards that allow us to connect the transmission media connector to our computer and form the physical path in order to communicate. The *Network Interface Board,* more commonly known as a Network Interface Card (NIC), has an internal transceiver that converts the information from the computer into a form that can travel across the medium.

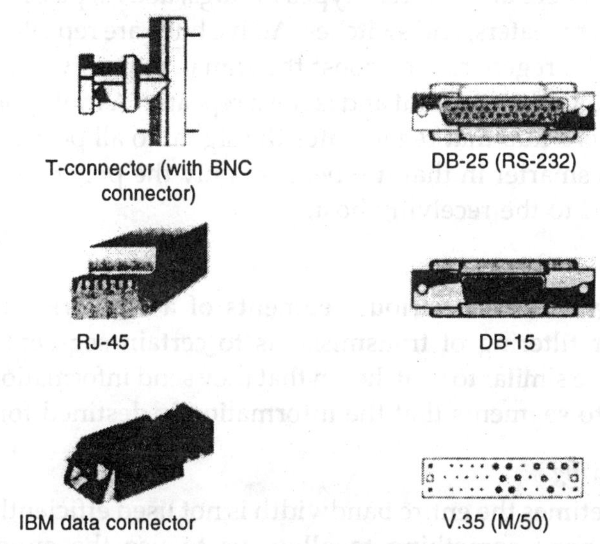

Fig. 6.6 Transmission Media Connectors

Modems

A *modem* stands for modulator/demodulator. The modem converts the digital signals from a computer into an analog signal that can transfer across a phone line or microwave transmission.

Repeaters

Earlier we looked at the limitations of some media used in today's networks. When attenuation occurs we need a way to increase the signal in order to reach the distance we need. A *repeater* boosts the signal in order to expand the total distance for what we need. Many hubs are repeaters.

Hubs

In order to connect various cable segments we need a central point to plug everything together. A *hub* brings all the cable segments together. A hub can be a multiport repeater. There are different types of hugs; active, passive, multiport repeaters, and switches. Active hubs are repeaters because the regenerate or boost the signal. A passive hub is just a connectivity point and is not a repeater. A multiport repeater is a hub that regenerates the signal to all ports. A switch is smarter in that it repeats to only the port that is connected to the receiving host.

Bridges

Bridges connect various segments of a network and allow for filtering of transmissions to certain segments. Bridges are similar to switches in that they send information only on to segments that the information is destined for.

Multiplexing

Sometimes the entire bandwidth is not used efficiently and we need something to allow us to use the entire medium by transmitting multiple signals. A *multiplexer* (MUX) combines signals onto one transmission medium.

Internetwork Connectivity Devices

With today's variety of networks, we need a way to connect them together. This is where internetwork connectivity devices come into the spectrum of network hardware. Here we all take a brief look at routers, brouters, and CSU/DSUs.

Routers and Brouters

Routers and brouters connect to logically different networks. A good example of this is a company's network that is connected to the Internet. Perhaps they receive stock market information from another company. In this scenario they would probably have two routers connected to their network. The separate networks are referred to as subnetworks or subnets. The collection of subnetworks makes up the internetwork. Figure 6.7 shows an example of what a network would look like with routers in place. Brouters are the same as routers except that they can also do bridging.

CSUs/DSUs

Similar to a modem, a *CSU/DSU* is used to transfer data to a special format. The difference, however, is that a CSU/DSU is a digital-to-digital converter. The modem is a digital-to-analog conversion device. CSU/DSU stands for Channel Service Unit/Digital Service Unit. The CSU/DSU prepares the information from a LAN to be transmitted across the WAN. They work in conjunction with routers in some cases.

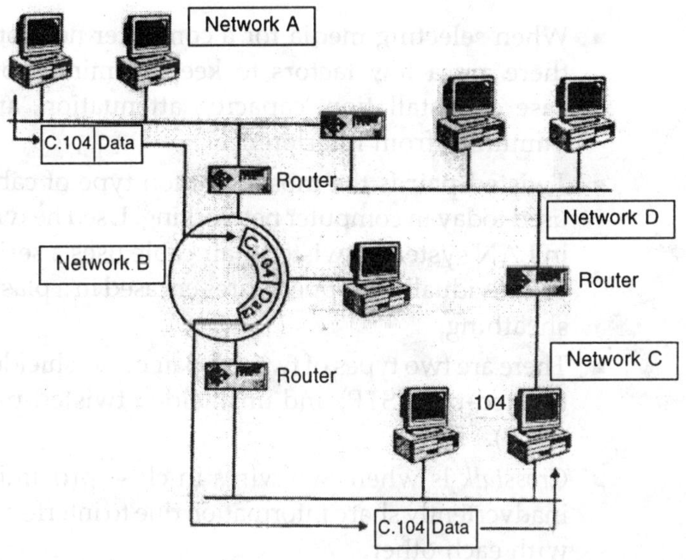

Fig. 6.7 An internetwork with routers

CERTIFICATION SUMMARY

In this chapter we looked at the different considerations we need to make when deciding on how to connect the network. For the exam you will see a few questions out of this chapter. The five big factors for network connectivity see cost, installation, capacity, attenuation, and interference.

We also looked at cable media. The different types include unshielded twisted-pair, coaxial cable, and fiber-optic cable. Wireless media includes the radio waves, microwave transmission systems, and infrared transmission systems.

We also took a brief look at the different network connectivity types from network cards to routers.

TWO-MINUTE DRILL

- When selecting media for a computer network, there are a few factors to keep in mind: cost, ease of installation, capacity, attenuation, and immunity from interference.
- Twisted-pair is the most common type of cable used today in computer networking. Used heavily in LAN systems, twisted-pair cable uses a series of individually wrapped wires encased in a plastic sheathing.
- There are two types of twisted-pair cable: shielded twisted-pair (STP) and unshielded twisted-pair (UTP).
- *Crosstalk* is when two wires in close proximity inadvertently share information due to interfering with each other.
- Fiber-optic cable is made up of a light conducting glass or plastic core. More reflective material,

called cladding, surrounds the core, and then the outer plastic sheath protects the inside.

- There are three classes of radio wave transmissions: low-power single frequency, high-power single frequency, and spread spectrum.
- Network Interface Boards are the logic boards that allows us to connect the transmission media connector to our computer and form the physical path in order to communicate.
- The *Network Interface Board,* more commonly known as a Network Interface Card (NIC), has an internal transceiver that converts the information from the computer into a form that can travel across the medium.

SELF TEST

The following Self-Test questions will help you measure your understanding of the material presented in this chapter. Read all the choices carefully, as there may be more than one correct answer. Choose all correct answers for each question.

1. Which of the following is not one of the five factors to consider when choosing a transmission media type?
   A. Ease of installation
   B. Capacity
   C. Insinuation
   D. Immunity from interference
2. What do you call the condition when a signal becomes weak as it travels along the medium?
   A. Distance Limitation Factor (DLF)
   B. Attenuation

C. Attenuation

D. Electromagnetic Interference (EMI)

3. What is the distance limitation of unshielded twisted-pair?

   A. 100 meters

   B. 500 meters

   C. 300 meters

   D. Unlimited

4. Which category of unshielded twisted-pair allows for data transmission speeds up to 20 Mbps? (Choose all that apply.)

   A. CAT 1

   B. CAT 3

   C. CAT 5

   D. CAT 2

   E. CAT 4

5. What is the inner conductor in coaxial cable made of?

   A. Aluminium

   B. Glass

   C. Plastic

   D. Copper

6. What is the the rating and size standard for Thin Ethernet?

   A. 50 OHM RG-8/RG-11

   B. 50 OHM RG-58

   C. 50 OHM RG-59

   D. 93 OHM RG-62

7. Which type of transmission media is made up of an inner core of glass or plastic?

   A. UTP

   B. STP

C. Coax
D. Fiber

8. Which form of wireless media falls into the 10 KHz to 1 Ghz range in the electromagnetic spectrum?
   A. Radio wave transmission
   B. Microwave transmission
   C. Infrared transmission
   D. Terrestrial transmission
9. What type of transmission media connector is commonly used with twisted-pair cabling?
   A. T-connector
   B. RJ-45
   C. DB-15
   D. V. 35
10. What type of network connectivity device is used to change a digital signal to analog?
    A. Router
    B. Bridge
    C. Network card
    D. Modem

NATURE OF COMPUTER CRIME

Introduction

The advent of computer technology has brought many kinds of opportunities and some of these, not surprisingly, are of a criminal nature. Computers may facilitate the commission of 'old-fashioned' crimes such as fraud or counterfeiting or give rise to new mischiefs such as computer hacking and the deliberate erasure of programs or data. Contrary to popular belief, the law is reasonably well equipped to deal with computer crime and has been substantially strengthened by the Computer Misuse Act 1990. The biggest stumbling block in practical terms, is detection and a considerable amount of thought must be given to the security of any computer system as, in this case, prevention is better than cure.

By far the greatest threat to a computer system comes from within - that is, from employees. One of the largest reported computer frauds ever attempted, which concerned the transfer of $70 million, involved in employee of the First National Bank of Chicago. Even when computer crime is detected and the persons involved are prosecuted and convicted, the penalties imposed seem relatively trivial when compared with other forms of criminal activity. In 1989, a teenage bank cashier who transferred nearly £1 million into his own and a friend's bank account, received only one year's youth custody.

The diversity of criminal activities associated with computers is remarkable and has given rise to a whole new vocabulary. Examples are computer hacking, time-bombs, logic-bombs and computer viruses. These terms will be defined at the appropriate sections of this Part of the boom, the purpose of which is to describe the criminal offences associated with computers, what remedies are available at law and to suggest how the threats posed by these activities can be avoided or, at least, minimised. In previous chapters the offences popularly described as 'computer fraud' are considered. In previous chapters the activity known as hacking is examined followed, by a discussion of the legal implications where a person erases programs or data from a computer system or leaves a virus on a system which later corrupts or deletes information. Other forms of criminal activity, such as blackmail, forgery and counterfeiting and piracy offences, are discussed in previous chapters. Computer evidence in criminal proceedings is dealt with in previous chapters and practical suggestions to prevent computer crime are contained in previous chapters which concludes with a summary of offences, their maximum penalties and scope, presented in tabular form.

The scale and nature of computer crime

Stories, often unsubstantiated, of massive computer frauds, widespread hacking and chaotic disruption to computer systems caused by viruses are legend. Cinema films such as *Superman III* and *War Games* fuel the imagination, and reporting in the media, warning of the Friday 13th virus, for example, adds to this. Determining the true scale of crime is an impossible task when considering conventional crime because of under-reporting (a great deal of crime goes unreported for a variety of reasons - this is known as the dark figure of crime) and this is even more so when it comes to computer crime. In some cases the crime will remain undetected or it may result in no action or disciplinary action rather than prosecution if the offender is an employee. It has been rumoured that some financial institutions attempt to cover up the fact they have been a victim of computer crime, fearing that publicity will damage their reputation.

Wild, exaggerated figures are sometimes quoted as the total cost of computer crime. In most cases, these can be taken with a pinch of salt because they are purely speculative. there is no foundation for them whatsoever. Of course, computer crime has been and remains a very serious issue and, fortunately, some realistic data is available as the Audit Commission for Local Authorities and the National Health Service in England and Wales carry out surveys triennially (Audit Commission Update, *Ghost in the Machine: An Analysis of IT Fraud and Abuse,* February 1998 and *Opportunity Makes a Thief: An Analysis of Computer Abuse,* Audit Commission, 1998). The latest survey covered the three-year period ending in December 1996 and, as before, involved both the public and the private sector. The survey was based upon responses from 900 organisations, reporting a total of 510 incidents. Table 7.1 shows a summary of the results of the surveys in 1987, 190 and 1993. Unfortunately, the forms of misuse do not exactly match the legal definitions of offences but the criminal law has changed significantly since the first survey was carried out in 1981. Due to a different format in the latest report, precise statistics are not available but Figure 7.1 shows the results from the latest survey in percentage terms.

There has been a significant increase in the reporting of incidents, particularly in respect of viruses. This may be a reflection of an increase in incidents of computer misuse but could be explained, at least partly, by an increase in awareness of computer crime. Nevertheless, just over half the incidents were detected by accidental means. Confirming that most computer crime comes from within: 85 per cent of reported incidents were perpetrated by internal staff, mainly administrative staff, although a proportion were committed by managers. The most common preventative measure taken by organisations was internal auditing followed by the adoption of an information technology security policy.

TABLE 7.1

Computer misuse (survey based on three-year periods)

Types of misuse	*1993*		*1990*		*1987*	
	No.	*Direct loss(£)*	*No.*	*Direct loss(£)*	*No.*	*Direct loss(£)*
Fraud	108	2904430	73	1102642	61	2526751
Theft[1]	121	196305	27	1000	22	34500
Hacking[2]	47	65500	26	31500	35	100
Viruses	261	30485	54	5000	0	0
Totals	537	3196720	180	1140142	118	2561351

[1] includes illicit private work, theft of data or software

[2] includes invasion of privacy and sabotage

Source of data: Audit commission, *Opportunity Makes a Thief: An Analysis of Computer Abuse,* HMSO,1994 and previous reports.

A report from the National Audit Office (*IT Security in Government Departments,* HMSO, 1995) also confirms a growing threat from computer misuse. Over 100 government departments and agencies were asked to provide information on incidents of computer misuse in the year 1993/4. Compared to the reported figures for 1992/3, the following increases were noted, as shown in Table 7.2. In the National Audit Office study, very little fraud was reported. Indeed, from 1990 to 1994 only 36 cases were reported and the total value was less then £250000, an average of only £7000 per incident. The average for the Audit Commission study in the three-year period to 31 December 1993 based on direct losses only was around £27000. In spite of all the publicity, big time computer fraud appears to be relatively rate! In the three-year period to 31 December 1996, total losses for the 900 organisations responding to the survey was £3.9 million.

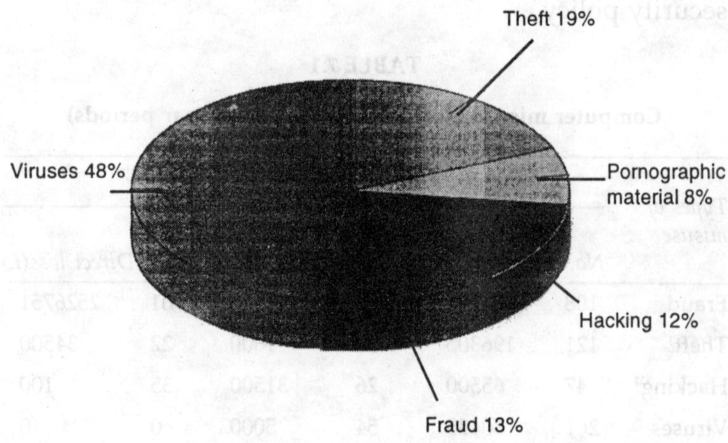

Fig. 7.1 Forms of computer abuse

TABLE 7.2

Computer abuse in government departments

Type of abuse	*Increase (%)*
Hacking	140
Viruses	86
Theft of IT equipment	60

Source of data: National Audit office, IT Security in Government Departments, HMSO 1995.

One thing that is apparent from the Audit Commission surveys is that a significant proportion of perpetrators are not prosecuted and, in many cases, no action is taken or the perpetrator, if an employee, is reprimanded, transferred to other duties or dismissed. In the case of *Denco Ltd* v *Joinson* [1991] IRLR 63, it was held that an employee who used an unauthorised password to gain access to information stored in a computer and which he knew he was not entitled to see was guilty of gross misconduct and could be summarily dismissed from his employment. The employer's security arrangements were criticised by the Employment Appeal Tribunal and the Industrial Tribunal which heard the case first (the employee had argued that he had been unfairly dismissed).

A disregard for basic control safeguards and ineffective monitoring were high lighted by the Audit Commission as still being prevalent. Recommendations made in the reports, accepting that prevention is better than cure, include:

- carrying out risk analysis reviews;
- developing and implementing secure and controlled environments;
- having rigorously implemented IT security policies;
- giving staff computer awareness training, focusing on risks and precautions to be taken;
- assigning responsibility for security and developing secure access control;
- making sure that the internal audit department has computer audit skills; and
- making the necessary financial commitment to security aspects of an organisation's computer systems.

An awareness of the criminal law and its applications to computer technology is an important part of implementing security strategies and it is also important that persons working with computers are aware of the potential seriousness of what might seem to them a trivial matter. Prevention will not, sadly, eliminate computer misuse altogether and the remainder of this Part of the book examines the criminal law in relation to computer crime.

The Prosecution of Criminal Offences

Before specific offences are examined, it will be useful to describe, very briefly the procedure for prosecuting offences, the classification modes of trial.

When a criminal offence has been committed, the normal procedure is for the police to be informed (the police detect very little crime themselves but depend on the public bringing incidents of crime to their notice). The police will then investigate the crime and, if they suspect a particular person or persons of having committed the crime, they may charge the person or persons and then pass the case over to the Crown Prosecution Service which decides whether to prosecute and what charges to bring. In coming to its decision, the Crown Prosecution Service uses guidelines which include the possibility of securing a conviction and the public interest. If the decision is made to proceed, the accused will appear before a Magistrates' Court where, depending on the nature of the offence and other matters, either his case will be dealt with, or he will be committed for trial in the Crown Court. It is possible to being a private prosecution if, for example, the Crown Prosecution Service declines to act. However, the Director of Public Prosecutions has the power to take over a private prosecution. Other bodies may bring prosecutions such as local authority trading standards officers, the Department of Social Security, the Data Protection Commissioner and HM Customes & Excise. Bringing a private prosecution is, in most cases, an extreme action, but it may be relevant to computer crime if the official bodies fail to take an interest in prosecuting certain behaviour, due perhaps to a lack of understanding of the problems involved or a feeling that the civil law offers sufficient remedies. Though this latter point may be true, it does not have the deterrent effect that a successful criminal prosecution can have.

Criminal offences are heard in either the Crown Court or Magistrates' Courts. The latter tend to deal with the less serious offences which make up the vast majority of criminal cases. Offences are classified according to how they may be tried. Relatively minor offences, such as exceeding the speed limit, may be tried only in Magistrates' Courts and these offences are described as being *summary* offences. Serious offences such as murder and robbery can only be tried in the Crown Court and these are called *indictable* offences. In between these two types of offence, there is vast number of intermediate offences which can be tried in either a Magistrates' Court or the Crown Court; these offences, of which theft is an example, are called *triable either way* offences. These may be tried summarily in a Magistrates' Court or, on indictment, in the Crown Court. Many of the offences which will be described in this part of the book fall into this category; they are offences which are triable either way, an example being the unauthorised modification of computer programs or data. On the other hand, computer hacking (unauthorised access to computer material) is triable summarily only.

When an offence is classified as being triable either way, the choice of mode of trial initially rests with the magistrates. They may decide that the nature of the case is such that it should be tried in the Crown Court; for example, if it is a serious example of the offence. If the magistrates decide that the case can be heard on their court, the accused person can then decide whether to proceed in the Magistrates' Court or to elect trial in the Crown Court. Certain other factors are important in deciding on the mode of trial apart from the seriousness of the offence. For example, the magistrates might consider that the accused, if found guilty, is deserving of a punishment greater than they can award (although they can commit a convicted person to the Crown Court for sentence if they feel that their sentencing powers are inadequate in the particular case), or the accused might think he stands a better chance of acquittal before a jury. In one case, a hacker was acquitted by a jury on the basis that he was addicted to hacking even though addiction is not a defence known to English law.

The maximum penalties available in Magistrates' Courts need to be mentioned. Providing the relevant statute does not contain a lower maximum, for a single offence the magistrates may send a person to prison for a term not exceeding six months and/or impose a fine not exceeding £5000. Other sentencing powers are available to the magistrates such as discharging the offender or imposing a probation order or a community service order. In the context of computer crime, the use of imprisonment and fines are the most likely punishments, although other forms of sentence may be appropriate in some circumstances.

8 COMPUTER FRAUD

Introduction

Computer fraud often makes headline news but it is thought that the number of cases of fraud detected and prosecuted are just the tip of the iceberg. Rumours abound about massive frauds which are not reported by the victims (usually large financial institutions) because of a fear of publicity. It does not help a bank's image of solid dependability to have employees prosecuted for computer fraud at regular intervals. All the major financial institutions throughout the world use computers to carry out their business and vast sums of money are transferred by computer (electronic funds transfer). As far as the criminal is concerned, the creation of an account in his own name, followed by instructions via a computer terminal to the main computer to transfer large sums into that account, is much more attractive than walking into a bank with a shotgun. There seems to be a feeling that no commit fraud by using one's won brains to defeat a computer system is something to be applauded and is not really serious crime. however, this form of crime causes great anxiety in the commercial world and is considered by the authorities to be very serious. The maximum penalties available are quite heavy and computer fraud can be dealt with by prison sentences of up to ten years.

Types of Computer Fraud

The phrase 'computer fraud' is used to describe stealing money or property by means of a computer: that is, using a computer is obtain dishonestly, property (including and cheques) or credit or services or to evade dishonestly some debt or liability. It might involve dishonestly giving an instruction to a computer to transfer funds into a bank account or using a forged bank card to obtain money from a cash dispenser (automated teller machine).

The types of activities described as computer fraud can be considered to be of two main types: data frauds and programming frauds. In the first type, unauthorised data is entered into a computer or data that should be entered is altered or suppressed. The main distinguishing factor in this type or fraud is that it is computer data, either input or output data, which is tampered with. Data fraud is probably the most common type or computer fraud (it is the most easily detected) and is relatively easy to carry out. The Audit Commission recognises four types of computer fraud (data fraud is sub divided into three categories):

- input fraud,
- data fraud,
- output fraud, and
- program fraud.

In the latest survey by the Audit Commission (*Ghost in the Machine: An Analysis of IT Fraud and Abuse,* Audit Commission Publications, 1998), fraud was the second most common form of incident reported. Routine auditing procedures should eventually expose most input, data and output frauds but this is not necessarily true of program frauds which may remain undetected for a long period of time. The sub-species of frauds are described below. Unless otherwise indicated, examples are taken from an earlier Audit Commission report (*Survey of Computer Fraud and Abuse*, HMSO, 1991) which, unlike the later reports, contained substantial detail of individual incidents in an informative and entertaining supplement.

Entry of Unauthorised Instruction (Input Fraud)

This is the unauthorised alteration of data prior to it being input into a computer. Typically, an employee preparing data to be entered into a computer by another employee will make incorrect entries on the relevant document or form. The employee who enters the data into the computer may be an innocent agent or, in some cases, may be an accomplice of the first person or conspiring with him. It is an easy form of fraud to attempt and requires no particular computer skills. The only intelligence required to succeed is in knowing the organisation's checking and auditing systems thoroughly and matching the fraud up with any shortcomings in those systems. This is a strong argument for organisations to continually review, modify and enhance their auditing systems.

In one case the perpetrator gave incorrect data input forms to a clerk who then entered the data which related to debits to customer accounts. The perpetrator misappropriated the money concerned - £100000. His actions were detected by internal audit and he was prosecuted under the Theft Acts 1968 and 1978, sentenced to four years' imprisonment and fined £10000 (Audit Commission Survey 1991, Supplement, p. 12).

Alteration of Input Data (Data Fraud)

In one case, a box office supervisor cancelled tickets which had been sold and then later resold them, keeping the cash. The box office supervisor falsified the audit trail but this was detected after problems with the software were investigated. The employee was prosecuted under the Theft Acts 1968 and 1978 and given six months' imprisonment (Audit Commission Survey, 1991, Supplement, p 38). In another case reported in the National Audit Office study a member of staff in an employment department entered false data in relation to a claim made by his brother resulting in the brother receiving girocheques to which he was not entitled for a total of £2933. The employee was dismissed and prosecuted and, on conviction, was sentenced to two months' imprisonment (National Audit Office, *IT Security in Government Departments,* HMSO, 1995, p.17).

Data fraud, as defined by the Audit Commission, differs from input fraud in that with data fraud it is the person entering the data into the computer that makes changes to the data. This form of fraud is also fairly common and is easily carried out, but it will be detected if appropriate checking procedures and auditing are adopted. Most organisations using computers are vulnerable to fraud perpetrated by employees preparing data for entry into a computer or authorised to enter data into a computer system and, consequently care must be taken in the selection of such employees and an effective way of checking systems for the occurrence of fraud should be used, bearing in mind that an audit trail can be vulnerable.

Suppression of Data (Output Fraud)

This particularly applies to output data - for example, printed reports generated by a computer system. These reports may be suppressed simply by tearing them up or not printing them out or, if printed, they may be altered. In either case, the motive will usually be to hide some criminal activity. For example, a person responsible for collecting money for club might destroy a computer printout, which would indicate that he had kept some of the money collected. Concealing information can be a criminal offence. For example, in *Adams* v *The Queen* (unreported) 4 November 1994, two company directors by the use of offshore companies and bank accounts concealed information relating to secret profits they had made from the company they worked for. One of the directors brought an appeal to the Judicial Committee of the Privy Council against his conviction in New Zealand for conspiracy to defraud. His appeal was dismissed.

An example of this type of fraud is reported in the Audit Commission survey. A cashier who had taken money from her till destroyed daily audit rolls from each printer at her place of work thinking that his would make it impossible to trace her as the thief. Unfortunately for her, she was unaware that a computer file was also used to keep a record of transactions and this identified her as the culprit. She was sentenced to 18 months' imprisonment (Audit Commission Survey, 1991, Supplement, p. 25).

Program Frauds

The second form of computer fraud (as opposed to fraud involving data in one way or another) is more sophisticated and dangerous, and this is where someone alters a computer program to effect the fraud. Program fraud is much harder to detect than data fraud and reported examples are few and far between. We have to go back to the Audit Commission survey published in 1988 to find a good example. Two computer programmers wrote some stock accounting software and concealed a routine in the software which suppressed certain details in reports generated, in order to reduce Value Added Tax liability (Audit Commission Survey, 1988, p. 58). The software was designed for use in video-hire shops and the routine was activated by a special password. The software was sold to 120 shopkeepers although only 12 had been informed of the secret routine. these 12 had defrauded Customs and Excise of £100,000. Each of the programmers was prosecuted and convicted. They were each imprisonment for nine months and were fined a total of £34000.

Another example of this form of fraud, of fraud, which was discovered in West Germany and made famous in the film *Superman III*, involved the alteration of a program to collect decimal fractions of financial transactions, such as half-cents which were normally rounded down and ignored. Instead, these fractions were placed in an account opened by the perpetrator of the fraud. This is known as a 'salami fraud' because it involves thin 'slices' of money.

Computer programmers, analysts and others involved in the commissioning or alteration of software present another source of danger in that many of them will have detailed knowledge about the security and password systems used and could pass such information on to persons intent on committing fraud. As a result of their knowledge of the computer systems, computer staff are also susceptible to involvement with would-be fraudsters.

The Computer as an Unwitting Accomplice

A computer system might be used to detect information which assists the criminal in the commission of his crime. For example, in the case of *R* v *Sunderland* (unreported) 20 June 1983, Court of Appeal, an employee of Barclay's Bank used the bank's computer to discover a dormant account and then forged the holder's signature to withdraw some £2100. The employee of the bank used the computer in a very simple way to detect an account which had not been use for a long period of time but which had some funds in it, a simple but effective way of stealing money although, eventually, the scheme was discovered when the holder of the dormant account attempted to make a withdrawal and discovered that the account contained less money than it should have done. This employee, who was of previous good character, was sentenced to two years' imprisonment, which was changed on appeal by the Lord Chief Justice who suspended 18 months of the sentence. He said:

> ... other people like bank clerks and bank officials need very little reminding that if they commit this sort of offence they will lose their job and to to prison, albeit for a comparatively short time.

This case illustrates the vulnerability of some computer systems to criminal activities. Of fundamental importance in the design of any computer system is the attention given to passwords and security, audit trails and the controls placed on employees.

Few of the activities described above require a great deal of computer expertise to carry out; often they will be committed by employees on low income engaged to perform relatively menial tasks such as data preparation and entry. Such frauds are fairly easy to detect by careful scrutiny, audit, spot-checks and occasional manual checks. Strong security measures will also have a major deterrent effect, especially if they are performed in a high-profile manner.

Fraud Offences

When discussing computer fraud, the word 'fraud' can be a little misleading, and the activities commonly described as computer fraud can involve criminal offences other than those traditionally described as fraud. Fraud comprises a collection of similar offences such as obtaining property or services by deception, false accounting, false statements made by company directors, suppression of documents and income tax fraud including cheating. Most of these offences are covered by sections 15 to 20 of the

Theft Act 1968 and sections 1 and 2 of the Theft Act 1978. Section 15A of the Theft Act 1968, obtaining a money transfer by deception, may also be relevant. Income Tax and Value Added Tax fraud are dealt with by specific legislation such as the Finance Act 1972 although the common law offence of cheating is still available for offences relating to the public revenue. Apart from this exception, cheating was abolished by section 32(1) of the Theft Act 1968. Certainly, some of these offences may be carried out using a computer, but it is with respect to those offences requiring deception that the greatest difficulty lies. Often, the most appropriate offence to charge is theft. Although theft (section 1 of the Theft Act 1968) is not normally considered to fall within the 'fraud' group of offences, there is an overlap between theft and fraud and, depending on the circumstances, a charge of theft might be more likely to lead to be successful prosecution. First, the deception offences will be considered.

Obtaining by Deception

At first sight, the offence of obtaining property by deception (section 15 of the Theft Act 1968) seems to be most appropriate to computer fraud as the culprit usually means to obtain someone else's money or other property by a deception or trick - for example, by pretending to have authority to carry out some transaction on the computer such as transferring money. There is no problem stemming from the intangible nature of money, credits or cheques as section 4(1) of the 1968 Act states that property includes money and things in action. Banker's cheques, money orders and bills of exchange are all examples of 'things in action'. This definition of property applies to the 1968 Act generally and therefore applies to section 15. There are several forms of deception provided for by the Theft Acts of 1968 and 1978 involving the obtaining of property or a pecuniary advantage or services, and the evasion of liability.

So far as obtaining property by deception is concerned, section 15(1) of the Theft Act 1968 defines the offence as follows:

> A person who by any deception dishonestly obtains property belonging to another, with the intention of permanently depriving the other of it, shall on conviction on indictment be liable to imprisonment for a term not exceeding ten years.

Dishonesty is an important requirement this affects the nature of the deception. The Theft Act 1968 further states that the deception can be 'deliberate or reckless', so if a person carelessly causes a computer system to transfer money into his own or a friend's account (an unlikely occurrence if he is no more than careless), he is not guilty of the offence as carelessness is not sufficient in this context, though recklessness is likely to be judged objectively.

In terms of computer fraud, the difficulty with this offence is that it requires a deception and this implies that it is an actual person that is being deceived, not a machine. In *DPP* V *Ray* [1974] AC 370, Lord Morris said:

> For a deception to take place there must be some person or persons who will have been deceived.

Other case law does not help very much and the question was left open in one case involving an automatic car park barrier (*Davies* v *Flackett*[1973] RTR 8). Bearing in mind that *DPP* V *Ray* was decided in the House of Lords, the better view is that the deception must work upon a human mind.

If a person gains access, whether with or without permission, to a bank's computer system and dishonestly instructs the computer system to transfer money from one account into another, then that person is 'deceiving' the computer or computer system: that is, he purports to have the authority to carry out such an act. Even if he has authority to transfer money from one account to another under normal circumstances as an employee would, that authority is nullified by his dishonesty. The main point is that it is the computer which is being 'deceived'. Under normal circumstances, no other human being is involved and, therefore, it would seem that the offence of obtaining property by deception is not made out. It would be different if, before the transfer was made, a message is displayed at someone's terminal requesting confirmation of the transfer. In that case, the other person would be subject to the deception as well a the computer and there should then be no difficulty related to the applicability of the offence involving deception.

The notion that a machine cannot be deceived is strengthened by the Theft Act 1978 which defines the offences of obtaining services by deception (services such as hiring a care or providing bed and breakfast) and evasion of liability by deception (such as where a debtor tells a lie to his creditor in order to let him off part or the whole of the debt) because the wording used strongly suggests that the deception must operate on the human mind. For example, section 1(1) states:

> A person who by any deception dishonestly obtains services from *another* shall be guilty of an offence [emphasis auded].

This interpretation is reinforced by other language used in the statute. An example of obtaining services by deception in the context of computers is where a person makes an unauthorised use of a system which is normally paid for such as PRESTEL. The problem of who has been deceived still exist, but if the person has deceived some other person by saying that he has permission to use the terminal used to access the system, then the offence of deception will have been made out under section 1 of the Theft Act 1978. There is a requirement for the services to be subject to payment, so the same act with respect to a 'free' service does not involve the offence - for example, if a person dishonestly uses a computer system in a library to locate a particular book.

Obtaining a Money Transfer by Deception

A new offence was inserted into the Theft Act 1968 as a result of the case of *R* v *Preddy* [1996] AC 815. Charges were brought against the accused persons under section 15 of the Theft Act 1968. They had made over 40 applications for mortgages by making false statements. Their plan was to use the money to buy houses with the intention of reselling them at a profit and redeeming the mortgages. They hoped to make a substantial profit as, at the time, property prices were rising quickly and there was something of a property boom. The lenders said that they would not have lent the money to the accused persons had they known the true motive for obtaining a mortgage. Some of the mortgage advances were made telegraphically or electronically, by electronic funds transfer, while others were made by cheque. The accused were convicted and their appeals to the Court of Appeal were dismissed.

The appeals to the House of Lords were allowed and the convictions were quashed. An account in a bank or building society is classed as a 'chose in action' (thing in action). As regards the telegraphic or electronic fund transfers, it was held that when payment was made from one bank or building society account in credit (the lender's account) to another bank account, the chose in action represented by the credit balance in the lender's account was extinguished or reduced and a new chose in action was created in the borrower's account (or the borrower's solicitor's account). Therefore, the borrower did not get the lender's chose in action. Consequently, the borrower did not obtain 'property belonging to another' as required by section 15(1) of the Theft Act 1968. The account itself, the chose in action, was not transferred to the borrower.

As regards the cheques, the chose in action represented by the cheque never belonged to the bank or building society as when it came into existence it belonged to the borrower - it was made out to the borrower or his solicitor who would then transfer the payment to the person selling the house. As the chose in action belonged to the borrower right from the start, no property belonging to another was obtained by the borrower. Although the cheque itself was a physical object (that is, the paper as opposed to the chose in action relating to the amount it was made out for) and was property belonging to another, the borrower did not obtain it permanently as it would be returned to be bank or building society after presentation to the borrower's bank (or his solicitor's bank). Therefore, even charging these persons with theft of the piece of paper on which the cheque was written would have been doomed to failure.

Section 15 of the Theft Act 1968 was inserted by section 1 of the Theft (Amendment) Act 1996. This provides that a person is guilty of an offence if by any deception he dishonestly obtains a money transfer for himself or another. A money transfer occurs when a debit is made to one account and a corresponding credit is made to another account and the credit results from the debit or the debit results from the credit. Both credit and debit relate to an amount of money and it does to matter if the credit and debit are exactly the same amount or whether the transfer results from the presentation of a cheque or by another method or whether there is a delay in the transfer process.

Nor does to matter whether either account is overdrawn before or after the transfer. The maximum punishment is imprisonment for a term not exceeding ten years on conviction on indictment. It is reasonable to assume that dishonesty is a matter or satisfying the *Ghosh* test, discussed later under the section on theft.

This new offence is very welcome. In the light of *Preddy,* anyone who carried out a fraudulent electronic fund transfer could possibly have escaped conviction not only for obtaining property by deception but also for theft as that offence also requires that the property which is stolen belongs to another. The diminution of the victim's bank balance and the corresponding increase in the fraudster's bank balance would not be an obtaining (or, for theft, an appropriation) of property *belonging to another.* The importance of plugging this loophone was reflected in the speed with which the new offence was brought into force. Other offences could be relevant such as under the Computer Misuse Act 1990, and if, two or more persons were involved, the common law offence of conspiracy to defraud, as described below, would be appropriate.

To summarise, an essential element for the deception offences contained in the Theft Acts is that a human being has been deceived. In such a case, the deception could be simply a person claiming to have permission to use a computer system to gain access to terminal or by pretending to be somcone else. Some related offences such as false accounting, where 'deception' is not an element of the offence, should cause no additional problems merely because the offence was committed by or facilitated by the use of a computer system.

Conspiracy to Defraud

Generally, a conspiracy is an agreement between two

or more persons to carry out an unlawful act. Conspiracy may be statutory or common law. A statutory conspiracy is when a person agrees with another or others to embark upon a course of conduct which will necessarily involve a criminal offence by section 1 of the Criminal Law Act 1977 as amended by the Criminal Attempts Act 1981. An example is where two persons agree to steal a computer; both will be guilty of a conspiracy to steal the computer even if they do not go on actually to steal it. Statutory conspiracy requires that the proposed act is itself a criminal offence and, in the case of obtaining by deception, difficulties remain relating to the concept of deceiving a machine, as discussed above.

However, at common law, the offence of conspiracy to defraud may be available. It appears that, in this context, 'deceit' is not an essential element of the offence and in *Scott* v *Metropolitan Police Commissioner* [1975] AC 819, Viscount Dilhorne said:

> ...'to defraud' ordinarily means... to deprive a person dishonestly of something which is his or of something to which he is or would or might but for the perpetration of the fraud be entitled.

In other words, it is not necessary to show that a person has been deceived. In the *Scott* case, the accused made an agreement with cinemas projectionists to make copies of films being shown in the cinemas and to sell those copies for profit. The original films were borrowed overnight, copied and then returned the next day. It was held that it did not matter that no person had been deceived and the appeal against conviction was dismissed.

The common law offence of conspiracy to defraud is separate and distinct from the fraud offences in the Theft Acts, although in many cases, such as where to or more persons agree to obtain goods or services by impersonating others, the offence of conspiracy to defraud and offences under the Theft Acts will be committed if the course of action is carried through to its conclusion. The maximum penalty for conspiracy to defraud is ten years' imprisonment.

The consequence is that if two or more persons agree to dishonestly operate a computer, perhaps entering a password they are not entitled to use, to transfer funds to their own accounts, they will be guilty of a conspiracy to defraud even through no human being has been deceived. Of course, a limitation of the scope of this offence is that it requires an agreement between two or more conspirators and it cannot apply when only one person is involved. Nevertheless, the offence is a useful weapon in the fight against computer fraud, especially if the act of transfering the funds in question is not completed and the circumstances are not sufficient to warrant a charge of attempting to steal. In the past, and particularly before the advent of the Computer Misuse Act 1990, the track record of conspiracy to defraud in terms of dealing with computer fraud was very good. Indeed, even now, it may be preferable to use this offence because of its inherent flexibility and freedom from the technicalities of the Computer Misuse Act. In one example, a junior bank clerk was imprisoned for five years after pleading guilty to conspiracy after trying to transfer £31 million to a bank account in Geneva (*Computing*, 2 March 1995, p.1).

At one time it was held that conspiracy to defraud and statutory conspiracy where mutually - that is, if the carrying out of the agreement would result in some offence being committed, however trivial, then a charge of conspiracy to defraud would be bad for duplicity. Section 12 of the Criminal Justice Act 1987 changed that rule and not it does not matter if carrying out the intended acts involves the commission of some other offence. The activities in the *Scott* case did not entail the commission of another offence. The conspirators were infringing copyright in a film, in those days a civil matter only. Now their activities would be a criminal offence under section 107 of the Copyright, Designs and Patents Act 1988 but this would not longer be fatal to a charge of conspiracy to defraud. Indeed, the conspirators could also be charged with a conspiracy to commit a section 107 offence.

Attempts

To be charged with an attempt, the person involved must have done an act which is 'more than merely preparatory to the commission of the offence' (section 1 of the Criminal Attempts Act 1981). The scope of the law of attempts is uncertain when it comes to computer fraud but it does not apply to conspiracies. It could be argued that a computer fraud which is not completed is an attempt to steal money. However, it depends on how far towards the completion of the theft the fraudster got and whether any of his acts were more than merely preparatory. It has been argued that a criminal attempt occurs when the person concerned carries out an act penultimate to the commission of the offence, that is, the last act before completion. In the end, however, the question is one for the jury to decide being a question of fact.

Consider the case of an employee at a bank who decides, on his own, to transfer money to his own account from a customer's a account. First, he switches on a computer terminal. Second, he enters the appropriate password to gain access. Then, he enters the instruction at the keyboard which causes the funds to be transferred. Finally, he draws the money out of the account. The problems arise when the bank employee fails to complete the offence of theft of the money for one reason or another. At what stage in the course of the events described do his actions become more than merely preparatory? A reasonable member of a jury might conclude that the offence of attempting to steal is not made out until the third act has been carried out - that is, the entry of instructions which cause the computer system to transfer the money to the employee's account.

Doubts about the applicability of the law of attempts in the context of uncompleted computer frauds were among the reasons why section 2 of the Computer Misuse Act 1990 was enacted. This creates an 'ulterior intent' offence, where someone commits the basic hacking offence with the intention of proceeding to commit a serious offence.

Computer Fraud as Theft

It might seem from the above that, unless a conspiracy or attempt can be proved, a person who dishonestly convinces a computer that he is authorised to do something when he is not in fact so authorised, and makes the computer transfer money into his own bank account, commits an offence only if some other person has been deceived. Unless a human being has been subjected to the deception, it might seem that a charge of obtaining property by deception would not succeed. However, the criminal law is not so easily defeated. Usually, the offence of theft will be committed, regardless of the interposition of a computer. The offence of theft is defined in sections 1 to 6 of the Theft Act 1968 and section 191) states:

> A person is guilty of theft if the dishonestly appropriates property belonging to another with the intention of permanently depriving the other of it...

The words 'dishonestly', 'appropriates', 'property' and the phrases 'belonging to another' and 'with the intention of permanently depriving the other of it' all have special legal meanings which are set out in section 2 to 6 of the Act.

As far as computer crime is concerned, there is no real difficulty arising from the meanings of these words and phrases although the following points should be noted:

(a) the definition of 'property' is very wide and will cover most things that can be stolen with the aid of a computer, but land does not usually come within the meaning of property not do wild mushrooms or flowers, fruit or foliage on a wild plant;

(b) property is deemed to 'belong to another' if that person has control of it or has any proprietary right of interest in it;

(c) 'appropriation' is the assumption of the rights of the owner;

(d) the 'thief' must intent to permanently deprive the other of the property; usually a mere 'borrowing' of an article is not theft, although it can be if, for example, it is for a very long period of time or if, when it is returned, there is no 'goodness' left in the property.

Point (d) above is quite interesting. What is the position if a person gains access to a bank's computer system, draws money from various accounts and puts the money in his own account for a few weeks, collecting interest on the money, and then transfers the money back from whence it came, less the interest earned? Although there has been an appropriation (the person involved has assumed the rights of the owners is respect of the money in the accounts), the account holders have not been permanently deprived of their money; it has merely been borrowed for a few weeks and what has been lost is the interest which the capital would have earned. Clearly, there is no theft of the capital which has been returned intact, but what about the interest - has this been stolen?

A case involving the borrowing of cinema films adds weight to the argument that a person who uses the computer to transfer funds temporarily into his own account does not commit the offence of theft. In *R* v *Lloyd* [1985] 2 All ER 661, a projectionist at a cinema, a association with two others, removed films from the cinema for a few hours so that they could be copied and then returned the films so that no one would know what had occurred. The pirated copies of the films were then sold, making a considerable profit for the pirates. A charge of theft (actually a conspiracy to steal in this case) was held to be inappropriate. As has been seen in the *Scott* case above, where the facts were very similar a charge of conspiracy to defraud would have been more likely to secure a conviction.

In the *Lloyd* case, it was obvious that there was no intention permanently to deprive the owners of the films or was the copyright in the films stolen (it is not altogether clear whether copyright can be stolen). As mentioned earlier, borrowing can be theft if the period and circumstances are equivalent to an outright taking or disposal of section 6(1) of the Theft Act 1968, and this would be when the 'goodness' or 'virtue' in the thing taken and gone from it. Examples would include when a person borrows a radio battery intending to return it when it is exhausted, borrows a bus pass intending to return it to the rightful owner when it expires. In the case of the films, however, there was still virtue in them when they were returned: they were still capable of being used and shown in paying audiences, so the pirates' convictions were quashed.

The fact that the owner of the copyright in the films had been deprived of potential 'sales' of the films by the circulation of pirate copies was not relevant to the offence of theft, but would it be relevant in a case of the temporary transferal of funds while interest is collected? Although the lawful owner of the money (or other things such as shares and invesments) has been deprived of he interest or earnings, it would appear on the basis of *Lloyd* that the law of theft cannot be invoked. Nevertheless, the person borrowing the money could still be deemed to have an intention to permanently deprive the owner by section 6(1) of the Theft Act 1968. This is expressed in terms of treating the thing as one's own to dispose of regardless of the rights of he owner and borrowing or lending may amount to so treating it if, in the circumstances, it is equivalent to an outright taking or disposal. However, it is hard to know whether this would apply to a short-term borrowing without permission as section 6(1) has been described as 'gobbledygook'. Even if it is not equivalent to an outright taking or disposal, the owner may be able to get some relief by obtaining damages for conversion at civil law. Other criminal offences, such as unauthorised access to computer material.

The meaning of 'dishonesty' for the purposes of theft needs also to be considered. The test used, derived from the case of *R* v *Ghosh* [1982] QB 1053, has two elements: first, was what was done dishonest according to the ordinary standards of reasonable and honest people? Second, did the person involved realise that what he did was dishonest by those standards? In there example above, where money is borrowed for a period of time for the purpose of collecting interest or as capital for a short-term investment, the second limb of the test could be difficult to prove beyond reasonable doubt as regards the obtaining of interest from the bank. Certainly, the actions as a whole are dishonest and should be criminal and it is likely that a jury would convict on the facts.

What if the money is borrowed for a very short period of time, however, and invested in a high-risk speculation which pays off and the borrower returns the capital and an amount to compensate for lost interest? There has been no intention to permanently deprive the owner of the capital. As far as the interest is concerned, that would seem to be a matter between the owner of the capital and his bank which is contractually bound to pay the interest. However, in *Chan Man-sin* v *Attorney-General for Hong Kong* [1988] 1 All ER 1, an accountant forged cheques drawn on company accounts and was charged with theft of the debt owned by the bank to the companies. The accountant argued that he had not committed theft because the companies had not been deprived of anything as the bank was contractually bound to the companies to replace the money. The Judicial Committee of the Privy Council rejected this argument because the accountant had purported to deal with company property regardless of the rights of the companies and that was within the meaning of an intention to permanently deprive the companies of their property.

Authority and Consent

A person committing fraud may have authority to use the computer system concerned. An employee whose duties include entering data into a computer system may alter the data to effect the fraud. Here, the employee is doing no more than carrying out his duties, albeit fraudulently. However, as discussed in the following, chapter, in a controversial case (*DPP* v. *Bignsall*), the court suggested that doing something authorised in an unauthorised way may still be deemed to be authorised.

In other cases, the employee who has permission to use a computer system might do things using the computer in a manner beyond his normal duties. How does the law of theft deal with such cases? The concept of authority or consent is an important one on theft, for how can a person steal something if he has permission to take the thing? In *R* v *Morris* [1984] AC 320, a case involving label-switching a supermarket (that is, substituting one price tag with another stating a lower price), it was said that an unauthorised act was required for the appropriation necessary to constitute theft. Switching price labels is obviously not authorised by the supermarket. An employee who attempts to commit a fraud using computers will be doing something outside the scope of his authority to use the computer system: for example, the person employed to input data into a computer system does not have authority to enter false data. If the other elements of the offence are present, such as an intention to permanently deprive, then theft will be committed.

Another case which reinforces and exapands this approach is *Lawrence* v *Metropolitan Police Commissioner* [1972] AC 626. An Italian visitor to England hired a taxi and at the end of the journey gave the taxi-driver a £1 note for the fare. The taxi-driver said that his was not enough (the correct fare was just over £0.50) and proceeded to help himself to an additional £6 from the visitor's wallet which was still open. The defence argued that the money had been taken with consent but it was held that the prosecution did not have to prove that the taking of the money was without the victim's consent. This is considerably wider than the *Morris* case and it is difficult to reconcile the two. Even if the narrower view is taken, however, it is difficult to think if a case of computer fraud where the person will not be guilty of theft when he exceeds or otherwise compromises his authority to use a computer system. The fact that the computer system 'consents' to the transaction should to be relevant, as in *Lawrence,* because it is consent obtained by deception. The restriction of deception operating on a human mind should not be relevant in these circumstances. In *R* v *Gomez* [1992] 3 WLR 1067, the House of Lords confirmed that the wider approach in *Lawrence* is the correct one. Therefore, any assumption of the rights of the owner in respect to any property where it is done with consent obtained by deception can amount to an appropriation for the purposes of theft.

Other Offences

Other offences which contain an element of fraud are provided for in the Theft Act 1968 - for example, false accounting (section 17), false statements by company directors, etc. (section 19) and the suppression of documents (section 20). There is nothing special about these offences in terms of computers except that their commission may be carried out with the aid of a computer.

The remaining part of the common law fraud-related offence of cheating is of interest. Cheating was abolished by section 32(1) of the Theft Act 1968, with the exception of cheating with respect to offences relating to the public revenue. If a person makes a false declaration concerning his Income Tax or Value Added Tax, whether by using a computer or not, he will be guilty of the offence of cheating in addition to any offence under the Finance Acts. This dual liability is useful because there is a higher ceiling on the penalty available for cheating, which can consequently be used for more serious examples of revenue fraud. For example, in *R* v *Mavji* [1987] All ER 758, the accused had evaded Value Added Tax of over £1 million and was charged with cheating; he was sentenced to six years' imprisonment and fined. If he had been charged under the Finance Act 1972, the longest sentence of imprisonment he could have received was two years. In the light of this case, it appears that no deception is required; the ommission to make a tax return is sufficient. According to the Theft Acts, it appears that the offence of deception requires a human being to be deceived, but in the case of cheating there is no such requirement. This leads to the conclusion that if a person has a computerised accounts system which incorporates Value Added Tax report generator, then suppressing or altering computer reports, and consequent failure to submit a return or submitting a 'doctored' return, means that the offence of cheating has been committed and the fact that a computer has been used should not cause any difficulty.

A final possibility is that the fraudster may be prosecuted under the Computer Misuse Act 1990. The section 2 offence is particularly appropriate where the fraud has not been completed, with the advantage that, if there is insufficient evidence of intention, the court or jury (if tried in the Crown Court) can return a verdict of guilty section 1 (the basic hacking offence). Even the section 3 offence may be applicable (unauthorised modification of computer material) and an example of a conviction for this in relation to fraud is given in the Audit Commission report, 1998. The Computer Misuse Act offences are discussed in the following chapters.

9 HACKING ILLEGAL ACCESS TO COMPUTER MATERIAL

The Problem in Perspective

Computer hacking is the accessing of a computer system without the express or implied permission of the owner of that computer system. A person who engages in this activity is known as a computer hacker and may be motivated by the mere thrill of being able to outwit the security systems contained in a computer. A hacker may gain access remotely, using a computer is his own home or office connected to a telecommunications network.

Hacking can be thought of a form of mental challenge, not unlike solving a crossword puzzle, and the vast majority of hacking activities have been relatively harmless. Sometimes, a hacker has left a message publicising his feat and this reflects the popular image of a hacker - a young enthusiast who is fascinated by computers and who likes to gain access to secure computer systems to prove his skills to himself or his peers. At worst, this form of hacking is no more than a nuisance although, once it is known that a hacker has entered a computer system, the system manager may have to carry out a significant amount of work to confirm that the hacker has not modified or erased data. Many hackers are motivated by a sense of achievement; the very act of breaking into a computer system using their own mental effort is reward enough for them. There is a danger, however, that such 'innocent' hackers can cause damage to computer systems inadvertently and they may pave the way for other more malicious, persons.

There is a more sinister side to computer hacking. Many computer systems concern what might be called 'high-risk' activities such as the control of nuclear power stations, defence systems, aircraft flight control and hospital records. These are known as 'safety-critical systems'. The dangers stemming from hacking into these systems are self-evident and the potential for terrorism is worrying. As terrorists are unlikely to be deterred by the criminal law, it is not just a matter of strengthening the law to deal with hackers. The key to overcoming the problems lies with those responsible for computer systems in these high-risk areas and it is essential that they do their utmost to make sure that the systems are as secure as possible. There is something to be said for the view that the enthusiastic young hacker has done the computer industry a great service by highlighting the deficiencies in the security aspects of many computer systems. Rather than subjecting these hackers to criminal proceedings, perhaps the computer industry should consider making use of their skill and expertise. In 1989, the co-founder of the Apple Computer Corporation made a donation to the University of Colorado for a computer hacking scholarship in the belief that it increased knowledge and understanding of computer systems.

Once the hacker has penetrated a computer system he might do one of several different things. He might read or copy information, which may be highly confidential, or he might erase or modify information or programs stored in the computer system, or download programs or data, or he might simply add something, such as a message boasting of his feat. He might be tempted to steal money or direct the computer to have goods sent to him, in terms of computer fraud is relevant. By their very nature and relative susceptibility to unauthorised access, computer systems pose different problems to those encountered with information stored on paper. In the days before computers, sensitive information was kept locked away in filing cabinets in locked rooms on the premises of the organisation holding the data. This way the sensitive information was relatively safe from being tampered with or copied. The biggest threat would then come from employees but, burglars and industrial spies apart, persons outside the organisation would find it extremely difficult to gain access to the information. By contrast, information stored on a computer that is linked to a telecommunications system is much more vulnerable. It is analogous to information stored in paper files kept in locked cabinets but left in a public place. It is just a matter of finding the right key to fit the cabinet and not only can a total stranger try the lock but, often, he can spend as long as he likes trying different keys with impunity until he finds one that turns the lock.

The House of Lords decision in the case of *R* v *Gold* [1988] 2 WLR 984 highlighted the problem of computer hacking and the case with which it could be done. After the case, which was taken by many to indicate that computer hacking was not a criminal activity, the computer industry became most dissatisfied with the scope of the criminal law and the perceived lack of haste on the part of Parliament to act. Concern at this position led to the Law Commission Working Paper No. 110, *Computer Misuse* (HMSO, 1988), examining the scope of the law in terms of computer misuse generally and proposing alternative suggestions for legal changes directed at the problem of computer crime.

Emma Nocholson MP introduced a private member's Bill to combat computer hacking in 1989 but withdrew it after a Government promise to legislate in this area. That promise was broken and, in 1990, Michael Colvin MP brought in another private member's Bill on computer misuse, which was successfully steered the rough Parliament and became the Computer Misuse Act 1990. This Act did not restrict itself to computer hacking but also dealt with some other problems such as the law of attempts, unauthorised modification of computer programs and data, as well as addressing problems of jurisdiction and extradition. This chapter deals specifically with the basic hacking offence and ulterior intent offence following a discussion of the decision in *R v Gold*.

The Case of *R v Gold*

Two computer hackers gained access into the British Telecom Prestel Gold computer network without permission and they altered data. One of the accused also got into the Duke of Edinburgh's personal computer files and left the message;

GOOD AFTERNOON. HRH DUKE OF EDINBURGH

The two accused hackers were journalists who claimed that they had hacked into the network in order to highlight the deficiencies in its security. They were charged under the Forgery and Counterfeiting Act 1981 on the basis that they and made a false instrument within section 1. This states that a person shall be guilty of forgery if he makes a false instrument, with the intention that he or another shall use it to induce somebody to accept it as genuine, and by reason of so accepting it to do or not to do some act to his own or any other person's prejudice.

It was claimed that the false instrument was the CIN (customer identification number) and password. Section 8(1) of the Act states that a false instrument may be 'recorded or stored on disc, tape, sound track or other device'. However, their lordships suggested that 'recorded' or 'stored' connoted a process of a lasting and continuous nature from which the instrument could be retrieved in the future. In this case, the CIN and password were held only temporarily in the computer system while they were checked for validity and, after the check, they were eradicated totally and irretrievably.

The accused had been found guilty at Crown Court - one being fined £750 and the other £600 - but their convictions were quashed by the Court of Appeal and this was confirmed in the House of Lords. In the Court of Appeal, the Lord Chief Justice, Lord Lane, said that the acts of the accused in gaining access to the Telecom Gold files by what amounted to a dishonest trick were not criminal offences. If the defendants' convictions had been upheld, the only rational interpretation of the effect of section 1 in the circumstances was that the defendats had deceived a computer. Bearing in mind that, in terms of the Theft Act offences, it does not appear to be possible to deceive a machine, the decision in the *Gold* case was eminently sensible.

The Basic Hacking Offence

Section 1 of the Computer Misuse Act 1990 is aimed directly at hackers who gain access to computer programs or data without any further intention to carry out any other act. It says that a person is guilty of an offence if:

(a) he causes a computer to perform any function with intent to secure access to any program or data held in any computer;

(b) the access he intends to secure is unauthorised; and

(c) he knows at the time when he causes the computer to perform the function that this is the case.

The intent does not have to be directed at any particular program or data or at programs or data of a particular kind or at programs or data held in any particular computer. The offence is triable summarily only (that is, in a Magistrates' Court) and the maximum penalty is imprisonment for a term not exceeding six months or a fine not exceeding level 5 (presently £5000) or both.

Section 17 of the Act contains definitions and other aids to interpretation but the Act does not define 'computer', 'program' or 'data'. Securing access is widely defined as causing a computer to perform any function, altering or erasing a program or data, copying or moving it to a different location in the storage medium in which it is held, using it or having it output from the computer in which it is held, and access to a program includes access to a part of a program. Note that the offence is made out if the hacker simply intends to make access regardless of whether he succeeds but he must know, at the time, that the access is unauthorised. Careless or reckless access will not suffice. Because copying is within the meaning of securing access, potentially it can be an office under section 1 to make a pirate copy of a computer program or other software or to download an unauthorised copy of a computer program. However, there may be some difficulty as to whether such an act is unauthorised for the purposes of the Act, as discussed later.

The language of section 1 is rather strange at first sight as it speaks of access to programs or data in *any* computer, presumably including the computer being used by the hacker. This has been subject to judicial scrutiny in *Attorney-General's Reference (No. 1 of 1991)* [1992] 3WLR 432, in which a former employee went to visit his previous employer, a wholesale locksmith, to purchase some articles. While alone (an assistant had temporarily left the room), the ex-employee entered instructions into the computer effecting a 70 per cent discount on the articles he had bought. There was no need for him to use a password. At the trial, the judge said that the wording of section 1 required that a second computer had to be involved. This was rejected on appeal to the Court of Appeal, where it was held that the wording of section 1, given its plain and ordinary meaning, was not limited to the use of one computer with intent to gain access to another computer. The offence was made out even if only one computer was used.

There have been a number of successful prosecutions under section 1 of the Act, the first being in March 1991 when a man was fined £900 for making unauthorised calls to the United States using Mercury Communications equipment. Because 'computer' is not defined, it is likely to be given a generous meaning by the courts and can include equipment which has computer technology built into it although it would not normally be described as a computer.

A tremendous amount of publicity was generated by the acquittal of Paul Bedworth following his prosecution for conspiracy to commit offences under sections 1 and 3 of the Computer Misuse Act 1990 (for example, see *The Times*, 18 March 1993, p.3). The defence counsel argued that Bedworth was addicted to computer hacking and, as a result, he was not capable of forming the necessary intent to commit the offences charged. Although addiction, *per se*, is not a defence to a criminal charge (although it could be a mitigating factor when it comes to sentencing) the jury acquitted him. This raised concerns that the Act was not doing its job and there were calls for it to be strengthened, presumably by watering down the requirement for intention. This is unnecessary and would cause more problems and could result in the imposition of criminal liability on careless, clumsy or inept computer operators who, without meaning so, gained access to material they were not authorised to. The only sensible explanation of the Bedworth decision is that the jury probably felt some sympathy towards the accused. Perverse jury verdicts are not unknown. Two other hackers who had been charged along with Bedworth pleaded guilty and received six-month prison sentences. Altogether, the activities of the three hackers cost the victims hundreds of thousands of pounds.

It is certainly possible for employees to commit the basic hacking offence when using their own computer terminals at work if they intend to gain access to any program or data in respect of which they know they do not have authority to access. The concept of authority is strangely defined in section 17 in terms of being entitled to control access or having the consent of such a person. If the person is not so entitled and does not have the necessary consent, his intended access is unauthorised. Of course, the hacker must know this and the implication is that employers must make it quite clear to employees which programs and data they are entitled to access. This also applies to others such as pupils or students and self-employed consultants. Ideally, a written statement as to access entitlement should be issued.

Authorised Access for an Unauthorised Purpose

An employee may have authorisation to use a computer system as a normal part of his duties to his employer. If the employee subsequently uses the system for an unauthorised use - for example, for his own purposes such as carrying out private work or retrieving information for other purposes unconnected with his employment - does the access become unauthorised for the purposes of the Computer Misuse Act 1990? An example of this form of unauthorised use is given by the Audit Commission. A nurse at a hospital had authorisation to use the patient administration system but used it to search for medical details relating to friends and relatives. She then discussed these details with other members of her family. The nurse was not prosecuted under the Act but given a written warning for this breach of patient confidentiality (Audit Commission, *Ghost in the Machine: An Analysis of IT Fraud and Abuse,* Audit Commission Publications, 1998, p.18).

Where authorised access is used for an unauthorised purpose, it seems that the access remains authorised. So it was held in a surprising judgment in *DPP v Bingnell* (1998) 1 Cr App R 1. Two police officers had used the police national computer to gain access to details of motor cars which they wanted for private purposes unconnected with their duties as police officers. They were charged with the unauthorised access to computer material offence under section 1 of the Computer Misuse Act 1990 and convicted at Bow Street Magistrates' Court but their appeals to Southwark Crown Court were allowed and this was confirmed by the Queen's Bench Divisional Court.

The sole issue was whether the access was authorised. The Divisional Court held that it was, even though the purpose of the access was not authorised. Whether access is unauthorised is defined in section 17(5) of the Computer Misuse Act 1990 in the following terms:

> Access of any kind by any person to any program or data held in a computer is unauthorised if -
>
> (a) he is not himself entitled to control access of the kind in question to the program or data; and
> (b) he does not have consent to access by him of the kind in question to the program or data from any person who is so entitled,
>
> but this subsection is subject to section 10.

Section 10 is simply a saving in respect of access carried out for purposes associated with any search warrant, etc.

The Court decided that as the police officers were, in fact, entitled to control access to the material within section 17(5) they were authorised to access the computer data even if this was for an unauthorised purpose. As part of their normal duties, the police officers were entitled to access such computer information. But being entitled to access computer material is not the same as being entitled to control access to such material. This is an important and crucial distinction which the court failed to make. Even so, whether entitled to access the material or entitled to control access, that entitlement is surely subject to it being for police purposes only.

This is clearly a worrying decision and it is probably wrong as to this aspect of the Act. Otherwise, any employee using his employer's computer system to which he has been given access cannot commit the section 1 offence (nor for that matter the section 2 offence) if he uses the system for his own personal or private purposes. For example, if Joe, who is employed by the Mammoth Bank plc and has access to the customer database, uses the database to discover details of famous customers and their accounts at the bank and divulges that information to the media, he will not be guilty of the unauthorised access offence. Of course, as pointed out by the judge in *DPP v Bignell*, there could be an offence committed under data protection law (see the offence under section 55(1) of the Data Protection Act 1998 discussed in Chapter 31). However, not all use of computer material for unauthorised purposes will be caught by this and, unless the data relates to a living individual who can be identified from that data, the Data Protection Act 1998 will not apply.

The decision in *DPP v Bignell* leaves an unsatisfactory gap in the Computer Misuse Act 1990. The judge drew support for his view of the Act from the Law Commission Working Paper No. 110, *Computer Misuse* (1988), which suggested that it would be undesirable for the hacking offence to extend to an authorised user who is using the computer for an unauthorised purpose. The Working Paper was far from unambiguous and put forward various options for dealing with computer misuse in all its various forms. It went on to give an example of a situation which should not be criminalised; where a word processor operator uses the office computer to produce private correspondence. That is not the type of behaviour at which section 1 of the Computer Misuse Act 1990 was directed and this is confirmed by the White Paper which preceded the Act (Law Com. No. 186, *Criminal Law: Computer Misuse,* 1989). This specifically acknowledged that employees may be liable for the basic hacking offence and stated (para 3.35):

> The thrust of the basic hacking offence is aimed at the 'remote' hacker, but the offence is apt to cover the employee or insider as well. For that reason it is particularly important ... that (in addition to defining 'access' to exclude merely physical access to the computer itself) the *mens rea* of the offence should catch only the case where the employee consciously and deliberately misbehaves.

That sentiment is most appropriate in the circumstances of the case before the Divisional Court and would certainly cover the situation where the accused knowingly exceeded the scope of his authorisation intending to access data for his own purposes. From the reported facts of the case, it would seem beyond doubt that the accused police officers had consciously and deliberately misbehaved in the sense suggested in the White Paper by using the police national computer to gain access to information to be used for their own private purposes.

One of the main aims of the Computer Misuse Act 1990 was to deter unauthorised access to computer programs and data. When one contemplates that most computer misuse comes from within an organisation, perpetrated by its own employees, the decision in *DPP v Bignell* significantly prejudices the effective operation of the Act. In the Audit Commission Report, *Opportunity Makes a Thief: An Analysis of Computer Abuse*, HMSO, 1994, no less than 85 per cent of reported incidents of computer abuse were carried out by employees.

All three offences in the Computer Misuse Act 1990 are seriously affected by this decision as they all depend on the concept of authorisation. The ulterior intent offence under section 2 requires a section 1 offence to be committed as a precursor to the ulterior intent and section 3 is couched in terms of an unauthorised modification, being defined in section 17(6) in terms of being entitled to determine whether the modification should have been made or having the consent of such a person.

The Ulterior Intent Offence

Apart from hacking pure and simple, other problems were identified by the Law Commission. The law of attempts was of uncertain application to computer fraud and it did not seem that a person who obtained services without permission using a computer committed a significant offence. Of course, if two or more persons were involved a charge of conspiracy might be apposite but, otherwise, there were problems. Section 2 of the Computer Misuse Act 1990 covers these situations and also provides a alternative and, perhaps, better route to conviction where other offices are intended by the hacker. The section 2 offence is described in the Act as unauthorised access with intent to commit or facilitate the commission of further offences. It is a preliminary offence, particularly useful where the offence to which the ulterior intent applies is not completed. Another way of looking at it is to say that it is an aggravated form of the basic hacking offence.

The further offence must be one for which the sentence is fixed by law (for example, murder or high treason) or one for which the maximum sentence is not less than five years. Thus, section 2 applies to theft, blackmail, obtaining property or services by deception, abstracting electricity and a great many other offences, all having maximum punishments of five or more years' imprisonment. If the further offence is completed, then that offence will normally be charged but section 2 is useful where, for one reason or another, this is not the case. An example is where a hacker attempts to gain access to a computer with the intention of sending a blackmail message to someone but is not able to get beyond the log-on screen. It is unlikely that a charge of attempted blackmail will succeed because he has not done an act which is more than merely preparatory, but a charge under section 2 will be more likely to result in a conviction providing the necessary intentions and knowledge can be proved - that is:

- the intention to secure access,
- the knowledge that the access is unauthorised, and
- the intention to commit blackmail.

The ulterior intent offence is triable either way and carries a maximum penalty of five years' imprisonment and/or a fine if tried in the Crown Court. Any person who is tried for a section 2 (or a section 3 offence) in the Crown

Court can, if found not guilty, be found guilty by a jury of the section 1 offence and sentenced accordingly (section 12). A person can be found guilty of a section 2 offence even if the commission of the further offence is impossible: for example, where a hacker intends to erase details of a debt he owes when the person to whom the debt is owed has already written it off or if the hacker is mistaken about owing the debt in the first place.

Jurisdiction

The international character of some computer crime has caused concern about the possibility of criminals escaping prosecution because of jurisdictional issues. For example, in *R v Tomsett* [1985] Crim LR 369, the accused sent a telex from London intending to divert funds from New York to the accused's account in Geneva. It was held in the Court of Appeal that, had the attempt been successful, the theft would have taken place in New York and the English courts would not have had jurisdiction to try the perpetrator. To prevent this type of problem (making it tempting for fraudsters to set up in England to carry out frauds abroad using computers and telecommunications systems), the Computer Misuse Act contains complex provisions relating to jurisdiction and extradition in sections 4 to 9. All that is required is a link with the home country - England and Wales, Scotland or Northern Ireland, as appropriate. That is, the ofence must either originate from the home country or be directed to a computer within it: for example, a person from within England attempts to carry out a computer fraud in Sweden or a person from Italy attempts to hack into a computer located in London.

A finally requirement is that of double criminality; that is, if the person operates from within any of the home countries intending to commit a further offence under section 2 in a different country, that offence is indeed a criminal offence in that other country as well as in the home country. Of course, in most cases this will not present any problems - most countries recognise theft and fraud.

Other Offences Associated with Hacking

Although it is to be expected that the Computer Misuse Act 1990 will be the main weapon in the fight against computer hacking (and some other forms of computer misuse), certain other areas of criminal law may be relevant. It is possible that these other offences will apply in situations outside the scope of the 1990 Act: for example, there could be a problem in proving that the hacker knew that his access was unauthorised. In such a case, recourse must be had to he pre-existing law and the possibilities are discussed below.

The Law of Theft

As we have seen, the offence of theft is defined by section 1 of the Theft Act 1968 as a dishonest appropriation of property belonging to another with the intention to permanently deprive the other of it. If a hacker gains access to a computer system without permission and then makes a printout of some information contained therein, has he committed theft? The fact that the owner of the information has not been deprived of it, because the hacker has only made a copy, is fatal to any charge of theft.

In *Oxford v Moss* (1978) 68 Cr. App R 183, it was held that confidential information odes not come within the definition of property for the purposes of theft. The case concerned the 'borrowing' of an examination paper by a student before the date of the examination. Although the authority of the case is weak, having been decided at first instance only, it is likely that it would be followed because the consequences of the decision are fundamentally sensible. After all, the owner still has the information unless the only copy was taken, but this is different from saying that the information is not property for the purposes of the Theft Act. Property is defined as including money and all other property, real or personal, including things in action and other intangible property' and it could fairly be argued that confidential information comes within the meaning of 'other intangible property'. A better construction of *Oxford* v *Moss* is that the taking of the examination paper could not be theft because there was no intention to deprive the owner of it permanently. For this reason a hacker who simply reads or copies information has not committed theft. Similarly, in the Scottish case of *Grant* v *Procurator Fiscal* [1988] RPC 41, an employee who offered copes of his employer's computer printouts to a competitor for £400 was acquitted. It was said that there was no authority for the proposition that the dishonest exploitation of the confidential information was a criminal offence.

If the information concerned is copied onto paper belonging to someone else, such as an employer, there will be an offence of theft committed with respect to the paper. Likewise, if a person copes information from a computer on to a disk which belongs to someone else and takes the disk, this would be theft of the disk of the other elements of theft are present such as the intention to permanently deprive the owner of the disk.

If the hacker goes further and not only makes a copy of the information but then, immediately after, goes on to erase the original from the computer system, is this more likely to be viewed as theft? An act of deliberate erasure will almost certainly be an offence under section 3 of the Computer Misuse Act 1990, as discussed in Chapter 26. In terms of theft, there will be a dishonest appropriation of property belonging to another but is there an intention to permanently deprive the owner of that information? The difficulty here will be if the hacker believes that the owner has another copy of that information, for, if he does to believe, there is no intention to permanently deprive. In the world of computers, back up copies of programs and data are the rule and it would be very reasonable for the hacker to believe that back-up copies have been made. Therefore, it would appear that unauthorised copying, even coupled with the subsequent destruction of the original, is unlikely to be theft.

There is an offence in the Theft Act 1968 which holds out some promise and that is the offence of abstracting electricity. The very act of hacking will result in the host computer (the computer hacked into - assessed without permission) performing work as it retrieves information from its store. If that information is stored on magnetic disks, the disk drive heads will physically move, tracking across the disks, locating and then reading the information which will then be moved into the computer's volatile memory by means of tiny electrical currents. More electricity will be consumed in transmitting the information to the hacker's computer terminal. The total amount of electricity used to perform these acts will be small but, nevertheless, a definite amount will have been used as a result of the hacker's actions.

Section 13 of the Theft Act 1968 describes the offence of abstracting electricity as its dishonest use without due authority, or its dishonest waste or diversion. The offence is committed regardless of the amount of electricity so used and the only difficulty concerns the concept of dishonesty. There is no definition of dishonesty in the Theft Act 1968 for the purposes of section 13, but case law provides some guidance. The test of dishonesty which is used for the offences of theft and obtaining by deception derives from the case of *R* v *Ghosh* [1982] QB 1053, and there is no reason no doubt that the same test would apply to the offence of abstracting electricity. Ultimately, the test must be resolved by the jury and while a jury would probably consider, objectively, that hacking was dishonest, the members of a jury might have more difficulty in deciding whether the accused hacker would realise that what he was doing was dishonest by the ordinary standards of reasonable and honest persons.

Communications Offences

Section 1 of the Interception of Communications Act 1985 makes it an offence to intercept a communication intentionally during its transmission through a public telecommunications system. This will only apply to a case where the hacker actually intercepts something (for example, the transmission of computer data over the BT network). In most cases, the hacker will initiate the transmission and will cause the sending of the information. This offence therefore applies only to the situation where the hacker is 'eavesdroping': that is, listening in for interesting communications to intercept.

Section 43 of the Telecommunications Act 1984 makes it a criminal offence to transmit messages which are grossly offensive, indecent, obscene or menacing by means of a public telecommunications system. Similarly, an offence is committed if false messages are sent by a person knowing of their falsity, or persistent use is made of the system for the purpose of causing annoyance, inconvenience or needless anxiety. The Act refers to messages, so if a pornographic diagram or picture is sent by the hacker the offence might not be applicable. It could be argued, however, that a picture is just another way of conveying a message, in which case section 43 of the 1984 Act would apply. It would seem that the Obscene Publications Acts of 1959 and 1964 do not apply because there must be publication or possession of an obscene article and the definition of article given by section 1(2) of the 1959 Act, as extended by section 2(1) of the 1964 Act, requires some tangible object. It would be different if a person distributes disks containing computer pornography; this would certainly fall within the meaning of the Acts.

Menacing messages could be linked to the offence of blackmail where the threat itself is transmitted by such means. The threat could concern the computer system - for example, where someone threatens to destroy information stored on the computer system. Alternatively, the threat may be of a less technical nature - for example, a threat to inform the IT Manager's wife of his adultery. This offence under the Telecommunications Act will only be committed where a public system is used. It would appear that a hacker who sends just one false message will commit the offence if he knows that the message is false and transmits it for one of the purposes mentioned - for example, to cause annoyance. The same applies if the hacker persistently sends messages, whether true or false with any of the motives mentioned above. Another possibility is a prosecution under the Protection from Harassment Act 1997, for example, if messages which cause alarm or distress are sent. A course of conduct is required, meaning more than one occasion.

A weakness has been found in the telecommunications statutes in a case concerning evidence of a telephone conversation involving a drug trafficker. In *R* v *Effick* (unreported) 22 July 1994, the accused had argued that a recording of the conversation was made in contravention of section 1(1) of the 1985 Act. Section 9 declares that evidence obtained in breach of section 1(1) is inadmissible. However, the House of Lords held that the signals transmitted from a cordless telephone handset to the base unit were not in a public telecommuniations system and intercepting the signals by means of a radio receiver was not caught by section 1(1) of Interception of Communications Act 1985. Unfortunately for the trafficker, this meant that the evidence was correctly admitted in his trial and the conviction was confirmed.

Data Protection Act 1998

This Act is described more fully in Part Four. However, there may be some scope for the Act in terms of computer hacking and therefore this aspect will be discussed here.

The Data Protection Act 1998 regulates the use and storage of personal data - that is, information relating to individuals who can be identified from that information.

A 'data controller' is a person who processes personal data and must notify the Data Protection Commissioner if the processing is carried out by automatic means (some forms of sensitive manual processing may also be required to be notified). Failure to notify is a criminal offence, triable either way, carrying an unlimited fine if tried in the Crown Court, or a fine not exceeding £5000 if tried in a Magistrates' Court.

If a computer hacker gains access to a computer system on which personal data is stored and then makes a copy of that data which he stores in his own computer, the hacker is guilty of the offence of processing personal data without having notified the Commissioner. There are a number of other offences under the Act, for which see Part IV of this book.

Postscript

In *R* v *Bow Street Magistrates' Court and Allison (A.P.) ex parte Government of the United States of America,* 5 August 1999, the House of Lords considered the concept of authorisation in the context of the Computer Misuse Act 1990. An employee, who was authorised to access customer accounts as part of her duties, accessed them for the purposes of carrying out fraud-related offences.

The House of Lords considered the decision in *DPP* v *Bignell* and the decision in the present case in the Divisional Court, and noted a misunderstanding of the concept of authorisation for the purposes of the section 1 offence. The error was to consider authorisation in relation to programs or data of a particular kind (control of the computer at a particular level) when what the Act required was to consider authorisation in relation to a particular program or to particular data. Lord Hobhouse said:

> Nor is s 1 of the Act concerned with authority to access kinds of data. It is concerned with authority to access the actual data involved.

Although the employee had authority to access the kind of data that she accessed, as part of her normal duties, she did not have authority to access the particular data she did access, as such access was made with a view to conspiring with others to commit theft and forgery.

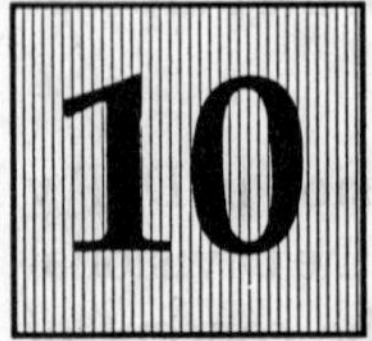

UNAUTHORISED MODIFICATION OF COMPUTER PROGRAMS OR DATA: (A Case Study)

The Law Before the 1990 Act

Prior to the Computer Misuse Act 1990, damage or erasure of computer programs or data was an offence under the Criminal Damage Act 1971. By section 1(1) of that Act, a person is guilty of an offence if, without lawful excuse, he destroys or damages any property belonging to another. The definition of the offence required that the person intended such consequences to occur or was reckless as to whether property would be so destroyed or damaged. In the case of *R* v *Caldwell* [1982] AC 341, it was held that whether a person had been reckless was an objective test-that is, whether the course of action undertaken by the accused created what would be an obvious risk of damage in the eyes of the ordinary prudent individual.

One potential difficulty with the Act is that property must be destroyed or damaged and property is defined by section 10 as meaning tangible property. This creates an immediate problem when programs or data stored on magnetic media such as a disk are erased. Programs or data are not tangible in this form, although the disk itself certainly is. The first case to tackle this apparent difficulty was *Cox* v *Riley* (1986) 83 Cr App R 54, in which the accused erased programs from a printed circuit card used to control his employer's computerised saw for cutting out timber sections for window frames. He was charged with criminal damage but argued that the programs were not tangible property within the meaning of the Act. Nevertheless, he was found guilty on the basis that the printed circuit card had been damaged and was now useless. It would require some work in reprogramming it before it could be restored to its former condition.

The 'Mad Hacker'

The Court of Appeal had an opportunity to examine the applicability of criminal damage when it heard the appeal against conviction of the self-styled 'mad hacker'. In *R* v *Whiteley* [1991] 93 Cr App R 381, the accused gained unauthorised access to the Joint Academic Network (JANET) and gave himself the status of Systems Manager. He deleted and added files, changed passwords and deleted audit files recording his activities. He was very skilled and even deleted a special program inserted to trap him. His activities caused serious disruption and he was convicted of damaging computer disks. The Court of Appeal rejected his appeal confirming that the value of the disks had been impaired. The Lord Chief Justice, Lord Lane,said that the Act required that tangible property had been damaged, not that the damage itself should be tangible.

The appeal in *R* v *Whiteley* had bene heard after the Computer Misuse Act 190 came into force but had to be decided on the basis of the prior law. The 1990 Act provides that, for the purposes of the Criminal Damage Act 1971, a modification of the contents of a computer is not to be regarded as damaging any computer or computer storage medium, unless its effect on that computer or storage medium impaired its physical condition (Computer Misuse Act 1990, section 3(6). This is to try and remove any overlap between the unauthorised modification offence under the Computer Misuse Act 1990 and the Criminal Damage Act 1971.

Current Position Under the Criminal Damage Act 1971

It would seem that the 1971 Act no longer applies to damage of programs and data stored in a computer. In *R* v *Whileley*, however, the conviction was based on the fact that the state of the magnetic particles on the disks had been altered. These particles, it could be argued, are tangible even if they a are not visible. This point may be of academic interest only as it is unlikely that a charge would be brought under the Criminal Damage Act 1971 in respect of damage to programs or data; the 1990 Act would be used instead. There is one occasion, however, when the 1971 Act might be helpful and that is when the accused denies an intention to cause damage because, under the 1971 Act, objective recklessness suffices. It goes without saying that a hacker moving around in a strange computer system without training or the appropriate documentation is being objectively reckless.

Unauthorised Modification Under the Computer Misuse Act 1990

One of the reasons for the replacement of criminal damage in relation to computer programs and data stored in a computer or on computer storage media was that there were doubts about the logical validity of the approach adopted in *Cox* v *Riley*. Section 3 of the Computer Misuse Act 1990 was intended to put the matter beyond doubt and states that a person commits an offence if:

> ... he does any act which causes an unauthorised modification of the contents of any computer; and at the time when he does the act, he has the requisite intent and the requisite knowledge.

The meaning of 'authority" applies in a way similar to that in relation to the section 1 offence - the modification is unauthorised if the person causing it is not entitled to determine whether the modification should be made and he does not have the consent of any person who is so entitled.

As mentioned in the previous chapter, there is a problem where a person who is authorised to access computer material uses his access for an unauthorised purpose. The same consideration could apply here: for example, where an employee is authorised to enter updated information into a customer database but deliberately changes some information to make it incorrect, he may escape liability as he is deemed to be entitled to determine whether any modification should be made. The better view is that *DPP* v *Bignell* is wrongly decided and an employee would not have *carte blanche* to make any modifications he wanted, only those in the course of his duties. Alternatively, as authority here relates to modification rather than access to programs or data, the concept of authorisation in *DDP* v *Bignell* does not apply in this context. It would be unthinkable if an employee could erase his employer's computer data as an act of revenge and escape liability under the Computer Misuse Act 1990. In practice, there have been a number of successful prosecutions under the Act for such activities. For example, a former operations manager who resigned from his post persuaded an operator in duty to give him access to the master operator terminal and loaded onto the computer system a malicious program which would have caused severe disruption had it not been discovered (Audit Commission, *Ghost in the Machine: An Analysis of IT Fraud and Abuse*, Audit Commission Publications, 1998, p.17).

'Modification' is extensively defined in section 17, the interpretation section, as the alteration or erasure of any program or data or the addition of any program or data to the contents of a computer. The latter covers situations where someone leaves messages on a computer without authority (a form of a computer graffiti perhaps) or the situation where a person introduces a computer virus into the system. It clearly covered the activities of the person who distributed disks claiming to contain advice for the prevention of Aids; after using one of these disks, data files on the computer were made inaccessible and a message was displayed asking for money in return for a cure. The culprit was arrested in the United States and convicted of blackmail.

For the purposes of section 3, the requisite intent is an intent to cause a modification to the contents of any computer:

- to impair the operation of any computer,
- to prevent or hinder access to any program or data held in any computer, or
- to impair the operation of any program or the reliability of any data.

It is immaterial whether the intent is directed at any particular computer, program or data or programs or data of a particular kind or at any particular modification or any modification of any particular kind. The requisite knowledge is knowledge that the intended modification is unauthorised.

The section 3 offence is useful in that it deals with the problem with precision and is wide enough to cover viruses, time-bombs and logic-bombs as well as dealing with immediate, direct modification. However, the need for the prosecution to prove that the accused possessed both of two states of mind - that is, having the requisite intent and the requisite knowledge - may make conviction less certain, particularly where employees are concerned. There seems to be no justification for narrowing intention in this way and the objective recklessness approach in criminal damage is preferable in this respect.

The offence is triable either way and the maximum penalties in the Crown Court are the same as for the section 2 offence: that is, imprisonment for a term not exceeding five years and/or a fine. The jurisdiction provisions apply to this offence as they do the section 1 offence.

There have been some successful prosecutions under section 3. For example, in June 1992 a free-lance typesetter tampered with a computer owned by a client thereby denying access to the client. He argued that the client owed him £2000 in fees but was, nevertheless, convicted of an offence under section 3 of the computer Misuse Act 190 and given two years' conditional discharge and fined £1650. The judge said that his crime was not particularly serious even though the client claimed to have lost £36000 in lost business as a result (*Computing*, 18 June 1992, p.2). In December 1993, a nurse hacked into the hospital computer and changed patients' drug prescriptions in a way that was potentially lethal. He was found guilty of two offences under section 3 and sentenced to 12 months' imprisonment. It is possible that a charge of attempted murder or manslaughter is appropriate in such circumstances but it might be difficult to prove the required intention. The same applies to the ulterior intent offence in section 2. The section 3 offence is much simpler as the intention only has to be directed towards the computer or programs or data stored in the computer.

If a prosecution is brought under section 3 it is important that there is sound evidence linking the alleged culprit with the unauthorised modification. In *R Vatsal Patel* (unreported) July 1993 (see *Computers and Law* (1994) 5(2),

p. 4), strange things started to happen on a project to write bespoke software. Database tables started to disappear and eventually development work was halted. The accused was a free-lance programmer and a member of the team writing the software and two 'wrecking programs' were found on his computer. One of the programs was named VAT which was the accused's nickname. A trap was set but nothing further happened - although the wrecking programs had been erased in the meantime. A charge was brought under section 3 of the Computer Misuse Act 1990 but, following a trial lasting six days, the jury acquitted the accused. The total losses to the client were in the order of £90000 and there was a suspicion that the accused had erased the tables in order to prolong his lucrative contract. However, any number of persons could have been responsible for erasing the data and, in addition, there had been problems with the hardware and the development platform itself had been highly unstable. In other words, there was no real proof that the accused was responsible. It was remarked upon that had he been responsible, he would have been unlikely to use his own nickname for one of the wrecking programs.

A person might modify computer records in order to cover up some other criminal or disreputable activity. In *R Sinha* [1995] Crim LR 68, a doctor at a medical practice in Cardiff was charged with manslaughter and attempting to pervert the course of justice. A 30-year-old female patent who suffered from asthma consulted the doctor and he prescribed a beta-blocker drug which induced a fatal asthma attack. The doctor later altered the computerised records relating to the patient to remove references to here suffering from asthma. However, although the references were no longer displayed they could still be retrieved from the computer disk. A charge was not brought under section 3 of the Computer Misuse Act 1990. As mentioned previously, because the doctor had authorisation to use the computer and access patient records, there could have been a problem with the issue of whether the modification was unauthorised. The offence of perverting the course of justice is more reliable in this respect and certainly applies to the destruction or concealment of evidence.

Computer Viruses

A computer virus is self-replicating program which spreads throughout a computer system, attaching copies of itself to ordinary programs. Often, by the time the virus is detected, many back-up disks also will have been infected. Rumours abound to the effect that viruses are far more likely to be on disks containing pirated software. There were no reports of computer viruses in the Audit Commission surveys prior to the one undertaken in 1990 where a total of 54 incidents were reported, accounting for some 30 per cent of all reported computer fraud and abuse (Audit Commission, *Survey of Computer Fraud & Abuse*, HMSO, 1991). The next survey showed a massive increase to 261 incidents (Audit Commission, *Opportunity Makes a Thief: An Analysis of Computer Abuse*, HMSO, 1994). In the latest survey, nearly 50 per cent of the organisations surveyed reported problems with viruses (Audit Commission, *Ghost in the Machine: An Analysis of IT Fraud and Abuse*, Audit Commission Publications, 1998).

There are literally, thousands of viruses and strains of viruses, some are relatively innocuous (though irritating) like the Italian virus which causes a bouncing ball to appear on screen but others are more pernicious and may completely corrupt a hard disk. The 'Aids' disk mentioned earlier was distributed as part of a blackmail scheme to over 30000 organisations worldwide. Obviously, viruses are going to remain a threat in the future but persons responsible for introducing them deliberately into a computer system are clearly guilty of an office under section 3 of the Computer Misuse Act 1990. This is so even if the perpetrator does not personally carry out the act causing the infection because section 3 states that the person is guilty if he does any act which causes the unauthorised modification and this will include distributing infected disks.

Publishing details of how to write computer viruses could fall within the law of incitement; that is, the person publishing the details could be inciting others to commit a section 3 offence. However, there must be an intention on the part of the inciter to bring about the criminal consequences and this may be difficult to prove, although, in May 1995, an unemployed man who called himself the 'Black Baron' became the first person to be convicted of incitement in respect of computer viruses (*Computing*, 1 June 1995, p.1). He was also convicted of 11 charges under the Computer Misuse Act 1990 and the judge warned him to expect a custodial sentence.

There is also a possibility of a charge as an accomplice but, again, intention must be proved. Obvious doubts about the applicability of the law of incitement and accomplices were confirmed by police fears concerning the then imminent publication of a book revealing virus techniques in 1992 (*The Times;* 12 June 1992). The same difficulties apply in regard to access providers on the Internet, though individuals responsible for posting details of how to write and spread viruses could be liable to prosecution. Bearing in mind the international nature of the Internet, however, jurisdiction and extradition will be problematic in many cases.

Blackmail

Blackmail is a serious and is triable only on indictment:

that is, in the Crown Court. The offence is provided for a section 21 of the Theft Act 1968 and carries a maximum penalty of 14 years' imprisonment. Basically, a person is guilty of blackmail if, with a view to gain for himself or another or with intent to cause loss to another he makes any unwarranted demand with menances. The menances are not restricted to threats of violence and include threats of action which is detrimental or unpleasant to the person to whom those threats are directed. An example is where a person threatens to reveal someone's previous financial difficulties unless that other person pays him some money. The 'protection racket' provides another example: that is, a shopkeeper's premises will be destroyed unless he makes certain payments.

So far as computers are concerned, a person would be guilty of blackmail who inserted a 'time bomb' into a computer system and demanded money in return for details of how to disable the time-bomb. If the owner of the computer system has already discovered and removed the time-bomb when the demand is made, it makes no difference; the offence has still been committed. The offence of blackmail will also have been committed even if the computer owner is not worried about the threat because he has a complete, up-to-date set of back-up copies of everything likely to be affected.

Blackmail may be associated with a virus. The fact a virus is present may focus the victim's mind more wonderfully than would be the case with a time-bomb where no harm would be done until a predetermined data. A virus starts its destructive work by immediatcly spreading throughout a system. If free-lance workers feel inclined to leave a virus or time-bomb behind to be used to pressurise a client into paying the agreed fee promptly, they should think again. A university lecturer carried out some consultancy work but when he was paid the client deducted part to pay for the telephone bill the lecturer had incurred. The lecturer retaliated by placing a virus in the client's computer with a message to the effect that he was owed money and that files were being modified and that the sooner the matter was settled, the less damage would be done. He was convicted of attempted blackmail and fined £500 (*Computing*, 8 October 1992, p.2)

The meaning of the word 'unwarranted' can cause problems. A demand is unwarranted unless the person making the demand does so in the belief that he has reasonable grounds for so doing and that the use of menances is a proper way of reinforcing the demand. In most cases the demand will plainly be unwarranted on the basis of this test, but there might be circumstances where this was not so. For example, a free-lance programmer has carried out a substantial amount of work for a company which, he believes, has substantially and deliberately underpaid him. In order to encourage the company to pay up, the programmer might tell the company that he has entered a computer virus into the computer system and he will not remove it unless the shortfall in his payment is made up. It appears from case law that the accused must be judged by his own standards when it comes to the interpretation of 'unwarranted' and a jury might acquit the programmer if it feels that the programmer genuinely believes that he has reasonable grounds for making the demand and that the means he employs are proper, in his subjective opinion. Although this is somewhat unsatisfactory in that an accused person is being judged by his own moral standards, this is the current state of the law. However, the case discussed above where a university lecturer used a virus as a means of securing payment shows how a jury is likely to react in practice . If the action threatened is of a very serious nature (for example, if it would result in the commission of a serious offence); a jury should be directed that the means cannot be proper.

Bearing in mind the serious nature of blackmail, any victim should not hesitate to inform the police. As with other forms of blackmail, a payment made to a blackmailer in return for not destroying computer data is likely to be followed by further demands in the future. Goods security and comprehensive back-up systems are the best defences against this insidious form of crime. At the same time as committing blackmail, the blackmailer may also commit other offences such as unauthorised modification of computer material, basic hacking, abstracting electricity and offences under section 43 of the Telecommunications Act 1984.

PIRACY AND OTHER OFFENCES

Copyright Law

We have already seen that infringement of copyright can give rise to a wide range of civil law remedies such as injunctions, damages and accounts of profits. Copyright is unique among intellectual property rights in that it is also well served by the criminal law. While patent law and trade mark law contain criminal sanctions, the rights prescribed by those branches of law are almost entirely enforced by the application of the civil law. Although it is true to say that the majority of copyright infringements will be dealt with in a satisfactory manner by the civil law, the criminal penalties available may be more appropriate in some circumstances.

Copyright law contains criminal penalties for may of the activities collectively known as 'secondary infringements'. The common denominator is that these activities can be thought of as being of a commercial nature and include the infringements of copyright commonly knows as 'computer software piracy' - an example would be importing or selling copies of computer software without the permission of the owner of the copyright in the software.

The criminal offences under copyright law are not restricted for cases of blatant piracy. In *Thames & Hudson Ltd* v *Design and Artists Copyright Society Ltd* [1995] FSR 153 the Design and Artists Copyright Society Ltd commenced private prosecutions against Thames & Hudson Ltd and its directors for offences under sections 107 and 110 of the Copyright, Designs and Patents Act 1988 on the basis that Thames & Hudson was selling and distributing a book knowing, or having reason to believe, that it contained material infringing copyright. (Section 110 imposes liability on officers of corporate bodies for offences under section 107.) An application by Thames & Hudson for a stay of proceedings until after the civil case had been heard was rejected by the judge who confirmed that section 107 does not differentiate between a reputable firm and a pirate. The activities which attract criminal penalties are listed in Table 11.1 with the appropriate maximum penalties.

As can be seen from Table 11.1, the scope of these criminal offences is fairly wide and will cover most forms of commercial exploitation. Of particular note is the fact that making an article designed to make copies is a criminal offence, as is being in possession of such a device if the intention is to make copies for sale or hire or use in the course of business. This would cover a piece of equipment specifically designed for this purpose but not a computer with a dual disk drive. Although the latter can be used for this purpose, computers are not designed for infringing copyright; they are designed for legitimate uses. The word 'article' is used in section 107(2) but is not defined in the Act in this context. Section 296 of the Act concerns devices and means to circumvent copy protection, but the word 'article' is not used in that section. It would seem unlikely that computer software designed to overcome copy protection, which facilitates the copying of other computer software, would fall within the meaning of 'article' and, therefore, producing such software may not be a criminal offence, although it would give rise to civil remedies.

TABLE 11.1

CRIMINAL OFFENCES AND COPYRIGHT LAW

Offence (Copyright, Designs and Patents Act 1988)	*Classification of offence (see below)*
Section 107(1)	
With respect to an article which the person concerned knows or has reason to believe is an infringing copy of a copyright work:	
(a) making for sale or hire	MC/CC
(b) importing into the UK (not for private or domestic use)	MC/CC
(c) possessing in the course of business with a view to committing any act infringing the copyright	MC
(d) in the course of a business:	
(i) selling or letting for hire	MC
(ii) offering or exposing for sale or hire	MC
(iii) exhibiting in public	MC
(iv) distributing	MC/CC
(e) distributing otherwise than in the course of a business to such an extent as to affect prejudicially the owner of the copyright	MC/CC
Section 107(2)	
With respect to an article specifically designed or adapted for making copies of a particular copyright work where the person concerned knows or has reason to believe that it is to be used to make infringing copies for sale or hire or for use in the course of a business:	
(a) making such an article	MC
(b) being in possession of such an article	MC

Classification of Penalties:

MC/CC - (triable either way). On summary conviction: Imprisonment not exceeding 6 months and/or a fine not exceeding £5000. On conviction on indictment. Imprisonment not exceeding 2 years and/or a fine (unlimited amount)

MC - (Summary trial only, i.e. in Magistrates' Court). Imprisonment not exceeding 6 months and/or a fine not exceeding level 5 (Presently £5000)

Alternatively, the software and the medium on which it resides might, taken together, be properly described as an article. The lack of clarity in section 107(2) is regrettable, although the primary purpose of this offence is the control of activities such as the making and use of plates for printing processes and the like. In fact, the Copyright Act 1956 talked in terms of a plate for making infringing copies. As discussed later in this chapter, however, the supply of software or devices to assist with the copying of computer software protected by copyright may be caught by the law of incitement.

The reason why the criminal law is relatively strong as regards copyright is the ease with which copyright works can be copied and the scale on which is can be done. In 1998, customes offices in Germany seized £37 million worth of pirated software in two warehouses (*Computing,* 13 August 1998, p. 4). Various estimates of the losses due to software piracy have been made: in 1990 the losses in Europe alone were estimated at $4.3 billion (*Computing,* 9 January 1992, p. 3). More recent estimates show that the losses may have peaked but world-wide losses stand at an estimated $12.8 billion (*PC Week,* 3 May 1994, p 4). Of course, such figures must be taken with a pinch of salt, but they do give some indication of the scale of the problem. It is a simple matter to copy most computer software, even if it is copy-protected, and, what is more, the investment required to do this and to market and sell the copies is relatively small. In contrast, to copy and sell an invention protected by patent law is likely to involve a substantial investment, requiring the acquisition of factory space, storage, expensive equipment, transport, etc. The scope and magnitude of criminal penalties have been gradually increased and strengthened to cater for the growing ease of copying with the advent of high speed photocopying, video recorders, twin-tap cassette players and computers.

The formula used for liability is that the person concerned 'knows or has reason to believe'. The meaning of this phrase was considered in*LA Gear Inc* v *Hi-Tec Sports plc* [1992] FSR 121, where the Court of Appeal said that the test to apply was on objective one - that is, whether the reasonable man, having the defendant's knowledge of the facts, would have believed that the copy was an infringing copy. Previously, the High Court had gone further saying that the phrase connoted the allowance of a period of time to allow the reasonable man to evaluate the facts and so form a reasonable belief. Although the Court of Appeal said the test was objective, it is truly so if it takes into account the facts known to the defendant. What if the defendant deliberately turns a blind eye to the facts; he suspects that copies are infringing copies but does to enquire into this?

The availability of equipment which facilitates copying has not gone unchallenged. In the United States of America, the film industry attempted, unsuccessfully, to prevent the sale of the Sony Btamax video recorder. In the United Kingdom the record industry argued unsuccessfully that the sale of the Amstrad twin-tape cassette machine was an incitement to infringe copyright (see *Amstrad Consumer Electronics plc* v *The British Phonograph Industry Ltd* [1986] FSR 159, and CBS *Songs Ltd* v *Amstrad Consumer Electronics plc* [1988] 2 WLR 1191). The way these machines were advertised did nothing to reassure the industry using phrases such as 'you can even make a copy of your favourite cassettes', and it is true that most purchases of such machines would use them to make unauthorised copies of music tapes and computer software, especially computer games on cassette tape. In the first Amstrad case above, it was held that supplying machines which would be likely to be used to unlawfully copy pre-recorded cassettes subject to copyright protection was insufficient to make the manufacturer or supplier an infringer of copyright. Neither could Amstrad be said to be authorising infringement of copyright because it had no control over the way its machines were used once sold. In the latter case, it was held that a claim that Amstrad, by its advertising literature, was inciting others to infringe copyright gave no legal remedies in civil law to the relevant copyright owner. In any case, Amstrad had printed a small warning about infringing copyright in its literature.

These two cases illustrate the difficulties in reconciling two distinct objectives - that is, encouraging technical innovation and making it available to the public on the one hand and protecting the interests of those willing to invest in music, films, computer software, etc. on the other hand.

Incitement is a common law offence and, with the exception of incitement to commit murder, is not to be found in Acts of Parliament. This gives the courts some flexibility in applying and interpreting this area of law. Although Amstrad, because of the use of a warning against copyright infringement, was not guilty of incitement, there may be other situations where a conviction might be more likely. For example, in the case of devices and computer software specifically designed to circumvent copy protection, the makers and sellers of such gadgets and software cannot point to legitimate uses unlike the Amstrad and similar twin-tape machines. They are designed to enable persons to make copies of software packages clearly against the wishes of the owners of the copyright in such packages. The Copyright, Designs and Patents Act 1988 specifically provides that civil law remedies should be available against persons responsible for the sale and distribution of such methods of overcoming copy-protection. It would appear that the criminal law offence of incitement also may be available against such persons.

A pirate who copies or imports copied software with a view to selling it may commit other offences apart from those under copyright law, depending on the circumstances. The Forgery and Counterfeiting Act 1981, the Trade Descriptions Act 1968 and section 25 of the Theft Act 1968 may be relevant. The pirate can also be pursued through the civil courts and the decision to pursue civil or criminal remedies, or both, will depend on the nature and scale of the infringement, the pirate's knowledge of the existence of copyright in the work and whether the pirate has any funds available to pay damages.

The Copyright, Designs and Patents Act 1988 has been used increasingly to prosecute computer software pirates and magistrates and judges are at last taking this form of crime seriously, using custodial sentences in some cases. For example, and Oxford computer dealer was imprisoned for six months and fined £5000 for making unauthorised copies of a popular word processing package with the intention of selling them (*Computing*, 11 August 1994, p.3). A few weeks earlier, a brother and sister pleaded guilty to 23 counts of software piracy and offences under the Trade Descriptions Act 1968 and were sentenced to 200 and 100 hours' community service respectively (*Computing*, 23 June 1994, p 14).

Forgery and Counterfeiting Act 1981

Section 1 of this Act states that:

> A person is guilty of forgery if he makes a false instrument, with the intention that he or another shall use it to induce somebody to accept it as genuine, and by reason of so accepting it to do or not do some act to his own or any other person's prejudice.

We have seen that the application of this offence to computer hacking has been a failure. If a computer software pirate makes copies of a popular package, however, dressing up the copies to look like the original and then selling them, he may be guilty of the offence contained in section 1 of the Act. It may seem strange to talk in terms of a 'false instrument' in relation to computer software, but section 8 of the ACt describes a false instrument as including:

> ... any disc, tape, sound or other device on or in which information is recorded or stored by mechanical, electronic or other means.

It would seem that every form or method of storing computer software will fall within this definition.

It could be argued that the person who buys a pirate copy of computer software will not be deceived and that he will know that, in the circumstances, the software he is purchasing is an unauthorised copy, especially if the price is considerably lower than usual, but this does not matter. The Act requires that the pirate intends the customer to accept the copy as being genuine and in one sense the copy will be genuine as it will be a direct copy of the computer programs. The programs themselves are the genuine programs. Section 1 requires that someone should accept the false instrument as genuine resulting in that person or another being prejudiced. Therefore, it does not matter if the person buying the copy is not prejudiced - after all he will have obtained a copy which works as well as the genuine article - it is sufficient that someone else has been prejudiced. That someone else is the owner of the copyright subsisting in the programs who will have been prejudiced because he has lost a potential sale as a result of the pirate's activities. If the customer himself believes that the software is genuine, then the pirate can be charged with the offence of obtaining by deception (Theft Act 1968, section 15) which carries a maximum of ten years' imprisonment, the same as under section 1 of the Forgery and Counterfeiting Act 1981. The choice between these two offences will have to be carefully considered in the light of the actual circumstances. In April 1991, a computer dealer was found guilty of obtaining by deception for selling pirate copies of software at the full retail price. He was sentenced to nine months' imprisonment, suspended for two years (*Computing*, 18 April 1992, p.3).

Trade Descriptions Act 1968

By section 1 of the Trade Descriptions Act 1968, any person who, in the course of a trade or business, applies a false trade description to any goods or supplies or offers to supply goods to which a false trade description has been applied, is guilty of an offence. A 'trade description' includes an indication as to the person by whom the goods are manufactured. Therefore, if a computer software pirate makes copies of a software package, without the permission of the copyright owner in such a way that the copies look like the genuine article, then the offence is committed. A person who sells or offers such copies for sale will a also be guilty of the offence. The rationale behind these provisions is to protect the public from being deceived into buying inferior gods rather than protecting the interests of copyright owners. Prosecution is normally undertaken by trading standards officers and the offence carries a maximum of two years' imprisonment and/or a fine if tried in the Crown Court or a fine not exceeding £5000 if the offender is convicted in a Magistrates' Court. The utility of this offence is that it is appropriate to pirated goods, including computer software, video cassettes, etc. sold in markets, often in the unofficial Sunday markets or car boot sales, which will be monitored by trading standards officers.

The offence can only apply if the copy carries the name or mark of the genuine maker, or a name or mark which is similar (false to a material degree). So a pirate can avoid the consequences of this legislation if he takes care to use a different name for the software and its maker and uses packaging which is different.

If the maker of computer software uses a registered trade mark (many of the names of popular software packages and the names of the makers of the packages are registered trade marks); someone who, without consent, applies a mark which is identical to or likely to be mistaken for the registered mark or sells or offers for sale, etc. goods which bear that applied mark, is guilty of an offence under section 92 of the Trade Marks Act 1994 if he does to with a view to gain for himself or another or with intent to cause loss to another. This also applies to such use of the mark on labels, packaging, business papers and advertisements and, with the requisite knowledge (knowing or having reason to believe), also to making or adapting articles to make copies of the trade mark or to be in possession of such an article. The penalties for this offence are relatively severe, reflecting the problems of imported counterfeit goods, ranging from pedal cycles to T-shirts to spare parts for vehicles to pharmaceuticals to computer software. On conviction on indictment the maximum term of imprisonment is ten years and/or a fine, while on summary conviction the maximum is six months' imprisonment and/or a fine not exceeding £5000. Computer software pirates would be well advised not to use a registered trade mark or anything remotely resembling a registered trade mark in connection with their pirated copies of software.

The offences mentioned in this chapter are not limited to computer software and could, just as easily, apply to hardware. For example, a person selling counterfeit computer equipment to which he has attached a registered trade mark without authorisation could be found guilty of both of the above offences.

Section 25 of the Theft Act 1968

Consider at software pirate travelling by car to car boot sale with a quantity of pirated software. He is stopped on the way by the police and the pirate copies are noticed. Has he committed an offence? He has not yet sold or offered any of the copies for sale. By section 25 of the Theft ACt 1968, he many be guilty of 'going equipped to cheat' and 'cheat' means the same as obtaining by deception (section 15). Therefore, if the pirate intends to sell the software as genuine to obtain payment, he is guilty of the offence. The maximum penalty is three years' imprisonment. It must be noted, however, that the software must look like the genuine article and it must be packaged to look like the real thing so that potential customers will be deceived.

Pornography

There has been considerable publicity about the availability of pornographic material on the Internet and it is clear that the courts treat this form of computer abuse seriously. The law is reasonably well provided with relevant offences though there may be difficulties in deciding whether something is obscene. Under section 1 of the Obscene Publications Act 1959, an article shall be deemed to be obscene if its effect is such as to tend to deprave and corrupt persons who are likely, having regard to all relevant circumstances, to read, see or hear the matter contained or embodied in it. By section 2, any person who, whether for gain or not, publishes an obscene article or who has an obscene article for publication for gain (whether gain to himself or another) commits an offence. There may be some difficulty with the requirement for an article but this is defined as any description of article containing or embodying matter to be read or looked at or both, any sound record, and any film or other record of a picture or pictures. There is no reason to doubt that it will include a magnetic disk or other form of electronic storage media.

Apart from the Obscene Publications Acts of 1959 1964, section 1 of the Protection of Children Act 1978 makes it an offence to take or permit to be taken any indecent photograph or a child or to distribute or show such a photograph or to have it in possession with an intention to distribute or show it. Indecent photographs are defined as including data stored on a computer disk or by other electronic means which is capable of conversion to a photograph (section 7 as amended by the Criminal Justice and Public Order Act 1994).

In *R* v *Fellows* (1997) 1 Cr App R 244, Fellows was a computer specialsit from Birmingham University who used a University computer to store indecent pictures of children and he printed copies. He also made the data available on the Internet. The Court of Appeal rejected the accused's argument that the computer data did jot comprise a photograph for the purposes of the Protection of Children Act 1978. It was claimed that Parliament could not have envisaged data being stored on computer so as to reproduce photograph which could be transmitted anywhere in the word when the relevant legislation was enacted. However, the Court of Appeal held that the images held in digital form were copies of photographs for the purposes of section 1 of the 1978 Act. The authority of an earlier case was accepted in which the court accepted that a video cassette was an article for the purposes of section 3(2) of the Obscene Publications Act 1959, *Attorney-General's Reference (No. 5 of 1980)* (1980) 72 Cr App R 71. In that case, the court found the accused guilty notwithstanding that it was accepted that Parliament probably had not envisaged that video cassettes would become widely available and provide a means of distributing obscene material.

In *Fellows*, Lord Justice Evans said that a computer disk was not a photograph but was a copy of a photograph which made the original photograph or a copy of it available for viewing by a person with access to the disk. Furthermore, under section 7 of the Protection of Children Act 1978, there was no restriction on the form of the copy of an indecent photograph and later contemporary copies were included. Fellows appeal, and that of a person who received material from Fellows' appeal, and that of a person who received material from Fellows' archive, were dismissed. Fellows had been sentenced to three years' imprisonment, demonstrating the seriousness with which such activities are regarded by the courts.

Section 1 of the Protection of Children Act 1978 also applies to pseudo-photographs (as does section 160 of the Criminal Justice Act 1988 - offence of being in possession of an indecent photograph). A 'pseudo-photograph' is defined as an image, whether made by computer graphics or otherwise, which appears to be a photograph. This extends to data stored on a computer disk or by other electronic means and which is capable of conversion to a pseudo-photograph.

If distributing or downloading pornographic material by the Internet can result in criminal prosecutions for the perpetrators, what is the position of Internet Service Providers? In Germany, an Internet Service Provider manager was sentenced to two years' imprisonment, suspended, for not censoring newsgroups which were making pornographic material available on the service (*Computing,* 4 June 1998, p.3). There are clear dangers for

Internet Service Providers and their managers as it is impossible for them to continually monitor what is being passed through their networks. Under English law incitement typically involves soliciting, encouraging, pressuring, or endeavoring to persuade another person to commit an offence. To be guilty of incitement, a person must intent that the offence will be committed though it appears that recklessness might suffice.

It would seem reasonable that, under English law, if an Internet Service Provider takes steps to prevent the use of his serviced to distribute pornographic material and removes it immediately if detected, he will not be guilty of incitement to commit an offence under the legislation dealing with obscenity. Some appropriate system of monitoring ought to be implemented, including the use of random checks and subscribers ought to be informed that distributing or downloading pornographic material using the service is a serious breach of the service agreement as well as attracting criminal liability.

Threatening E-mails

We have seen that sending a threatening or malicious message by a public telecommunications system, including by e-mail, can constitute an offence under the Telecommunications Act 1984. A much wider piece of legislation was brought in to deal with the problem of stalking and other antisocial behaviour such as that emanating from 'neighbours from hell'. The Protection from Harassment Act 1997 may apply where threatening messages are sent by e-mail or other forms of communication. It provides for criminal penalties as well as a civil remedy.

The relevant provisions of the Act came into force on 16 June 1997. Under section 1, pursuing a course of conduct which amounts to harassment of another, and which the person responsible knows or ought to know amounts to harassment of the other, is an offence. Whether a person 'ought to know' is an objective test based on a reasonable person in possession of the same information. If such a person would think the course of conduct amounted to harassment of the other, that is sufficient. By section 7, references to harassing a person include alarming the person or causing the person distress and a 'course of conduct' must involve conduct on at least two occasions though not necessarily the same conduct. 'Conduct' includes speech.

It can be seen that the offence can be committed relatively easily, Just sending two e-mails which objectively would cause in a reasonable person alarm or distress should be sufficient. For example, if Rodney sends two messages threatening to harm Wendy that should be an offence. The same applies if Rodney makes unelcome sexual advances of an unpleasant nature to Wendy by e-mail. As it appears that the conduct does not have to be the same variety. Rodney could also possibly commit the offence by sending one threatening e-mail and making one telephone call to Wendy.

The threshold for the offence may be relatively low if the Lord Chancellor's view is accepted. He approved of a description favoured by Lord Russell (*Hansard*, HC Deb, 24 January 1997) to the following effect:

> He said first, it [the conduct] is driving me round the bend. That is harassment. It is a continuation of the matter. Secondly it was unwelcome: that is an important criterion. He said that the activity went on and on. That makes for a course of conduct. He also said 'I did not want it'. Those are the elements of harassment.

The offence is triable in the Magistrates' Courts only and carries a maximum penalty or imprisonment for a term not exceeding six months and/or a fine not exceeding level 5 on the standard scale.

A more serious form of the offence is covered by section 4 of the Act. This is where the course of conduct causes another to fear violence on each occasion. The person pursuing the course of conduct must know or he ought to know that the other person will fear violence. Whether a person ought to know is based on an objective test - whether a reasonable person with knowledge of the same information would think it would put the victim in fear of violence. The offence is triable either way and, on conviction on indictment in the Crown Court, the maximum penalty is imprisonment for not more than five years and/or a fine.

In terms of the civil remedy, an actual or apprehended breach of section 1 is sufficient to give a right of action. The use of the word 'apprehended' makes it clear that it is the victim's perception which is important. Damages are available and there is provision also for injunctions, for example, prohibiting the person responsible from continuing the conduct.

There are some specific defences to the offence of harassment and it does not apply to a course of conduct if the person who pursued it shows that it was pursued for the purpose of preventing or detecting crime, that it was pursued under any enactment or rule of law or to comply with any condition or requirement imposed by any person under any enactment, or that in the particular circumstances the pursuit of the course of conduct was reasonable. For the section 4 offence the defences are the same except the last one which is to the effect that the conduct was reasonable for the protection of the person pursuing the conduct or another or for the protection of his or another's property. Note that the burden of proof is on the person responsible for the conduct (this will be satisfied on a balance of probabilities - the usual criminal standard of proof, beyond reasonable doubt, does not apply to defences).

12 COMPUTER EVIDENCE AND CRIMINAL PROCEEDINGS

Introduction

Criminal evidence is a complicated subject, littered with rules and exceptions to rules. One of the rules governs the admissibility of hearsay evidence; that is, a statement other than by a person giving oral evidence in the proceedings is not normally admissible or any fact or opinion contained in the statement. In relation to civil proceedings, this rule has all but been abolished but it remains firmly in place in criminal cases. The rule against hearsay evidence developed as a way of excluding evidence of which a witness did not have direct knowledge and so could not be effectively examined and cross-examined on it. The original maker of a statement is in the best position to give evidence of it. (Note that the law on the admissibility of evidence in criminal proceedings is different in Scotland and neither the relevant provisions of the Police and Criminal Justice Act 1984 nor the Criminal Justice Act 1988 apply there.)

There are many exceptions to the hearsay rule such as dying declarations, statements in public documents, depositions given before a magistrate, documentary evidence, etc. Without these exceptions, the person responsible for the statement in question must attend court and make the statement in person. In the case of computer documents there has to be some exception to the hearsay rule as, in many cases, it will not be possible to identify the person or persons who entered the information in question. The information may have passed through the bands of a chain of employees, a number of whom may have been responsible for its final form into the computer. The law of evidence has to be flexible enough to cope with the realities of the modern business world, otherwise persons committing criminal offences (particularly those involving dishonesty and fraud) would escape conviction all too easily. It must also be recognised, however, that computers are not infallible and some fundamental requirements have to be satisfied before computer documents can be admitted in evidence in criminal proceedings under in exception to the hearsay rule.

Main Provisions

The relevant statutory provisions are contained in section 69 of the Police and Criminal Evidence Act 1984 and in section 24 of the Criminal Justice Act 1988 which replaces section 68 of the 1984 Act. Section 24 applies to 'business documents'. In basic terms computer-generated documents and computer printouts are admissible in evidence if created or received by a person in the course of a trade, business, profession or other occupation, or as the holder of a paid or unpaid office. Furthermore, the information contained in the document must have been supplied by a person having, or reasonably supposed to have, personal knowledge of it. An additional requirement is that the person who supplied the information cannot reasonably be expected to have any recollection of the matters contained in that information. This will obviously be the case in a large organisation where employees are dealing with many transactions each working day. If, however, the person supplying the information can be identified and does remember it, then that person can give evidence of it, in which case his evidence will not be hearsay but will be first hand and directly admissible.

Section 24 of the 1988 Act is subject to section 69 of the Police and Criminal Evidence Act 1984 which expresses that a statement produced by a computer is not evidence of any fact stated in it, unless it can be shown that there are no reasonable grounds for believing that the statement is inaccurate because of improper use of the computer and that the computer was operating properly at all material times or, any failure was not such as to affect the production of the document or the accuracy of the contents.

It might be thought that a failure of a computer to operate properly would make any evidence in a statement produced from the computer completely inadmissible. If there is a problem with the computer it might reasonably be thought to cast grave doubts on the veracity of any information stored or processed by the computer. However, the wording of section 69 suggests that a computer statement may be admissible as evidence notwithstanding some problem with the operation of the computer.

The meaning of the section was fully explored until the House of Lords case of *Director of Public Prosecutions* v McKeown [1997] 1 WLR 295 in which appeals against a decision of the Queen's Bench Divisional Court quashing convictions for driving after consuming alcohol in excess of the legal limit contrary to section 5(1) of the Road Traffic Act 1988 were allowed. It was accepted that the Lion Intoximeter, a breathalyser device, was a computer for the purposes of section 69 of the Police and Criminal Evidence Act 1984. In the cases before the House of Lords, the clock on he breathalyser device was approximately one and a quarter hours slow. However, the police sergeant operating it had properly tested and calibrated it.

Lord Hoffmann said that the words in section 69 were not meant to be taken too literally. Of course, the discrepancy resulted in the accuracy of the printout being affected in that the time shown on the printout was wrong. However, the section accepts that a computer may not have been operating properly at all material times but the evidence may still be admissible if that was not such as to affect the production of the document or the accuracy of its contents. An example of a fault which caused the document to be printed in lower case when it should have been in upper case was given by Lord Hoffmann who thought a rule which excluded such a document would be totally irrational. The purpose of the rule had to be considered to give effect to what Parliament had intended. He thought the purpose of section 69 was a relatively modest one and did not require the prosecution to show that the statement was likely to be true. That was a question for the jury. All the section requires is that there is positive evidence that the computer had properly processed, stored and reproduced whatever information it received. If the information it received was wrong, that did not make the evidence inadmissible. In otherwords, the processing accuracy of the computer was the critical factor. As the old adage goes, garbage in - garbage out. The production of garbage by a computer does not mean to say it has not been operating properly.

During the trial in the Magistrates' Court, the justices had a statement from the police sergeant identifying the document and describing the manner in which it was produced, giving particulars of any device involved in the production of the document and dealing with matters mentioned in section 69(1), that is, to the best of his belief that there were no reasonable grounds for believing that the statement was inaccurate because of improper use of the computer and that it was at all material times operating properly or, if not, was not such as to affect the production of the document or the accuracy of its contents (PACE, Schedule 3, paragraph 8).

Lord Hoffmann said that a computer is a device for storing, processing and retrieving information. An error in clock display would not have anything to do with whether the computer itself was operating properly and, in any case, he doubted that the clock mechanism itself would constitute part of the computer for the purposes of section 69(1). Instead it was likely to be something which supplies information to the computer.

Where computer evidence is involved, it is an attractive proposition to attack the admissibility of computer evidence, particularly if that evidence has significant probative value from the prosecution's point of view. However, following *DPP* v *Mckeown*, the courts seem to be taking a more robust view and are more prepared to admit computer evidence. In *Reid* v *Director of Public Prosecutions, The Times*, 6 March 1998, minor typographical errors in a printout produced by a breathalyser device did not alter the validity of the results of the analysis of the breath specimen produced by the machine when it had been properly calibrated and was functioning properly. The errors were the omission of the second half of the first character and second character in every line and, in one version, the top line was printed in smaller font than the rest of the printout. The evidence was admissible under section 69 and the court referred to the outcome in *DPP* v *McKeouen* [1997] 1 WLR 295, making it more difficult for unmeritorious and unattractive claims to succeed. The printer malfunction did not alter the way in which the machine processed, stored or retrieved information used to generate the statement. 'Getting off on a technicality' no longer seems possible where computer evidence is involved.

Evidence is show that it is safe to rely on the documents produced by a computer may be tendered in two ways. One way is by a certificate which must be signed by someone who ws qualified so as to be in a position to give reliable evidence of the operation of the computer - in other words, a computer expert. The other way is by oral evidence given by a person familiar with the operation of the computer who can give evidence of its reliability. So it was held in *R* v *Shephard* [1993] AC 380 by the House of Lords. In that case, a woman had been convicted of theft for shoplifting. Various goods had been found in her car. She did not have any receipts, claiming that she never kept receipts anyway. However, the store detective from the ship where she claimed to have bought the goods went through the till rolls (produced by cash tills connected to a central computer) but found no record of any sale of the goods in question. The till rolls had been submitted in evidence. It was clear that the store detective was familiar with the workings of the tills and computer though not an expert. The House of Lords in upholding the conviction confirmed that it would rarely be necessary to call expert witnesses and in most cases, the requirement in section 69 could be satisfied by calling a witness who was familiar wi th the computer and who knew what it did and who could confirm that it was operating properly at the relevant time.

If oral evidence is given by someone familiar with the computer in question, it must be so as to confirm that the computer was operating properly and not simply to conform what the computer did. Convictions for carrying excess weight in lorries were quashed by the Queen's Bench Division in *East West Transport Ltd* v *Crown Prosecution Service* (unreported) 15 February 1995. Here a weighbridge had been used to measure the axle load of the lorries but the weighbridge operators gave oral evidence only about the function performed by the computer, nothing else. At the trial in the Magistrates' Court, the magistrates had erred by considering that the evidence from the computer was admissible without proof of accuracy, in the absence of evidence that the machine was not functioning properly. In another weighbridge case, *Connolly* v *Lancashire County Council* [1994] RTR 79, evidence that the weighbridge (being a computer for the purposes of section 69) had been tested regularly and was found to be working properly before and after the date on which the offences were alleged to have been committed was deemed to be sufficient. The judge confirmed that in most cases a certificate will be submitted and in other cases oral evidence will suffice. He went on to say that in some cases circumstantal evidence would lead to a legitimate inference.

Section 25 of the Criminal Justice Act 1988 gives the court a discretion to refuse to admit hearsay evidence, including computer documents, if the court is of the opinion that the statement ought not to be admitted in the interests of justice.

The application of the provisions relating to the admissibility of computer documents has not proved easy for the courts and in the case of *R* v *Harper* [1989]1 WLR 441, the Court of Appeal laid down some guideline. This case involved the interpretation of section 68 of the Police and Criminal Evidence Act 1984 which has now been replaced by section 24 of the Criminal Justice Act 1988, but the principles should be the same. If anything, section 24 is a less stringent provision. The guidelines suggest the following approach:

1. Section 24 of the Criminal Justice Act 1988 and section 69 of the Police and Criminal Evidence Act 1984 are not independent tests but should

both be satisfied notwithstanding that section 69 applies to all computer documents whereas section 24 is more limited as was confirmed in*R* v *Shephard*.

2. Although the 'personal knowledge' requirement of section 24 might prove difficult to show in practice because it might not be possible to identify the exact persons involved in a large organisation, circumstantial evidence of the usual habit or routine regarding the use of the computer might suffice, based on a presumption of regularity. The same applies to the requirement that the person who supplied the information cannot reasonably be expected to have any recollection of the matters contained in the information concerned.
3. The total judge should critically examine any suggestions that any prior malfunction of the computer or its software has any relevance to the reliability of the particular computer records submitted in evidence.
4. If the judge decides that the computer evidence is admissible, he should direct the jury that the weight to be attached to such evidence is a matter for the jury to assess.

These provisions are not notable for their clarity and the flowchart in Fig. 12. 1 will help to explain them. It is based on the assumption that both section 24 and section 69 apply. Some computer printouts may be admitted as direct evidence and not subject to section 24 such as where the computer supply keeps a record of some physical characteristic such as air temperature.

An example might also help no clarify the position. Joe Smith alters his building society passbook to show a balance of £1000, when he should only have a balance of £100, and this is the figure recorded on the computer along with a record of transactions on his account. Joe is prosecuted for forgery and attempting to obtain property by deception after he tries to withdraw £500 from the building society. The prosecution wishes to submit, in evidence, a computer printout showing details of his account and the transactions on it.

Referring to the flowchart, the first test is easily satisfied because the building society is acting in the course of business. The second test is more difficult because the employees of the building society who supplied details of the transactions entered into the computer system cannot be identified with any certainty. It can be presumed, however, from the regular business of the building society (that is, the third test) that staff supplying the details would have personal knowledge, at the time, of those details, so this provides sufficient circumstantial evidence. The fourth test, concerned with the recollection of the matters in the information, can be answered in the negative for it is self-evident that the person who made the statement would not in the normal way be able to remember the information. If, however, there was something very unusual about it these individuals would be able to be identified and so could give evidence directly.

The sixth and seventh stages of the flowchart concern the use and operation of the computer system. Say that in the example concerning Joe Smith there have been problems with the computer software which resulted in errors in the recording of certain transactions, but there is evidence that the problems were quickly overcome and that Joe Smith's account was not in use at the time of the problems. Furthermore, a computer hacker has penetrated the computer system but it is claimed that the system is now

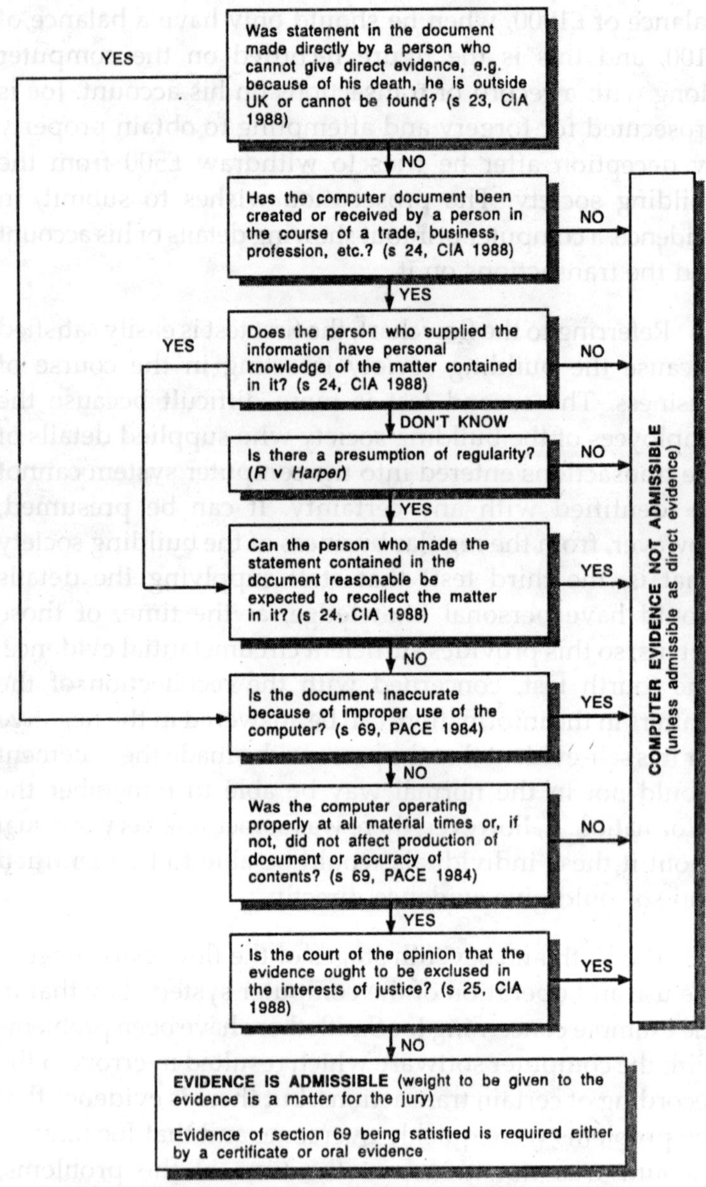

Fig 12.1 Adimissibility of computer evidence in criminal proceedings

secure and, again, Joe Smith's account was not affected. On the basis of the foregoing, it is likely that the trial judge would allow the computer printout to be admitted in evidence, but he would direct the jury that the weight to be attached to this evidence was a matter for them to assess in the light of the problems experienced with the computer system.

Once, more the importance of maintaining a secure computer system can be seen. If a jury is satisfied that the computer system has been professionally operated and maintained, it is more likely to believe that the computer printout is accurate and truly reflects what happened. It is vital that nothing should detract from the admissibility or weight to be attached to computer evidence in view of the now widespread use of computers to handle and record information. The ability of hackers to penetrate a computer system coupled with poor hardware and software monitoring and maintenance procedures is likely to destroy the admissibility of computer evidence, or, at the very least, reduce its credibility.

A hacker or fraudster can make his subsequent prosecution and conviction more difficult by altering or destroying programs or data stored in a computer system. The insertion of a computer virus would be especially effective. The best way to prevent or nullify this is to keep back-up copies of the programs and data and, preferably, several copies providing an historical record of the state of programs and data. Of course by modifying the contents of the computer, offences under section 3 of the Computer Misuse Act 1990 would also be committed.

Section 23 of the Criminal Justice Act 198 also provides for the admissibility of computer evidence in criminal proceedings applying where the statement in the document has been made directly by the person concerned.

An example might be where a person writes some notes concerning an assault he has witnessed, using a word processor, and that person cannot give direct evidence for any one of the following reasons:

(a) the person has subsequently died or is unfit to give evidence because of his bodily or mental condition;

(b) the person is no longer in the United Kingdom and it is not reasonably practicable for him to attend as a witness; or

(c) the person cannot be found, after taking reasonable steps to find him.

Section 23 is also subject to the provisos in section 69 of the Police and Criminal Evidence Act 1984; that is that the document is accurate because there has been no improper use of the computer and the computer has been operating properly at all material times. Section 25 also gives the judge a discretion to exclude evidence which is admissible under section 23.

Section 69 of the Police and Criminal Evidence Act 1985 also applies to extradition hearings. In *R* v *Governor of Brixton Prison, ex parte Levin* [1997] 3 All ER Levin was alleged to have used a computer terminal in St Petersburg, Russia to gain unauthorised access to a computerised funds transfer service at a bank a New Jersey, USA in order to make fraudulent transfers of funds from the bank to accounts which his associates controlled. He was charged before a Federal District Court in the USA and arrested in the United Kingdom. There followed an application to extradite him from the United States government which submitted evidence that included computer printouts. Levin argued that section 69 did not apply to extradition proceedings and, consequently, the printouts were inadmissible as evidence.

The House of Lords held that for the purposes of the Police and Criminal Evidence Act 1984, extradition proceedings were criminal proceedings on the basis of section 9(2) of and paragraph 6(1) of Schedule 1 to the Extradition Act 1989 which required extradition proceedings to be conducted as nearly as may be as if they were committal proceedings before magistrates. Therefore, the normal rules of evidence and procedure applied to extradition proceedings. In any event the printouts were not hearsay as they were tendered to prove the transfers of funds which they recorded and did not assert that the transfers took place. They were direct evidence.

As technology moves on, part from issues of admissibility of computer evidence, there complexity of the evidence itself may be lost on a jury. For example, in *R v Adams (No.2), The Times*, 3 November 1998, the defence led evidence expressed in mathematical probability and the jury were invited by the defence to pay attention to Bayes Theorem. This is a method of combining a number of independent observations or results to derive an overall probability of a given hypothesis, a technique regarded by some as controversial. The Court of Appeal ruled that, in the absence of special cases, such evidence was a recipe for confusion and misunderstanding and misjudgment, possibly among counsel, probably among judges and almost certainly among jurors.

Reform of Hearsay Rule

The Law Commission has investigated the requirement to prove, in effect, the infallibility of computers in court before evidence produced or stored in them can be admitted. The Commission cited one case where 20 hours were spent trying to prove that four computers were working properly. There is a suggestion that some lawyers have been using section 69 of the Police and Criminal Evidence Act 1984 as a device to obstruct the course of justice. The Law Commission recommended, therefore, that section 69 be repealed (*Computing*, 13 July 1995, p.2). In view of the fact that a growing number of jury members are likely to have some experience in the use of computers, this would be a sensible move, and a jury should be left to make to own mind up about the weight to be given to computer evidence. If there have been problems with the computer, or if there is a suspicion that this is the case, it should be up to the defence of put this to the judge who could then rule whether or not the evidence should be admissible, and, if so, give an appropriate warning to the jury.

COMPUTER CRIME—CONCLUDING REMARKS

Suggestions to Prevent or Minimise Criminal Activities

There are several things which the owner or operator of a computer system can do to prevent or minimise the possibility of criminal activities being successfully perpetrated against the computer system or the data or software stored therein. The main principle is to avoid complacency; it would be a very brave IT manager who considers his system so secure that it is safe against criminals and malicious employees. To some extent, strong security can foster complacency and can even present the would-be criminal with an enjoyable challenge. However, the golden thread running through the suggestions below is that security is a most important means of protection and great care must be taken to develop a strong,yet workable system of passwords and hierarchical access. Persons using the computer system should only be able to obtain access to those parts of the system which they will use. Different modes of access might be appropriate for different operators. For example, if the computer system contains a database, some users will only need to view and inspect the data, while some will be allowed to add to the data; yet others may be entitled to delete or edit the data or parts of the data. The scope of access granted to various people should reflect their responsibilities and be no more than is necessary for them to carry out their duties. Access will be by way of numbers, spouse's names, etc. should be avoided. Passwords need to be changed frequently and the use of a two-password system, one password or identifier unique to each user and another for his level of access, should be considered.

A log of access to the computer system must be kept which notes user identification and and times of ingress and egress, and these must be checked with users periodically. Furthermore, it must be made as difficult as possible for ordinary users to enter the computer's operating system. It is wise to invent some time and effort in making computer systems secure, appointing specialist staff or consultants for this purpose. Although this will require financial commitment it should be remembered that the consequences of poor security can be dire, not just in terms of direct costs but also in relation to the costs associated with detection and prosecution and in validating that a system is now free from viruses. For example, in the Audit Commission Survey of 1990, the average cost of detection and prosecution was £3468 per single incident.

With this general advice in mind, some more suggestions, related to specific criminal threats, are described below.

Fraud and Theft

The largest threat is from within - that is, from employees. Therefore, employees' attention needs to be drawn to the fact that security is taken seriously and incidents will be reported to the police. This must be reinforced by the operation of a system of audits and spot checks and systems for double-checking (including manual systems). These systems should be varied from time to time as variety is the criminal's greatest enemy and someone considering using the computer to commit a fraud wil usually do so only after they have become cognisant of the systems in operation. Changes will frustrate attempts to do this. Spot checks should be carried out on accounts chosen at random and on any unusual transactions - for example, sudden movement in an account that has been dormant for some time.

As regards supplier/sub-contractor accounts and wages systems, it must be ensured that any new accounts are genuine and that they have performed the work for which they are being paid. A data processing systems and to use a high profile when it comes to checking that everything is as it should be.

Hacking

Obviously, security is very important here too. The location of passwords must be carefully considered: as they in a text file stored on the computer which can be easily inspected by a person working in the operating system? Some form of code for any passwords which must, of necessity, be stored on the computer system should be considered. If a computer system is being installed or expanded, the need for linking that system with a telecommunications system must be carefully considered. Is it essential to have remote access to the system? Would it be feasible to have computers at branch offices which are updated by being sent new copies of the data on disk or tape from time to time? Security needs to be made a high-profile matter at branch offices.

Educating employees should be seen as a priority. The need to take care of their passwords and change them frequently should be stressed. It may be better if the software is designed so that password changes are forced on employees after a period of time Employees should be made aware of the dangers of accessing software they are not entitled to access and they should be given express instructions as to what they can and cannot access and what they are allowed to do where they have access.

Unauthorised Modification (Including Time-Bombs and Viruses)

The danger here can come from hackers, employees, freelance programmers and sub-contractors. Employees who have been dismissed or have been given notice of termination of their employment represent a significant threat of damage to a computer system for such a person may seek revenge. If an employee has given notice to leave his employment, or has been dismissed, that employee should be denied access to the computer system and should perhaps be given salary in lieu of notice. Passwords and security generally will need to be reviewed and changed depending on the employee's familiarity with the computer system. It should be borne in mind that the employee may have found out a considerable amount about the computer system during his employment - perhaps more than he should know for the purpose of performing his duties. It is worthwhile keeping a separate set of back-up copies of important programs and data in write-protected form. For example, when a new software package has been obtained the original disks need to be write-protected immediately and duplicates made which can be used as working copies.

Again, it needs to be clear that security is taken seriously and that the computer system is constantly being monitored. A potential source of computer viruses is pirated software which is to be avoided at all costs as should any software of doubtful pedigree. If a computer is attended to by a maintenance engineer, his diagnostic disks should be checked to ensure that they are write-protected for, if not, he may have collected a virus on his rounds which could be passed on to any computer. The acquisition of suitable 'anti-virus' software is a must and should be updated as new versions are available in an effort to keep up with the ever increasing number of viruses. Executable files must not be downloaded by remote access, especially on the Internet, unless hey are known, positively and absolutely, to be free from viruses. Particular caution should be exercised with unsolicited e-mails.

Intellectual Property Offences

So far as these offences are concerned, little can be done in terms of prevention apart from pursuing the pirates ruthlessly and using the full weight of the civil law as well as the criminal law. Copy-protection can be counter-productive. Users should be educated about the important benefits of using genuine software such as support and the availability of updates. Care must be taken to prevent employees copying software and distributing it as this could breach the terms of the employer's licence agreement, allowing the licensor to revoke the licence and claim damages.

Evidence

Sloppy computer management could result in vital evidence of criminal activity being declared inadmissible. IT managers should be aware of the requirements for admissibility and they should ensure that there is a detailed record of the computer's operation. Some months or even years into the future, the IT manager may have to sign a certificate confirming that the computer was operating properly at the material time or, if not, that any failure was not such as to affect the accuracy of the document in question. Even ordinary computer operators, or at least their managers, should note in their desk diaries changes to software (for example, installation of an updated operating system), virus checks and audits and the results of these as well as anything untoward. It is important to build up a picture of the computer's operation. Historical back-up copies of programs and data should also be kept together with a record of when they were last altered is very useful but only if the computer's clock is accurate. This includes taking account of British Summer Time. In one case, an argument that a printout from a breathalyser device should not be admitted as evidence because the time was incorrectly set was accepted and a conviction for 'drunk driving' was quashed (*Gerrard Jones* v *Director of Public Prosecutions* [1995] Crim LR 69). However, this was overturned on appeal to the House of Lords, as discussed in the preceding chapter in the case of *DPP* v *McKeown.*

Audit Commission Recommendations

The Audit Commission reports, *Ghost in the Machine: An Analysis of IT Fraud and Abuse* (Audit Commission Publications, 1998) and *Opportunity Makes a Thief: An Analysis of Computer Abuse* (HMSO, 1994), contain many recommendations to improve security on the basis that prevention is better than cure. All persons having responsibility for the management of computer installations of whatever size would do well to read the reports. The reports identify a number of characteristics as being important in terms of an IT security policy; these are summarised below:

- an IT security which fits in with business strategy;
- a clear statement by management of the importance it places on IT security;
- a statement of staff responsibilities to protect the investment in IT and in respect of the computer data they use;
- a statement of the relevant legislation confirming that it will be enforced (this applies not only in

terms of computer crime but also software piracy and data protection law);

- a statement indicating the steps taken by management to encourage and enforce high security standards;
- the steps taken to minimise computer abuse (adequate division of duties, secure password systems, etc.);
- the procedures relating to the acquisition of new hardware and software to ensure completeness and accuracy of data processing;
- the internal control mechanisms for monitoring that the policy is working and being adhered to; and
- the role of internal audit and other monitoring agencies in the organisation.

The reports recommend the use of codes of practices such as the British Standard for Information Security Management (BS 7799). The British Standard proposes ten key controls over information, including having an information security document, education and training, allocating responsibilities as to security, reporting incidents, having virus controls in place, controls over copying software, data protection and complying with security policy. The latest report goes on to suggest a checklist of questions that should be asked by management, which include questions as to 'all risks', fraud, viruses, sabotage, private work, theft of data and software, the Internet, hacking, illicit software and misuse of personal data. The questions include individual issues such as whether:

- management has issues an IT security policy and, if so, whether this is known to all staff,
- regular audit and security reviews are carried out of all key systems,

- staff are instructed not to use externally acquired disks,
- procedures are clear when disgruntled employees resign,
- risks posed by the Internet have been reviewed and steps taken to prevent access to the internet or unauthorised and improper purposes,
- records at password guessing are monitored,
- attempts at password guessing are monitored,
- staff are aware of the Data Protection Act and have been warned against misusing personal data.

The seriousness of computer misuse cannot be overstated and the consequences of poor controls and procedures can be very costly. As more reliance is placed on IT systems, it is vital that effective and workable security policies are established and reviewed regularly and implemented in an effective manner. The importance of good security can be put into perspective when one reflects on the annual UK budget for information technology spending, which is in the order of a staggering £26 billion (Audit Commission, *Ghost in the Machine: An Analysis of IT Fraud and Abuse,* Audit Commission Publications 1998, p.3).

Organisations should develop their own code of practice and ensure that it filters down to all departments. Probably the most important aspect is raising staff awareness and obtaining the commitment and support of staff at all levels in developing and maintaining secure computer systems. Good security will come from delegation of responsibilities and developing in ethos of manual commitment rather than by the imposition from on high of time-consuming and awkward procedures with little explanation of their importance and rationale.

Summary

It has been shown that a wide variety of criminal offences can be committed using or involving computer technology. Other offences may also be carried out. For example, murder or manslaughter can be committed by interfering with a 'safety-critical system' such as an air traffic control computer or a hospital computer monitoring the treatment of patients. Of course, some offences are not relevant to computer technology and it would be difficult to envisage a situation where rape could be carried out using a computer. However, given the ingenuity of the criminal mind, there are certain to be other forms of crime which will be attempted in the future.

The criminal law is now quite strong in relation to all forms of computer crime following the enactment of the Computer Misuse Act 1990 and computer programs and data are relatively well protected by the criminal law. On the whole, the legal environment in the United Kingdom has struck a reasonable balance between the interests of industry and commerce and the private individual. At least we do not execute computer hackers as happened in China a few years ago. Although the Computer Misuse Act has been welcomed by many in the computer industry and financial institutions, the presence of stronger laws should not be seen as a substitute for strong security measures and effective systems of auditing. Those organisations which store confidential information concerning individual members of the public or which have safety-critical systems have a moral duty (and in some circumstances a legal duty) to protect their computer systems from criminal activities, whether perpetrated from outside the organisation or within it.

Finally, the fact is that only the minority of offences result in prosecutions. Of the 537 reported incidents in the Audit Commission report published in 1994 only 58 of the culprits were prosecuted. There were 519 incidents reported in the 1998 report from 900 organisations. In terms of all IT fraud and abuse around 20 per cent resulted in dismissal and/or prosecution. As regards computer fraud over 40 per cent of detected incidents led to prosecutions. One welcome sign is that judges seem to be more prepared to take computer crime seriously and a number of offenders have been imprisoned. This now seems to be the most likely outcome where fraud, large-scale piracy or a serious case of hacking is involved. Other penalties imposed include large fines, suspected sentences and community service orders.

Table 13.1 gives a summary of offences together with their maximum penalties and some comment concerning their scope. It should be noted that, in most cases, a fine is also possible in addition to a prison sentence. Of course, subject to the maximum penalty, the courts have a full range of other disposals available to them such as probation orders, community sentences and absolute or conditional discharges.

TABLE 13.1

Summary of Offences

Offence	*Description*	*Maximum penalty*	*Comment*
Fraud/theft related			
s 15 Theft Act 1968	Obtaining property by deception	10 years	Difficulty with respect to machine being deceived (requires a human to be deceived)
s 15A Theft Act 1968	Obtaining a money transfer for deception	10 years	Designed for, but not restricted to , 'mortgage

Offence	*Description*	*Maximum penalty*	*Comment*
			frauds', applies to electronic funds transfers as well as cheques
s 1 Theft Act 1968	Theft	7 years	Will cover most cases involving computer 'fraud'
ss 17-20 Theft Act 1968	False accounting etc.	7 years	No particular difficulties with computer technology
s 2 Computer Misuse Act 1990	Basic hacking plus ulterior intent	5 years	Useful for attempts and not restricted to fraud
Conspiracy	Common law	10 years	2 or more persons
Cheating	Common law	Imprison-ment and/ or fine without limit	Only available for inland Revenue and VAT frauds
Hacking and damage			
s 1 Computer Misuse Act 1990	Basic hacking offence	6 months	Triable only in MC. Search warrants available from circuit judge
s 13 Theft Act 1968	Abstracting electricity	5 years	May be difficulty with respect to 'knowledge'
s 1 Interception of Communi-cations Act 1985	Interception of com-munication during its transmission through a public telecommunic-ations system	2 years	Suitable for computer 'eaves-dropping'. If tried in MC, max. is a fine of £5000
s 43 Telecom-munication Act 1984	The transmission of grossly offensive, indecent obscene or menancing messages	Fine max. £1000 summary trial only	Can only be tried in MC Must be public telecommunications system
s 3 Computer Misuse Act 1990	Unauthorised modific-ation of computer material	5 years	Replaces criminal damage in relation to programs and data
s 21 Theft Act 1968	Blackmail	14 years	Unwarranted demand with menances. Triable in CC only
Intellectual pro-perty related			
s 107 Copyright, Design & Patents Act 1988	Secondary infringement generally making pirate copies for sale or 'dea-ling' with pirate copies		See Table 1 for penalties

Offence	*Description*	*Maximum penalty*	*Comment*
s 1 Forgery and Counterfeiting Act 1981	Making a false instrument	10 years	Requires someone to believe it to be genuine
s 1 Trade Description Act 1968	Applying false trade description, etc.	2 years	Trade description includes an indication of the manufacturer of the goods
s 92 Trade Marks Act 1994	Applying a registered trade mark etc. without consent	10 years	It is a defence if the person concerned reasonably believed that the use did not infringe
s 25 Theft Act 1968	Going equipped to cheat	3 years	'Cheat' has some meaning as 'obtaining by deception'
Other			
s 21 Data Protection Act 1998	Processing personal Datas without having notified	unlimited fine	Strict liability; failure to notify changes is also an offence subject to a due deligence defence
s 55 Data Protection Act 1998	Obtaining, disclosing or procuring the disclosure of personal data without the consent of the data controller	Unlimited fine	Some defences apply. Selling such data is an offence. For further offences under the Data Protection Act, see Part Four of this book
Obscene PublicationActs 1959 & 1964 (s 2 of the 1959 Act as amended	Publishing obscene article or having obscene for publication for gain	3 years and/or a fine	Would apply with respect to a computer disk containing pornographic images or information but some doubt about transmission over network
s 1 Protection of Children Act 1978	Taking, or permitting to be taken, an indecent photographic of a child, distributing, showing or being in possession with intent to distribute or show such a photograph	3 years	Possession of an indecent photographic without intent is triable in the MC only and subject to a fine not exceeding level 5 on the standard scale (s 160 Criminal Justic Act 1988)
s 84 Criminal Justice and Public Order Act 1994	Obscene and indecent photographs of children extended to 'pseudo-photographs'	3 years	'Pseudo-photograph' covers computer graphics images and covers data stored on disk or electronically
s 1 Protection from Harassm-	Pursuing a course of conduct which causes	6 months and/or a	A course of conduct (more than one

Offence	*Description*	*Maximum penalty*	*Comment*
ent Act 1997	alarm or distress on at least two occasions	fine not exceeding level 5 on the standard scale	occasion), could include sending threatening e-mails
s 4 Protection from Harassment Act 1997	Pursuing a course of conduct causing another to fear violence on at least two occasions	5 years and/or fine	Course of conduct as for s 1 offence
Incitement	Encouraging, persuading, suggesting, proposing to someone to commit a criminal offence	At the court's discretion if tried in CC	Could apply particularly to material posted on the internet, for example, describing how to make a bomb, how to write a computer virus

Note: CC = Crown Court, MC = Magistrates' Court.
Unless otherwise indicated, offences can be tried in either a Magistrates' Court or in the Crown Court and, if tried in a Magistrates' Court, the maximum penalty available is 6 months' imprisonment and/or a fine not exceeding £5000.

Data Protection

Computer technology heightened fears about a society of the kind portrayed in George Orwell's 1984, because of the power of computers in terms of information processing. Even now, there remains a popular feeling that computers underline human skills and that the growth of computer technology heralds the dawn of an austere and coldly logical society. Certainly, the power of computers can be misused and there needs to be system of checks and balances to prevent abuse of this power. In particular, computers raise concerns about individuals and their privacy.

There is no general right to privacy in English law although some legal remedies may be available in some circumstances. For example, disclosure of confidential information may be actionable as will be the publication of defamatory material. There are rights of privacy in relation to certain photographs or films made for private sand domestic circumstances under copyright law. Other examples exist where a right to privacy may be affected indirectly. The absence of a general right to privacy has been criticised but English law has striven to strike a balance between interests and freedom of speech.

We are now entering a new era in terms of protecting rights to privacy. The Data Protection Act 1984 made a start but this only applied to personal data which were processed automatically. However, two major developments occurred in 1998. The first was the passing of the Data Protection Act 1998 which will replace the 1984 Act. The importance of this Act should not be underestimated. It marks a watershed in relation to privacy and personal data and gives individuals much greater rights than they had under the previous Act. It is also important in that it extends data protection law much more than before to manual files. The second development has been the passing of the Human Rights Act 1998. This incoporates the European Convention on Human Rights into United Kingdom law. Of particular interest is Article 8 of the Convention which states that everyone has the right to respect for his private and family life, his home and his correspondence. At the time of writing, the Data Protection Act 1998 is not yet in force (apart from some provisions dealing with definitions and the like). The Government has announced that it will come into force on 1 March 2000. The Human Rights Act 1998 looks a little further away at this stage but it should be implemented in the next year or so.

This Part of the book focuses on the Data protection Act 1998, with comparisons to the equivalent provisions under the 1984 Act where appropriate. The next chapter looks at the background to the Act, the main definitions in it, the data protection principle,s which are central to data protection law, and the role of the Data Protection Commissioner (the new name for the Data Protection Registrar) and the Working Party set up under the 'Data Protection Directive'. The following chapter looks at the Act from the perspective of the person who processed personal data, the data controller. There is then a chapter on the Act from a data user's point of view, followed by a chapter on the parallel legislation in the telecommunications field and the United Kingdom implementation of the 'Privacy in Telecommunications Directive'. Appendix 2 to this book contains a summary of data protection law under the 1984 Act for reference.

Note: Unless otherwise mentioned, all statutory references in this Part are to the Data Protection Act 1998.

14 INTRODUCTION AND BACKGROUND TO THE DATA PROTECTION ACT 1998: (A Case Study)

Introduction

Data protection law affects everybody. Most persons process information about individuals, even if it is simply name, address and telephone number. Many do this by computer and only those who use a computer for little more than straightforward word processing will fail to be regulated under data protection law. A great many people have manual filing systems containing information relating to individuals. These may be in the form of a card index system or even a simple address book. Until now, data protection law has not covered manual systems, but, with the advent of the new law, this is about to change. Even if we do not process personal information, the chances are others process information relating to us. Indeed, their can be very few persons who are not affected by data protection law as being the subject of data processed by others. Data protection law, therefore, has two main impacts. First, those who process information concerning individuals are subject to regulation and constraint. Second, as individuals we all have rights under data protection law. As this area of law is changing, the rights of individuals are given more prominence and a key phrase is 'transparency of processing'. Individuals should be better informed as to who is processing data relating to them, what the purpose of the processing is and what other processing activities are involved. They also have a right to more information than before in response to a request for access and greater rights to control processing activity.

There are many horror stories about people who have had information wrongly attributed to them and stored on computer. For example, a man with an impeccable character and without any convictions at all was arrested and charged with driving while disqualified because of incorrect information stored on the police national computer. Details about the disqualification had been entered against his name by mistake. He lost his job and had his car impounded. It took him four months to trace the man to whom the previous conviction related and who had a very similar name before the could clear his name (*The Times,* 8 May 1990, p.4). Another problem has been the lack of control of organisations who pass on personal information to others, resulting in many people having been inundated with unsolicited mail. A more sinister aspect of computer-stored information is a direct result of the powerful processing capacity of computers and the ability to use computers to target certain groups of individuals. The dangers of permitting the use of sensitive information stored on computers to continue unchecked are manifold.

As computer technology becomes progressively powerful and more use is made of computers, the dangers are set to increase. Numerous concerns have been expressed in the past by Data Protection Registrar and others. For example, some data may be very sensitive and may cause considerable harm if its use is not strictly controlled such as data relating to genetic information or illnesses and diseases. Other concerns flow from the use of 'while data' showing that a person has a good credit record and the activities of private investigators has caused concern in the past. Other issues relate to the balance between freedom of speech and individuals' right to privacy, two areas of apparently diametrically opposed interests always very difficult to reconcile. Nor is computer technology the only threat. The Economic League was an organisation which retained details of individuals who had been active trade unionists or members of the Communist Party. All this data was kept on paper. The Data Protection Act 1984 had no effect upon such data processing - it had to be by automatic means. Structured manual files can pose just as many problems as automated processing activities.

The Data Protection Act 1984 received the Royal Assent at an appropriate time in Orwellian terms. It was designed to control the storage and use of information about individuals stored and processed by computer. Control of processing was provided for by a system of registration with penalties for failing to register and for acting beyond the scope of the registration. Additionally, the Act introduced a set of *Data Protection Principles* which must be followed by persons who store or process information, using computers, about living persons. Computer bureaux providing services to those who process such information were also controlled and were required to register under the 1984 Act. Individuals, about whom information is stored on computer, were given rights of access and a right to have inacccurate records corrected or deleted. Under certain circumstances, individuals had a right to compensation.

The history leading up to the 1984 Act was relatively long and there were several Parliamentary Bills, Reports and White Papers concerning privacy and data protection. The Lindop Report (*Report of the Committee on Data Protection*, Cmnd 7341, HMSO, 1978) was important in respect of moves towards legislation. In the late 1970s several countries introduced data protection laws, in particular the United

States of America, Sweden and Germany. The final impetus was provided by the Council of Europe's Convention on Data Protection which was signed by the United Kingdom in 1981. The convention included principles for data protection and proposed a common set of standards. In 1982, a White Paper was published, outlining the Government's intentions (Cmnd 8539) and following this a Bill was introduced in the House of Lords. However, this failed to become law because of the general election of 1983 and a new Bill was introduced after the election and eventually received the Royal Assent in July 1984. The Data Protection Act 1984 was implemented in stages, the last of which mainly concerned individual's rights of access and which came into effect on 11 November 1987.

In this chapter, following a brief discussion of the Data Protection Directive, the background to the Data Protection Act 1998 is described. Next the *Data Protection Principles* are stated and there follows a look at the definitions contained in the Act. The work of the Data Protection Commissioner is then considered, followed by material on the Data Protection Tribunal and the Working Party set up under the Data Protection Directive.

The Data Protection Directive

In the context of a Single European Market, it is essential that there should be no barriers to the transfer of information between member states. The principle of freedom of movement of goods and services has been largely achieved and it would be unthinkable if, in this age of information technology, the same freedom of movement did not apply to computer data. However, not all the member states complied with the European Convention on Data Protection. Being conscious of the possibility that member states of the European Community could erect barriers to the flows of computer data on the basis of insufficient protection for individuals in other member states, the Commission worked towards a Directive laying down a basic framework for the protection of personal data while stressing the freedom of movement of personal data. The argument is that, if all member states adhere to the minimum standard of protection, there should be no barriers to the movement of personal data within the Community.

A proposal for a Directive on the protection of individuals in relation to the processing of personal data was published in 1990 (COM(90) 314 final - SYN 287, OJ [1990] C277/30 and provided a complex system differentiating between the public and private sector as was then the position in some countries such as the Netherlands. A further proposal was published in 1992 (COM (92) 24 final—SYN 393, OJ [1992] C311/38). The distinction between the public and private sector disappeard but this particular proposal was perceived by data users as being unduly restrictive and extremely onerous to comply with. Particular concerns were directed at the extension of data protection law to manual files, the requirements to inform data subjects and, in some cases, the need to seek data subjects' consent to processing. A survey carried out for the Home Office in the United Kingdom indicated hat compliance would cost the 625 organisations included in the survey at least £2 billion (*Costs of implementing the Data Protection Directive: Paper by the United Kingdom.* Home Office (1994) while the Department of Health estimated that it would be necessary to inform every member of the population that it held personal data concerning them and that this would cost over £1 billion (*Draft EC proposed Directive on data protection: analysts of costs,* Department of Health (1994)).

The Commission responded to some of the concerns of data users and changes were made to reduce the financial burden while retaining the principle of protecting the individuals' rights of privacy. Furthermore, a survey carried out for the Commission by the author of this book and a number of colleagues at Aston university and the university of Leiden indicated that the above costs were exaggerated. Eventually, the Directive was adopted in July 1995 although the United Kingdom abstained in the vote. The full title of the Directive is Directive 95/46/EC of the European Parliament and of the Council on the protection of personal data with regard to the processing of personal data and of the free movement of such data (OJ [1995] L281/31). In this and the remaining chapters in this Part of the book it will simply be referred to as the 'Data Protection Directive'.

Model of Data Protection Under the Directive

The Directive has, by Article 1, twin aims which at first sight appear to be incompatible. It states:

1. In accordance with this Directive Member States shall protect the fundamental rights and freedoms of natural persons, and in particular their right of privacy, with respect to the processing of personal data.
2. Member States shall neither restrict nor prohibit the free flow of personal data between Member States for reasons connected with the protection afforded under paragraph 1.

In other words, providing member states have complied with the requirements of the Directive-there must be freedom of movement of personal data throughout the Community.

Although the Directive marks a significant change in data protection law, it has at its heart data protection principles in Article 6. These derive from the European Convention on data protection and provide a common link between the new law and that under the 1984 Act. Thus, fir and lawful processing must be ensured, personal data must be processed only for specified purposes, the data must be adequate, relevant and not excessive, they must be accurate and up to date and not kept in a form which permits identification of the data subject for longer than necessary. Nevertheless, and reflecting the changes to data protection law, the mechanism of protection under the Directive is, it is fair to say, more complex than that under the Data Protection Act 1984. It is shown in Figure 14.1.

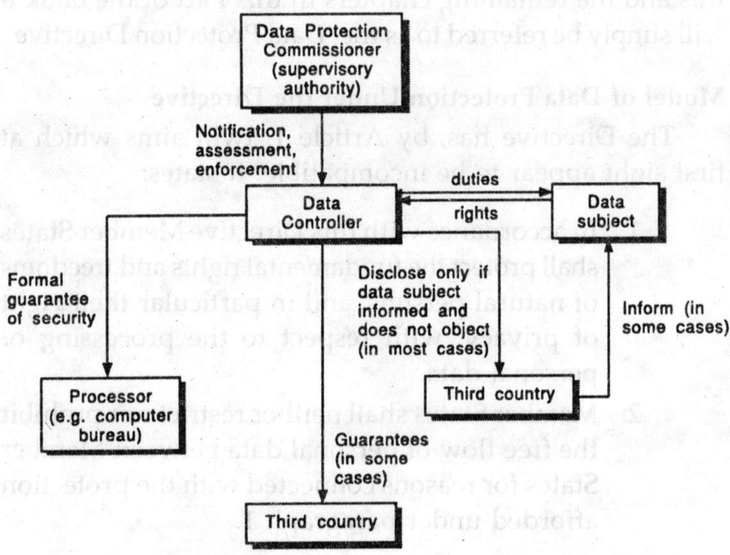

Fig 14.1 Model of data protection under the Data Protection Directive

Although the definitions used in the Directive and the Data Protection Act 198 are described below, for the purposes of understanding the diagram, suffice it to say that the data controller is the person who decides the purposes and manner of processing, the processor is a person who processes personal data on bahalf of the data controller, the data subject is the individual to whom the personal data in question relate, a third country is a country outside the European Economic Area (the EEA comprises the EC member states plus Iceland, Liechtenstein and Norway). The Data Protection Commissioner is responsible, among other things, for supervising compliance with the Act and a third party is any person other than a data controller, processor or employee or agent of either.

Data controller are required to notify their processing activities to the supervisory authority (the Data Protection Commissioner in the United Kingdom). Where the processing in question is likely to pose specific risks to rights and freedoms, the processing operation must be examined before it can commence. The Directive permits exemption from or simplification of notification where the processing is unlikely to affect the rights and freedoms of data subjects or where an 'in-house' data protection official is appointed under national law. Data controllers can only process personal data if they fall within one of a number of conditions. One of a further number of conditions must be satisfied where the personal data are 'sensitive', for example, relating to racial or ethnic origin, health, political or religious beliefs. Further duties are imposed on data controllers to inform data subjects and, in some cases, to seek their consent. Data subjects are given rights of access and rights to object to processing and to prevent processing in some cases. They are also given certain additional rights in respect of automated decision taking and rights of rectification, erasure or blocking of data the processing of which does not comply with the Directive.

Security obligations are imposed on a data controller and, where a data controller engages a processor, such as a computer bureau or a company to provide IT facilities management services, equivalent security obligations must be imposed on the processor. This must be by contractual means or by some other legal act and be in writing or equivalent form. Transfers to countries outside the European Economic Area may be prohibited or allowed only under certain conditions if the country in question does not have adequate protection for personal data.

The Directive also applies to structured manual files which, because of their structure, make it easy to access personal data belonging to a particular individual. However, there are a number of important derogations and options provided for in the Directive which allow for its impact to be lessened some what. Particularly important are the derogations allowing member states to delay the implementation of the Directive to processing already under way at 24 October 1998 (the date the Directive should have been implemented into domestic law) and to further delay the impact of certain parts of the Directive on manual processing.

A feature of the Directive is that the definitions used are fairly wide. For example, it is clear that personal data can include image data or sound data. The definition of processing is breathtakingly wide, including:

> ....collection, recording, organisation, storage, adaptation or alteration, retrieval, cosultation, use, disclosure by transmission, dissemination or otherwise making available, alignment or combination, blocking, erasure or destruction.

The presence of the word 'storage' indicates that simply being a possession of personal data is processing for the purposes of the Directive.

To summarise, issues flowing from the Directive which caused particular concern were:

- the extension of data protection law to some manual files,
- the requirement to inform data subjects on collection of data or otherwise,
- the possibility of data subjects objecting to processing,
- having to seek data subjects' consent to processing in some cases,
- the introduction of conditions for processing to proceed,
- possible constraints over transfers of personal data to third countries (outside the EEA),
- security of processing of personal data, and
- controls over automated decision making.

In the remainder of this chapter nd the following two chapters, the provisions of the Data Protection Act 1998 will be examined. Where appropriate, the provisions of the Directive will be discussed though, generally, it must be noted that the 1998 Act appears to be a reasonably faithful implementation of the Directive. The United Kingdom has taken advantage of many (though not all) of the derogations and options available in the Directive. Of course, mention will be made of the 1989 Act where appropriate and particularly where the new law is significantly different. The data protection cases mentioned were, if course, decided under the 1984 Act but remain. Some are no longer relevant: for example *R* v *Brown* [1996] 1 AC 543, an unsatisfactory decision under the 1984 Act by the House of Lords which has been overtaken by the wider definition of processing. But others remain very valuable in determining the scope of the new law: for example, *Innovations (Mail Order) Ltd* v *Data Protection Registrar* (unreported) 29 September 1993, concerning the provision of information to data subjects in the context of fair processing.

The Data Protection Act 1998

The Data Protection Bill was introduced in the House of Lords in January 1998. During its passage through the Lords and later, through the House of Commons, it underwent many changes. For example, as first printed, the Bill had no specific provisions for transitional arrangements and there was no control over enforced subject access. The Act finally received the Royal Assent on 16 July 1998. Some provisions came into force immediately, being primarily concerned with the definitions under the Act and the arrangements to make regulations under the Act. A number of regulations must be made before the bulk of the Act can come into force. For example, there must be regulations to deal with the fine detail of the notification requirements.

Before looking at the Data Protection Principles, the definitions and other provisions of Act, it must be noted that the Act is not the only source of constraints and controls on the collection, processing and use of personal data. Other areas of law may be highly relevant. For example, a person holding personal data may have an obligation of confidence not to disclose the data or a fiduciary duty in relation to them. Disclosure may be allowed only in a limited number of situations as is he case in banking where rules concerning when personal data may be disclosed were laid down in *Tournier* v *National Provincial* [1924] 1 KB 461. In that case, it ws held that disclosure of confidential information could proceed where the interests of the bank required disclosure. However, it is an old case and it is arguable whether it would be applied in the present climate of greater respect for individuals' rights and freedoms. Disclosure may otherwise be lawful if the individual consents or where the disclosure is in the public interest or where it is required by law. The laws of copyright and defamation may also restrict the use and disclosure of information relating to individuals.

The Data Protection Principles

The Data Protection Principles are at the root of protection law and they are contained in Part I of Schedule 1 to the Act. Part II of the Schedule provides interpretation of the Principles. The Principles appear much as before although there are some important differences. They are as follows.

1. Personal data shall be processed fairly and lawfully and, in particular, shall not be processed unless-
   (a) at least one of the conditions in Schedule 2 is met, and
   (b) in the case of sensitive personal data, at least one of the conditions in Schedule 3 is also met.
2. Personal data shall be obtained only for one or more specified and lawful purposes and shall not be further processed in any manner incompatible with that purpose or those purposes.
3. Personal data shall be adequate, relevant and not excessive in relation to the purpose or purposes for which they are processed.
4. Personal data shall be accurate and, where necessary, kept up to date.
5. Personal data processed for any purpose or purposes shall not be kept for longer than is necessary for that purpose or those purposes.
6. Personal data shall be processed in accordance with the rights of data subjects under this Act.
7. Appropriate technical and organisational

measures shall be taken against unauthorised or unlawful processing of personal data and against accidental loss or destruction of, or damage to, personal data.

8. Personal data shall not be transferred to a country or territory outside the European Economic Area unless that country or territory ensures an adequate level of protection for the rights and freedoms of data subjects in relation to the processing of personal data.

While these are very similar to those under the 1984 Act, Principle 8 is new and reflects concerns about transfers of personal data to countries which do not have adequate protection. Furthermore, the first Principle now refers to conditions for processing. Again this is new. Of course, the first Principle is without a doubt the most important - that processing shall be fair and lawful - and it could be said that the rest of data protection law merely fleshes this out and provides the detail of just what fair and lawful processing is.

There have been a number of cases on the Data Protection Principles under the 1984 Act, particularly in respect of the first Principle and these are discussed in depth in the next chapter. Some of the other Principles have also exercised the Registrar who was quite active at the time of the introduction of the Community Charge ('Poll tax') following concerns that a number of local authorities were collecting unnecessary information about persons and that the information was excessive in terms of that required for the purposes of the Community Charge. In *Rhondda BC* v *Data Protection Registrar* (unreported) 11 October 1991, the Tribunal upheld the Registrar's interpretation of the fourth principle (third principle under the 1998 Act) and confirmed the enforcement notice issued against the officers in charge of collecting information.

They had been asking for individuals' dates of birth. In *CCRO of Runneymede BC* v *Data Protection Registrar* (unreported) 1990, Data Protection Tribunal, information relating to the type of property in which the poll tax payer resided was deemed excessive.

The seventh Principle is concerned with security (it was the eighth Principle under the 1984 Act) and, following a number of thefts of computers from doctors' surgeries, the Data Protection Registrar warned general practitioners to review their security arrangements otherwise they could be in breach of that Principle (*The Times*, 2 December 1992, at p.3). The worry here was that the information stored could be used to blackmail individuals. One criticism of the 1984 Act (and the same applies to the 1998 Act) is that there was no express requirement to report the 'theft' of data and a spate of 20 such thefts over a six-month period could be just the tip of the iceberg.

The principles and their interpretation will be discussed in greater depth in the following chapters. It is considered to be useful, however, to let readers have sight of them now and to stress that it is the Principles which underpin the new law, as they did the previous law under the 1984 Act.

Definitions

The definitions are very significant and they set out the scope of the new law. The most important definitions are contained in section 1 of the Act. Some are similar to those under the 1984 Act, though others are much wider, First, the definition of data is given.

> *'data'* means information which-
>
> (a) is being processed by means of equipment operating automatically in response to instructions given for that purpose,

(b) is recorded with the intention that it should be processed by means of such equipment,

(c) is recorded as part of a relevant filing system or with the intention that it should form part of a relevant filing system, or

(d) does not fall within paragraph (a), (b) or (c) but forms part of an accessible record as defined by section 68.

Data within (a) and (b) above are those which are being or are to be processed by automatic means; in other words, computer data. Data within (c) are those in structured manual filing systems ("relevant filing system" is defined below). These are the data to which data protection law will now extend. The inclusion of such data was seen as one of the most costly provisions in the new law to implement.

Accessible records within (d) above are health records and certain educational and local authority records, which are caught by the new law even if they are processed manually and are not structured within the meaning required for a relevant filing system. The inclusion of such data is to incorporate the effect of the Access to Personal Files Act 1987 within the new law. This Act gave a right of access to certain local authority files such as social services files and housing files and is repealed in full. Access to health records which was covered by the Access to Health Records Act 1990 is also included in the new law. Where local authority files or health records are processed by computer, they are treated in the same way as other data under the 1998 Act.

Automatically processed data are treated somewhat differently than data in relevant filing systems within (c) above and accessible records within (d) above. In particular, only automatic processing need be notified (although in rare cases, manual processing may be subject to a preliminary assessment before processing can proceed). There are also provisions delaying parts of the new law specifically directed towards manual processing.

> *'personal data'* means data which relate to a living individual who can be identified—
>
> (a) from those data, or
>
> (b) from those data and other information which is in the possession of, or
>
> likely to come into the possession of, the data controller, and includes any expression of about the individual and any indication of the intentions of the data controller or any other person in respect of the individual.

There are some doubt as to whether the Directive intended to restrict personal data to living individuals but the 1998 Act puts this beyond doubt. The definition confirms that it is not necessary for all the identifying data to be subject to the processing activity. It is enough for there to be further information which the person processing the data has or will obtain and which, together with the data being processed, provides identification. For example, a computer database may not include names but might, instead, operate on individuals national insurance numbers. If the person processing the data also has a card index which contains national insurance numbers and the names of the individuals to whom they belong, that is sufficient for the data being processing by computer to be classified as personal data.

Personal data now include expressions of opinion and any indication of intentions. The latter was expressly excluded from the meaning of personal data under the

1984 Act. However, some of the exemptions from the subject access provisions will compensate for this change. In any case, it might be difficult to distinguish between an expression of opinion and a statement of intention. 'The performance of Joe Bloggs as a sale executive indicates that it is unlikely that he will be promoted in the near future' is an example.

> *'relevant filing system'* means any set of information relating to individuals to the extent that, although the information is not processed by means of equipment operating automatically in response to instructions given for that purpose, the set is structured, either by reference to individuals or by reference to criteria relating to individuals, in such a way that specific information relating to a particular individual is readily accessible.

The equipment is that personal data are easily accessible because of the structure, such as in the case of *pro forma* application form. This is confirmed in the Directive and its recital 15, which emphasises ease of access by virtue of structure. Clearly a card index system where each card bears an individual's name on the top, the cards being stored in name order will be a relevant filing system. It would appear that a file relating to a specific individual containing, for example, only correspondence to and from that individual will not be deemed to be a relevant filing system. The Home Office view was that some internal structure also is required. However, it is possible that a simple address book set out in alphabetical order is caught by the new law. If this contains name, address, telephone number and e-mail address it is at least arguable that it is a relevant filing system as it enables ease of access to information relating to any particular individual. Furthermore,it probably will have some form of internal structure: for example, it may have two columns, the left hand column containing a name followed below by an address; the right hand column might have telephone numbers and the like. Fortunately, if a simple address book is a relevant filing system, as such it does not have to be the subject of formal notification to the Data Protection Commissioner, as we shall see. Note that accessible records in the definition of data are caught by the new law whether or not the data are in structured files.

> *'data controller'* means ... a person who (either alone or jointly or in common with other persons) determines the purposes for which and the manner in which any personal data are, or are to be, processed.

Data controllers are the equivalent to 'data users' under the 1984 Act. Note that there may be two or more data controllers in respect of a single collection of personal data: for example, where an association of builders mutually share and are responsible for a central database of sub-contractors and suppliers. The significance of the phrase 'jointly or in common with other persons' is that if two or more data controllers agree between themselves as to the purposes and manner of processing, then they determine these matters jointly. However, if two or more data controllers have access to a central database, say a data warehouse, but they each have their own individual purposes and manner of processing, then they determine these matters in common. For example, Company A has a data warehouse (a massive collection of data relating to individuals where the information has been obtained from a number of sources). Company A uses this to extract information relating to creditworthiness of its customers. Company A also allows Company B to access the data warehouse. Company B has its own computer programs which are used to identify potential customers for a marketing campaign and to print out envelopes with the selected persons' names and addresses.

As before under the 1984 Act, a *'data subject'* is simply an individual who is the subject of personal data. He is the person to whom the personal data relate or refer.

'Processing' is very widely defined (much more than under the 1984 Act) and, in relation to information or data, means:

> obtaining, recording or holding the information or data or carrying out any operation or set of operations on the information or data, including-
>
> (a) organisation, adaptation or alteration of the information or data,
>
> (b) retrieval, consultation or use of the information or data,
>
> (c) disclosure of the information or data by transmission, dissemination or otherwise making available, or
>
> (d) alignment, combination, blocking, erasure or destruction of the information or data.

Obtaining, recording, using or disclosing data extends to the information contained within the data and it is immaterial if the processing or inclusion in a relevant filing system takes place outside the European Economic Area (EEA).

The definition extends to holding personal data (the Directive uses the term 'storage' instead). This means that simply being in possession of personal data will be processing for the purposes of the Act. Even if the data are stored in structured paper files kept as archive material in a dusty basement, the person responsible will be processing those data. Under section 1 of the 1984 Act, a data user was defined by being a person who holds personal data. Holding data was hen defined in terms of the data being part of a collection processed or intended to be processed by automatic means and the person holding the data alone or jointly or in common with others controlled the contents and use of the data. The definition also extended to data which were not at the time in a form ready for processing. Although 'holding' is not defined in the 1998 Act, one view is that, if the data are in a store and not subject to current processing activity, there must be an intention to process the data in the future. Given the very wide definition of processing, there would be little point in keeping data without having such an intention.

The definition of processing covers every conceivable use of data and its width is enhanced because of the operation referred to are not intended to be exhaustive because of the insertion of the word 'including'. The House of Lords case of *R* v *Brown* [1996] 1 AC 543, heard under the 1984 Act, shows the importance of having a wide definition of 'processing'. In that case, a police officer worked in his spare time with a friend in their debt collection agency. The agency was engaged by a third party to recover a debt. The police officer used the police national computer to obtain information concerning the debtor. He denied that he had used the computer for non-police purposes and said that he accessed the data because he had noticed that the debtor's car was without a tax disc. Furthermore, he claimed that he had only accessed the data and had not 'used' it subsequently. He was convicted at first instance for an offence under section 5(2)(b) of the Data Protection Act 1984 which made it an offence to hold or use personal data for a purpose which had not been registered.

The police officer's conviction was quashed by the Court of Appeal and this was confirmed in the House of Lords, which dismissed the appeal by the Crown by a 3:3 majority. The majority confirmed that the word 'use' must be given its ordinary dictionary meaning and simply retrieving the information in computer readable form from the database was not using the information so recorded. The majority judges thought that the word 'use' should be liberally interpreted so as to achieve the purpose of the Act otherwise there would be a serious gap in the law.

The definition of 'processing' takes on special significance when we look at the meaning of a *'data processor'* which is:

> any person (other than an employee of the data controller) who processes data on behalf of the data controller.

A computer bureau, processing data on behalf of a data controller, will certainly be a data processor. However, unlike the old law, computer bureaux do not have to register under the 1998 Act. But, as the meaning of processing is very wide, it is worth considering the types of persons who will be classed as processors under the new law. There follow some examples (it is assumed that the persons involved are not employees of the data controller-they may be self-employed, freelances or independent organisation):

- persons collecting data, such as market researchers accosting individuals in a shopping precinct,
- mail order catalogue agents,
- a small IT company providing data entry services,
- a company providing disaster recovery services or other back-up services,

- a company engaged to carry out database quality control by verifying, checking and, where necessary, correcting inaccurate information,
- a person engaged to prepare reports for a client using the client's database,
- an Internet Service Provider which provides Web pages or e-mail services to a client who includes personal data on those Web pages or e-mails,
- a company providing IT facilities management services to a client who has 'outsourced' his IT function,
- a company engaged to remove and destroy old computer printout or archived files containing personal data.

The significance of being classified as a processor is that they must be subject to security obligations which are in writing.

Further definitions are contained in sections 2 and 3 and elsewhere in the Act. A very important definitions is that of *'sensitive personal data'* which are, by virtue of section 2 of the Data Protection Act 1998, personal data consisting of information as to:

(a) the racial or ethnic origin of the data subject,
(b) his political opinions,
(c) his religious or other beliefs of a similar nature,
(d) whether he is a member of a trade union....,
(e) his physical or mentla health or condition,
(f) his sexual life,
(g) the commission or alleged commission by him of any offence, or
(h) any proceedings for any offence committed or alleged to have been committed by him, the

disposal of such proceedings or the sentence of any court in such proceedings.

Sensitive data are treated somewhat differently from other personal data. As far as all personal data are concerned, they can only be processed if one of a list of conditions in Schedule 2 to Act is present. For sensitive personal data, there must also be present a condition from a list of further conditions in Schedule 3. These are considered further in the following chapter.

The Act contains comprehensive provisions aimed at protecting freedom of speech. There is an obvious tension between this and the powers of the Data Protection Commissioner which are severely constrained where processing is for the special purposes, defined in section 3 as any one or more of the following:

(a) the purposes of journalism,

(b) artistic purposes, and

(c) literary purposes.

Further definitions are buried away in section 70. They include:

> *'recipient'*, in relation to any personal data, means any person to whom the data are disclosed, including any person (such as an employee or agent of the data controller, a data processor or an employee or agent of a data processor) to whom they are disclosed in the course of processing the data for the data controller but does not include any person to whom disclosure is or may be made as a result of, or with a view to, a particular inquiry by or on behalf of that person made in the exercise of any power conferred by law.

This is relevant in terms of notification of processing activity as recipients must be described in the particulars notified to the Data Protection Commissioner. Note that employees and agents of the data controller and any data processor must be mentioned. The latter part of definition is intended to excuse the notification of recipients who cannot easily be predicted but to whom personal data may be required to be disclosed to by law. A particular example is where a government department makes a particular one-off enquiry to a local authority where the person concerned is based.

> *'third party'*, in relation to personal data, means any person other than-
> (a) the data subject,
> (b) the data controller, or
> (c) any data processor or other person authorised to process data for the data controller or processor.

The relevance of the identify of third parties is that, under certain circumstances, where data are disclosed to a third party, there is an obligation to inform data subjects of this. For example, where data controller A sells a copy of his customer list to data controller B, he should inform all the data subjects concerned unless they are already aware that this would happen.

Now that the main definition have been introduced, it is useful to reflect on the identity of the various involved in data processing and this is set out in Fig. 14.2.

Application of the Act

The Data Protection Act 198 applies to the United Kingdom and extends to Northern Ireland. By section 5, except as otherwise provided for by or under section 54 (which concerns the Commissioner carrying out designated functions to enable the government to give effect to any international obligations of the United Kingdom), the Act applies to a data controller in respect of any data only if:

(a) the data controller is established in the United Kingdom and the data are processed in the context of that establishment, or

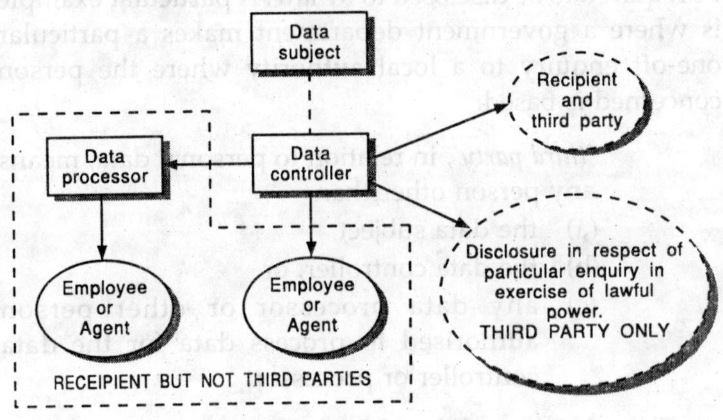

Fig. 14.2 Persons involved in processing activity

(b) the data controller is established neither in the United Kingdom nor in any EEA State but uses equipment in the United Kingdom for processing the data otherwise than for transit through the United Kingdom.

In the last case, the data controller must nominate a representative established in the United Kingdom. Thus, an English company processing data in connection with its business operations is subject to the 1998 Act. A Spanish company which engages a French company to process personal data on its behalf will be subject to the Spanish implementation of the Data Protection Directive under Spanish law. An Australian company using the services of a computer bureau situated in Scotland and using equipment situated there will be subject to the United Kingdom Act and must nominate a representative in the United Kingdom. In this case, it can be expected that it will be the Scottish company which will be the representative. Of course, in the latter case, the Australian company must notify the Data Protection Commissioner of the processing activity carried out in Scotland. If a Brazilian company transfers personal data to Japan via a computer situated in the United Kingdom the United Kingdom Act will not apply unless the data are processed in the United Kingdom for any any purpose other than the purpose of transit to Japan. This latter point is particularly important in terms of transmission via public telecommunications systems including by e-mail and the Internet. It obviates the need for the data controller to notify in all the members states of the EEA if the data is likely to pass through any or all of them (which it is by the nature of transmission over the Internet).

Role of the Data Protection Commissioner

The Data Protection Registrar under the 1984 Act is presently Elizabeth France. She will be the first Data Protection Commissioner under the new law. The Commissioner is required to act in an independent manner and is appointed by Her Majesty by Letters Patent. The role of the Commissioner can be seen as being concerned with the following major functions:

- consultation and dissemination of information,
- investigation,
- intervention,
- enforcement, and
- co-operation.

Consultation and Dissemination of Information

As required by the Data Protection Directive, the Commissioner must be consulted as regards administrative measures and regulations relating to the protection of individuals' rights and freedoms with regard to the processing of personal data. Thus, under section 67 of the Data Protection Act 1998, the Secretary of State shall consult the Commissioner before making an order under the Act (except for an order bringing parts of the Act into force) or before making any regulations under the Act except for the notification regulations

Under the 1984 Act, the Data Protection Registrar was very active in the dissemination of information concerning the Act and compliance with it. This included advertising and the publication of an excellent set of Guidelines, written in plain English. Anyone interested in seeing these and various other reports and other information should visit the Registrar's Website at http://www.open.gov.uk/dpr/dprhome.htm which also gives access to the register and is well worth the time taken to visit. Under the 1998 Act, the responsibility for the Commissioner to disseminate information continuous and is extended.

As before, the Commissioner is given general duties to promote good practice by data controllers and to promote observance of the Act. This includes the dissemination of information about good practice and about other matters within the Commissioner's functions under the Act. The Commissioner may give advice to any person as to any of those matters.

As before, there is a duty to lay a report before Parliament annually. Other reports may be placed before Parliament as must be codes of practice ordered to be prepared by the Secretary of State who may direct the Commissioner to draw up and disseminate codes of practice after consultation with trade associations, data subjects or persons representing data subjects. The order will describe the personal data or processing to which the code is to relate and may also describe the persons or classes of persons to whom it is to relate. The Commissioner may also draw up codes of practice where she considers it appropriate.

A new function is that the Commissioner will disseminate Community findings as regards the adequacy of protection for personal data in third countries (countries or territories outside the EEA) and decisions under Article 31(2) of the Directive made for the purposes of Article 26(3) or (4) as regards measures to be taken in respect of adequacy of protection in third countries and contractual clauses considered to offer sufficient safeguards and such other information relating to processing of personal data outside the EEA.

Investigation

The Commissioner has wide-ranging powers of investigation aimed at determining that processing complies with the Data Protection Principles and whether there has been otherwise any contravention of the Act. The powers of investigation are exercised through:

- information notices,
- special information notices, or
- powers of entry and inspection,

Before looking at these individually, it should be noted that any individual who considers that he is directly affected by any processing may, under section 42, apply to the Commissioner for an assessment as to whether or not it is likely that the processing has been or is being carried out in compliance with the Act. The Commissioner must, upon receipt of such a request, make such assessment, providing she has been furnished with sufficient information to identify the person making the request and the processing in question. The Commissioner may take into account the following factors to determine the manner of the assessment:

- the extent to which the request appears to the Commissioner to raise a matter of substance,
- any undue delay in making the request, and
- whether the person making the request is entitled to make a subject access request.

The Commissioner shall notify the person whether an assessment has been made as a result of the request and any view formed or action to be taken, having regard in particular to any exemption from subject access enjoyed by the data controller. In particular, a request for an assesssment may cause the Commissioner to serve an information notice.

Information Notices

An information notice may be served as a result of a request for assessment from an individual or if the Commissioner has reasonable grounds for suspecting that the data controller has contravened or its contravening any of the Principles. The notice requires the data controller to furnish the Commissioner with information relating to the request within the specified time and in such form as may be specified. The notice must include a statement that the notice has been served in response to a request from an individual if that is the case or, otherwise, with a statement that the information requested is regarded to be relevant in determining whether the data controller has complied or is complying with the Principles, together with reasons why the information is regarded as relevant. The notice must also contain particulars of appeal.

Normally, the time to reply should not be less than the

time during which an appeal may be brought (not specified in th4e new Act but likely to be 28 days as under the 1984 Act) except where the Commissioner considers that the information is required as a matter of urgency where the time limit can be seven days. The Commissioner must state the reasons why the information is required as a matter of urgency. The data controlled is excused fro providing information which is privileged or would reveal evidence of an offence other than an offence under the Act.

Information notices may not be served on a data controller in respect of processing for the special purposes (journalism, artistic or literary expression) unless a determination has been made and has taken effect under section 45 where it appears to the Commissioner that the personal data are not being processed only for the special purposes or are not being processed with a view to publication by any person of any journalistic, literary or artistic material which has not previously been published by the data controller. This provision is intended to prevent undue interference with freedom of speech. Figure 14.3 shows when an information notice may be served by the Commissioner.

Section 45 determinations are important also in respect of special information notices and enforcement notices, as described later. The Commissioner must serve on the data controller notice of the determination which must include particulars of the right to appeal and must not take effect until the end of the period for an appeal or, if an appeal is pending, until the appeal has been determined or withdrawn. Thus, if processing is for the special purposes only or with a view to publication, the Commissioner's powers are curtailed until a determination has taken effect. Note that publication can be by any person; presumably this includes the data controller, and of any personal data

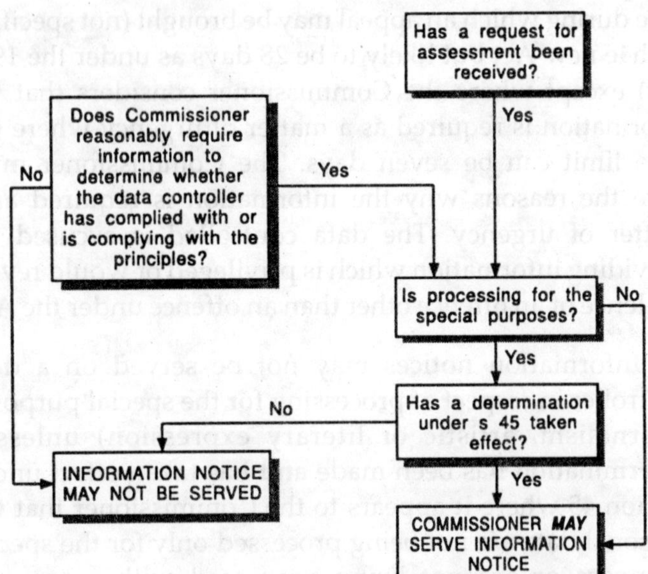

Figure 14.3 Information notice

not previously having been published by the data controller, and of any personal data not previously having been published by the data controller. Thus, if the data controller has already published material including the personal data in question, he cannot rely on the restrictions to the Commissioner's powers if he is now processing the data with an intention that he should re-published it or that another should now publish it. Even so, the Commissioner would still need to make a determination under section 45.

Special Information Notices

These notices relate to processing for the special purposes (journalism, literary and artistic purposes). These provisions are, in many respects, similar to those for information notices. Under section 44, the notice may be served if the Commissioner has received a request for assessment from an individual under section 42 (the Act is silent on whether there must be, on its face, an issue in the request relating to the special purposes) or if the Commissioner has reasonable grounds for suspecting that, in a case where proceedings have been stayed under section 32, the data are not being processed only for the special purposes for with a view to publication for the first time by the data controller.

A stay under section 32 may be ordered by the court where the data controller claims that the processing is only for the special purposes and with view to publication by any person of any journalistic, literary or artistic material which, at the time 24 hours immediately before the time of the claim, had not previously been published by the data controller.

The proceedings referred to in section 32 are in relation to subject access, processing likely to cause damage or distress, automated decision taking or rights in relation to inaccurate data. The stay applies until the Commissioner makes a determination under section 45 or the data controller withdraws the claim.

Unless the notice is sent after a request for assessment is made, the notice may only be sent where a data controller has used the exemption under section 32 (special purposes) as a shield in any proceedings to obtain a stay. The purpose of the notice is to obtain information to determine whether the exemption for the special purposes does indeed apply. Figure 14.4 shows when a special information notice may be served.

Entry and Inspection

The Commissioner has powers of entry and inspection, which are very similar to those under the 1984 Act. The powers are contained in Schedule 9 to the Data Protection Act 1998 and can be exercised by her after obtaining a

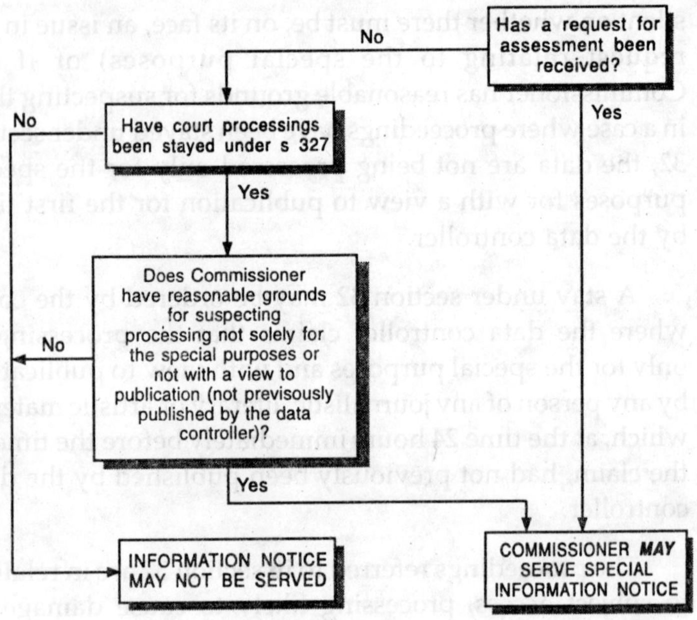

Fig. 14.4 Special information notice

warrant from a circuit judge who will grant the warrant if he is satisfied by information supplied by the Commissioner on oath that there are reasonable grounds for suspecting that a data controller has contravened or is contravening any of the Data Protection Principles or that an offence under the Act has been or is being committed. If the processing is for the special purposes, a warrant must not be issued a determination under section 45 has taken effect. The warrant must be executed within seven days of the date of its issue.

A judge must not issue a warrant (except if satisfied that the case is urgent as discussed below) unless he is satisfied that the Commissioner has given the occupier of the premises in question seven days' notice in writing demanding access and such access was demanded at a reasonable time and was unreasonably refused or although entry was granted the occupier unreasonably refused to comply with a request to permit the Commissioner or her officers or staff to do anything within the powers of entry and inspection, and the occupier, after such refusal, has been notified of the intended application for a warrant and has had the opportunity to be heard by the judge concerned. However, where the case is urgent and the judge is also satisfied that to comply with the above provisions would defeat the object of entry, he may issue a warrant without those preconditions being present.

A warrant will permit the Commissioner or her officers or staff executing the warrant to use such force as is reasonably necessary to enter and search the premises within seven days to inspect, examine and operate any test respecting any data processing equipement on the premises and to inspect and seize any documents or other materials (presumably including items such as magnetic disks and tapes) which may be evidence of an offence or contravention of the Data Protection Principles. Warrants are not available in the case of personal data which are exempt from any provisions of the Act under the national security provisions under section 28.

Intervention

The Data Protection Directive requires that the supervisory authority shall have effective powers of intervention. This requires the Commissioner to carry out a preliminary assessment of processing operations likely to pose specific risk to the rights and freedoms of individuals. The types of operations concerned will be specified by the Secretary of State and such processing must not proceed until the Commissioner has made the assessment to ensure that the processing will comply with the Act: section 22. In the normal course of vents, the Commissioner should inform the data controller of the results within 28 days of notification by the data controller. The period can be extended for a further period not exceeding 14 days.

In is unlikely that a preliminary assessment will be required in many cases. Indeed, the Directive states in recital 54 that the amount of processing likely to pose specific risk should be very limited. The Home Office has indicated that it might apply in the case of genetic data, data matching (that is, where personal data from different sources are matched to find any discrepancies which might indicate that the person concerned is involved in fraudulent applications for credit) and processing by private investigators. The key should be whether the particular description of processing is likely to cause substantial damage or substantial distress to data subjects or to otherwise significantly prejudice the rights and freedoms of data subjects. Processing may not proceed until the 28 days (as extended, if applicable) has expired or the data controller has received a notice from the Commissioner permitting processing.

Another from of intervention is that the Commissioner may require a data controller to rectify, block, erase or destroy inaccurate data as part of an enforcement notice and the Commissioner may also require the data controller to inform third parties to whom the data have been disclosed, having regard, in particular, to the number of persons who would have to be notified.

Enforcement

The Commissioner has two ways of enforcing the new data protection law. One is through enforcement notices, the second is by bringing a prosecution under the Act. In England and Wales and Northern Ireland, prosecutions normally will be brought by the Commissioner. Otherwise a prosecution may be brought by or with the consent of the Director of Public Prosecutions (or Director of Public Prosecutions for Northern Ireland). Presumably, in Scotland, prosecutions are brought by or with the leave of the Procurator Fiscal. The offences, of which there a several, are set out in the following chapter.

Under section 40, if the Commissioner is satisfied that the data controller has contravened or is contravening any of the Data Protection Principles she may serve a notice requiring the data controller to take or refrain from taking specified steps within a specified time and/or refrain from processing after a specified time:

- any personal data,
- personal data of a specified description, or
- for a specified purpose or purposes or in a specified manner.

As mentioned above, where an enforcement notice relates to a breach of the fourth Data Protection Principle (in that the data are inaccurate), the Commissioner may, if reasonably practicable, require the data controller to notify third parties to whom the data have been disclosed. Regard is to be had to the number of persons who would have to be notified. The court also has similar powers in respect of inaccurate data that record accurately information provided by the data subject or a third party.

In deciding whether to serve the notice, the Commissioner is to consider whether the contravention has or is likely to cause any person damage or distress. The provisions as to the service of enforcement notices are subject to restrictions as regards processing for the special purposes (journalism, literary and artistic purposes). Here, the provisions envisage that a court must give leave to serve the notice. In particular, the notice shall not be served unless a determination under section 45 has taken effect and the court has granted leave for the notice to be served. Such leave will only be granted if the Commissioner has reason to suspect a contravention of substantial public interest, and, except in cases of urgency, the data controller has been given notice in accordance with the rules of court for the application to the court for leave to serve the notice. Figure 14.5 shows when an enforcement notice may be served.

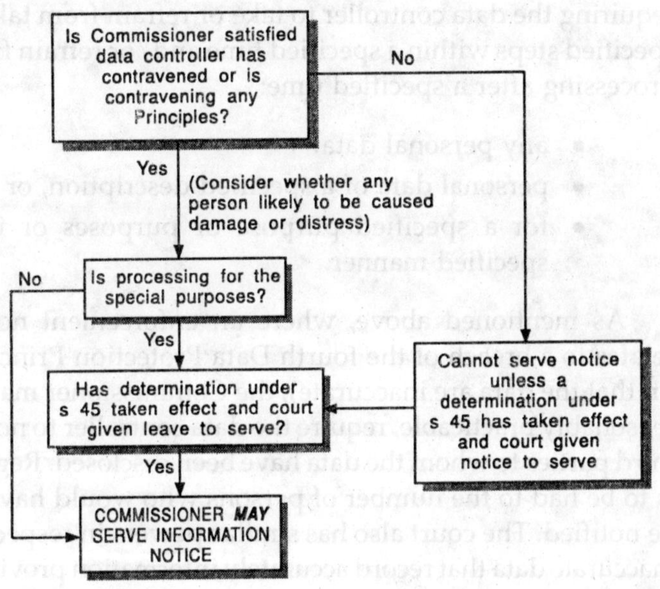

Fig. 14.5 Enforcement notice

Enforcement notices cannot take effect until the period for appeal has expired (expected to be 28 days) or pending an appeal unless the case is a matter of urgency, in which case the time for compliance is seven days. An enforcement notice may be cancelled or varied by the Commissioner. This may be done on the Commissioner's own initiative or following a written application by the data controller after the period for appeal has expired where he can show by reason of a change in circumstances some or all of the provisions of the notice need to be complied with to ensure compliance with the data protection principles: section 41.

Under the 1984 Act, in *British Gas Trading Ltd* v *Data Protection Registrar* (unreported) 24 March 1998, the Data Protection Tribunal held that the Registrar was right to serve an enforcement notice under the 1984 Act rather than accept an undertaking from British Gas Trading Ltd. Under the 1984 Act, there were other forms of enforcement, by de-registration notices and transfer prohibition notices. These find no direct equivalent under the new Act. The Data Protection Registrar had developed a preliminary notice with the approval of the Data Protection Tribunal. It is likely that an informal preliminary notice system might be used under the new law, where it can operate as a useful 'Yellow Card' system, except where processing is, or is alleged to be, for the special purposes.

Co-operation

All the supervisory authorities in the EEA are required to co-operate with each other in respect of exchanging all useful information and to the extent necessary for the performance of their duties. Furthermore, each member state shall designate a representative of its supervisory authority (or a joint representative if the member state has more than one supervisory authority, unlike the United Kingdom) to be a member of the Working Party set up under the Data Protection Directive, discussed later in this chapter.

Co-operation is also implicit in the drawing up of cods of practice, which may be required by the Secretary of State or may be developed as a result of the Commissioner's own initiative. Another provision is that the Commissioner can, with the consent of the data controller, assess processing for the observance of good practice. The Commissioner may, with the consent of the Secretary of State, charge for this service. This is not to be confused with requests for preliminary assessments which will be required in specified cases posing risks to rights and freedoms of data subjects before processing can commence.

Where an individual is an actual or prospective party to proceedings under one of a number of provisions, being in respect of:

- a failure to comply with a subject access request,
- a failure to cease processing likely to cause substantial damage or substantial distress,
- a failure to comply with the provisions an automated decision taking,
- an application to have inaccurate data rectified, erased, blocked or destroyed, or
- the compensation provisions,

that individual can apply to the Commissioner for assistance where the processing relates to processing for the special purposes (that is, journalism, artistic or literary expression.) The Commissioner shall provide assistance where it appears to her to involve a matter of substantial public interest under section 53. The assistance provided may be in the form of legal advice or assistance from a solicitor or counsel or assistance during proceedings. The Commissioner has a first charge on any costs or award in respect of the expenses in providing assistance.

The Commissioner will continue to be the designated authority for the purposes of Article 13 of the European Data Protection Convention 1981 and will be the supervisory authority for the purposes of the Data Protection Directive. Orders may be made for the Commissioner to co-operate with the European Commission and supervisory authorities in other EEA states and to carry out data functions to enable the government to give effect to international obligations in the United Kingdom.

The Tribunal and Appeals

The Data Protection Tribunal is the first line of appeal f rom notices served by the Commissioner or a determination by the Commissioner under section 45. The Tribunal is made up of:

- a chairman appointed by the Lord Chancellor after consulting the Lord Advocate (being a lawyer of at least seven years' standing),
- such number of deputy chairmen as determined by the Lord Chancellor (also being lawyers of at least seven years' standing), and
- such number of other members appointed by the Secretary of State (being persons representing the interests of data subjects or persons representing the interests of data controllers).

Under section 48, a person may appeal to the Tribunal on grounds related to the following:

- enforcement, information or special information notices,
- a refusal by the Commissioner to cancel or vary an enforcement notice,
- where a notice contains a statement that the notice must be complied with as a matter of urgency within seven days, the Commissioner's decision to include the statement or the effect of the inclusion of the statement as regards any part of the notice, or
- a determination under section 45.

The Tribunal may:

- allow the appeal,
- substitute another notice if it considers that the notice is not in accordance with the law,
- where it involved an exercise of discretion by the Commissioner, rule that the discretion ought to have been exercised differently,
- cancel or vary a notice,
- rule on a statement made by the Commissioner that compliance is required as a matter of urgency,
- cancel a determination of the Commissioner.

The rules of procedure will be made under powers on Schedule 6 to the Act (replacing the Data Tribunal Rules 1985) which also deals with the constitution of the Tribunal (a chairman or deputy chairman plus an equal number of persons representing the interests of data subjects and the interests of data controllers), *ex parte* proceedings in cases involving certificates in relation to national security, and the power to remit to the High Court for contempt. The Tribunal may review any determination of fact on which the notice in question was based. Appeals from the Tribunal on a point of law go to the High Court in England or Wales.

The Working Party

A Working Party on the Protection of Individuals with regard to the Processing Personal Data ('the Working Party') was established under the Data Protection Directive. It is an independent body with an advisory status. The Working Party is composed of a representative from the supervisory authority of each member state. Where a member state has more than one supervisory authority (for example, where one looks after the public sector and another looks after the private sector), a joint representative is nominated. A representative of the authority or authorities established for the Community institutions and bodies and representative of the Commission are also members of the Working Party. A chair is elected every two years and decisions are taken by a simple majority of representatives of supervisory authorities. The Working Party considers items placed on its agenda by the chairman, either on his own initiative or at the request of a representative of the supervisory authorities or at the request of the European Commission.

The brief of the Working Party is set out in Article 30 of the Directive and is to:

- examine any questions covering the application of national measures implementing the Directive so as to contribute to the uniform application of such measures,
- give the Commission an opinion on the level of protection afforded in the Community and in third countries,
- advise the Commission on any proposed amendment to the Directive, on any additional or specific to safeguard rights and freedoms with regard to the processing of personal data and to advise on any other proposed Community measures affecting such rights and freedoms,
- give opinions on codes of practice drawn up at Community level.

Furthermore, the Working Party must inform the Commission if it finds disparity between the laws of member states in respect of the protection of individuals with regard to the processing personal data. It may, on its own initiative, make recommendations on all data protection matters. An annual report, which will be made public, is to be drawn up dealing with the protection of natural persons with regard to the processing of personal data within the Community and in third countries. The Commission must inform the Working Party in the action it takes in response to its opinions and recommendations. This is to be done in a report forwarded to the European Parliament and the Council and will also be made public.

The Fourteenth Annual Report of the Data Protection Registrar (The Stationery Office, 1998) contains in Appendix 10 some of the documents and recommendations of the Working Party. There is a working document on assessing adequacy of protection in third countries, and another setting out preliminary views on the use of contractual provisions in the context of transfers of personal data in third countries. These transfers are a minefield and, at the time of writing, there are important discussions between the United States and the Commission trying to solve the problem that the United States has a different approach to data protection, being based on a more fragmented, self-regulatory system. There is also a working paper on whether self-regulation makes a meaningful contribution to the level of data protection in third countries and a recommendation on airline computerised reservation systems. In relation to the latter, recommendations include providing consumers with clear information about processing, obtaining excess consent where there data are sensitive (for example, disability, status or religion), responding quickly to subject access requests, archiving data off-line no more than 72 hours after completion of the journey and destroying the data within three years (during this period, the data can only be consulted for billing dispute reasons; the data can be kept longer if needed in a particular case to settle a claim for damages or if necessary to comply with a legal obligation for example, for tax of accounting purposes).

15 DATA CONTROLLERS AND THE DATA PROTECTION ACT 1998: (A CASE STUDY)

Introduction

It is upon the data controllers, those who process personal data, that the main burden of data protection legislation falls. In spite of some changes to the text of the 1992 proposed Directive and the significant use by the United Kingdom of derogations permitted by the Directive, costs of implementing the new law are still likely to be substantial. The financial memorandum to the Data Protection Bill put the figures as shown in Table 15.1.

TABLE 15.1

Financial Impact of the New Law

Sector	*Start-up costs (£ m)*	*Annual recurring costs (£ m)*
Central government	90	46
Local Government	104	29
Private sector	836	630
Voluntary sector	120	37

Although these figures are worryingly high, there is a lot data controllers can do to ease the burden of complying with the new law. By understanding data protection law, data controllers are in a much better position to develop systems and procedures to minimise the financial impact of compliance.

The purpose of this chapter is to explore the model of data protection law under the 1998 Act from the perspective of the data controller. The discussion will involve further consideration oft he Data Protection Principles which, with their interpretative provisions, are very important. Some of these latter provisions contain some of the most important and potentially onerous elements of he Directive. First, the notificaticn requirements will be described From a data controller's point of view, this is arguably of most immediate impact. This will include a look at the requirements to provide data subjects with information when data are obtained from them and in other cases. Following this, the constraints on processing activity are discussed. These include the conditions for processing which cannot proceed unless one of the conditions applies for normal data and, in the case of sensitive data, a further condition also is satisfied. These conditions are a new departure for the United Kingdom except in so far as processing was required to be fair under the 1984 Act.

The security provisions are, to some extent, similar to those under the 1984. Act but there are important requirements where data processors are engaged. Following the discussion of security, the exemptions are described. Although a number of exemptions are similar, on the whole, there are considerable differences to those under the 1984 Act, some of the which disappear including the 'word processing' exemption and those relating to unincorporated members' clubs and mailing lists. Next there is a brief look at enforcement from the data controller's viewpoint. This builds up on the description of the Data Protection Commissioner's functions in the previous chapter. The offences under the Act are then described in summary, as many will have been dealt with previously. Finally, the complex, though important, transitional provisions are discussed. One advantage of studying these is that some aspects of the transitional arrangements show how the new law differs from that under the 1984 Act.

Notification and Informing Data Subjects

The Data Protection Act 1998 exempts from notification all manual processing of data, that is data that are part of a relevant filing system or accessible record as defined in section 1. Unless exempt, all automated processing must be notified. However, even if required to be notified, processing may still be subject to a preliminary assessment where it poses specific risks and the Secretary of State has made the appropriate order requiring such assessment before processing can commence. Exemption from formal notification to the Data Protection Commissioner is not all good new s as the data controller must still furnish information to any person making a written request, as we shall see later. Further exemption from notification is possible by order of the Secretary of State. This may be possible in the future for payroll, personnel and work planning, purchase and sales administration, general administration, unincorporated members' clubs and certain non-profit-seeking bodies.

Under section 4(4) a duty is placed on every data controller, unless exempt, to comply with the Data Protection Principles. This applies whether or not he has notified his processing activities. Section 19 states that personal data must not be processed until registered, except in the case of manual processing which is not subject to a preliminary assessment (which will usually be the case) or if the processing is of a particular description to be exempted by notification regulations or if the sole purpose of the processing is the maintenance of a public register—for example, the electoral roll. Unless exempt from the notification requirements, section 18 requires data controllers to notify the 'registrable particulars' together with a general description of security measures. The information to be contained in the registrable particulars is set out in section 16(1), being in relation to a data controller:

(a) his name and address,
(b) if he has nominated a representative, the name and address of the representative,
(c) a description of personal data being or to be processed by or on behalf of the data controller and of the category or categories of data subject to which they relate,
(d) a description of the purpose or purposes for which the data are being or are to be processed,
(e) a description of any recipient or recipients to whom the data controller intends or may wish to disclose the data,
(f) the names, or a description of, any countries or territories outside the European Economic Area to which the data controller directly or indirectly transfers, or intends or may wish directly or indirectly to transfer, the data.

As regards security measures, one possible approach might be for data controllers to signify their adherence to BS 7799, Information Security Standard and Certification Scheme.

Where relevant, Where relevant, a statement must also be included of the fact that the notification does not extend to personal data being processed, or intended to be processed, but not subject to notification. This will apply to manual processing exempt from notification where the data controller has not chosen to notify such processing. For example, if a data controller has a computer data base containing personal data, he must notify that. If he also has a card index system processed manually, that is likely to be exempt from the notification requirements. The data controller.may choosen not to notify his card index system and, if he so chooses, he must include a statement in his notification of his automatic processing that he also processes personal data not subject to notification. This simply flags the fact that there is other processing being carried on and a person altered to that fact may wish to obtain further information from the data controller in respect of such processing, as discussed below. Alternatively, the data controller may decide to notify his manual processing also, in which case he need not provide a supplementary statement. The rationale is that of transparency of processing. Individuals should be able to see what processing is being carried out by consulting the register and, if altered to the fact that there is non-notifiable processing also going on, he can find out what that is also.

The Act states that notification will last for 12 months, although the mechanism is included to modify this period. Under the 1984 Act, the period of registration was three years.

Under the 1984 Act, the Registrar could refuse to register anyone as a data user if it appeared that the processing would contravene the Data Protection Principles or insufficient information had been furnished to allow the Registrar to determine this. Furthermore, the Registrar could issue a de-registration notice if satisfied that the processing has contravened or in contravening any of the Data Protection Principles. This link between registration and policing has disappeared under the 1998 Act and it appears that, providing the applicant has provided the registrable particulars and a general description of security measures and tendered the fee (to be announced) the Commissioner must enter the relevant details on the register. Of course, if it appeared that the processing did contravene the Data Protection Principles, the Commissioner could then exercise her enforcement powers under the Act or bring a prosecution, as appropriate. The only proviso to this apparent removal of checking the registrable particulars for compliance is that notification regulations, yet to be made at the time of writing, may make some provision for checking though there appears to be no specific power for this under the Act. One exception is that, in relation to processing of a description or descriptions to be specified by the Secretary of State, a preliminary assessment by the Commissioner to ensure compliance with the Act will be required before processing can proceed.

Under section 19, the Commissioner will maintain a register of data controllers, available for public inspection free of charge. Certified copies may be obtained for a prescribed free, expected to be £2. The general description of security measures is not available to the public. The existing register under the 1984 Act is available through the Data Protection Registrar's Website at

http:/www.open.gov.uk/dpr/dprhome.htm

and it is expected that the register under the 1998 Act will also be available in this useful form. One significant difference is that, under the 1984 Act, data users could have more than one register entry. The 1998 Act only allows one entry per data controller. This could ease the task of individuals carrying out subject access requests.

Failure to notify is an offence of strict liability. Even if the person processing personal data had never heard of data protection law, he will be guilty of the offence. There is a further duty on the data controller to notify changes in the registrable particulars by virtue of section 20. However, failure to notify any changes is a criminal offence which is subject to a due diligence defence.

The basis of a due diligence defence is that, generally, liability is strict unless the accused makes out a defence. Such a statutory defence presumes that the fault is the responsibility of another person and that the accused has exercised due diligence to prevent the wrongful act from occurring. One way a data controller may prove that he has exercised due diligence is to show that he had installed systems or procedures aimed at preventing the wrong occurring. This might be by training employees or agents as to the importance of data protection law and providing them with clear information as to what the scope of their duties was. In terms of failing to notify charges, a data controller might escape liability if he can show that clear instructions had been given to an employee responsible for data protection within the data controller's business.

Under the transitional provisions contained in Schedule 14 to the Act, existing registrations under the Data Protection Act 1984 continue to be effective until they expire, providing they expire before 24 October 2001.

Requirement to Provide Information to any Person on Request

Where a data controller has not notified his processing activity because he is not required to do so and has chosen not to do so, he must still be in a position to supply information equivalent to the registrable particulars (as per (a) to (f) above) to any person who submits a written request for such information. The information must be provided within 21 days of the written request otherwise the data controller commits an offence, subject to a due diligence defence under Section 24. No charge can be made for providing this information and the person making the request does not have to be a data subject in relation to the data controller, Specific exemption from this requirement may be made by notification regulations.

The main implication of this provision is that it may suit a data controller to notify processing which he is not required to. A further point is that, if a data controller has not notified all his processing which is within the scope of the Act, he ought to consider implementing a procedure for dealing with such requests although, for many data controllers, they are likely to be quite rare.

Preliminary Assessment (Prior Checking)

In cases, to be specified by the Secretary of State, processing will be subject to a preliminary assessment by the Commission (known as 'prior checking' in the Directive) and the processing must not proceed until the Commissioner has made a preliminary assessment to ensure that it will comply with the Act section 22. Where a preliminary assessment is required, in the normal course of events, the Commissioner should inform the data controller of his assessment within 28 days of notification by the data controller. The period can be extended for a further period not exceeding 14 days. No distinction is made between automatic and manual processing for a preliminary assessment. The Secretary of State will, by order, detail the descriptions of processing for which preliminary assessment is required. It is likely to be required in relatively few cases where it appears to the Secretary of State that a particular description of processing is likely to cause substantial damage or substantial distress to data subjects or to otherwise significantly prejudice the rights and freedoms of data subjects. Processing genetic data, data matching, endangered life databases and other sensitive processing operations are likely to be caught. Processing may not proceed until the 28 days (as extended, if applicable) has expired or the data controller has received a notice from the Commissioner permitting processing. Otherwise a criminal offence of strict liability is committed.

The preliminary assessment provisions contain no power for the Commissioner to prohibit processing. The intention is that they enable the Commissioner to give a view on whether the processing is likely to comply. It will then be up to the data controller to decide whether or not to proceed. Of course, if the Commissioner considers the processing unlikely to comply with the Act, she may use her powers of enforcement if the data controller decides to go ahead.

Data Protection Supervisors

In some member states, a system of internal data protection supervisors is in place. In-house officials oversee compliance with data protection law. The Directive provided the opportunity for other member states to adopt such a system which should permit the exemption or simplification of notification and allow internal preliminary assessments to be made, reducing the time delay in introducing new forms of sensitive processing. Data protection supervisors will not come in with the first wave of the new law but the Act contains the mechanism to introduce them at a later date. Under section 23 of the Data Protection Act 1998, the Secretary of State is given the power to make orders providing for personal data supervisors. They are to be responsible in particular for monitoring, in an independent manner, the data controller's compliance with the Act/. There are likely to be duties imposed on personal data supervisors owed to the Commissioner who may be given functions in respect of them. It may be some time before we see data protection supervisors in the Untied Kingdom. Perhaps the first place they may be allowed is in the public sector.

Informing Data Subjects on Collection and in Other Cases

The provisions on interpretation of the Data Protection

Principles require that, for the first principle, the method of obtaining the data and whether the person from whom they were obtained was deceived or misled as to the purpose or purposes of processing are factors in determining whether the processing is fair (although data obtained or supplied under statutory authorisation is automatically deemed to be fairly obtained). Transparency is obviously important here and the individual should know what personal data relating to him are to be used for. This principle of openness is developed further in the interpretative provisions which place further duties on data controllers to provide specific information to an individual on collection of personal data and in other cases, especially where the data are disclosed to a third party.

These obligations to inform data subjects are derived from ARticles 10 and 11 of the Data Protection Directive and have no equivalent under the 1984 Act, except as developed by case law such as in *Inovations (Mail Order) Ltd.* v *Data Protection Registrar*, 29 September 1993, Data Protection Tribunal. In that case, Innovation operated a large mail-order business, advertised through catalogues, newspapers and television. It also had a lucrative business selling its customer lists to other retailers and service providers (an activity known as 'list trading'). Customers ordering goods from Innovations were not told of the list trading activity at the time they placed their orders. It was only when they received a written acknowledgement of their orders that they were informed by way of notice on the rear of the acknowledgement form. The notice informed customers that they could have their names removed from the lists if they applied formally, sending in details of their name and address.

The Data Protection Registrar took the view that this was a breach of the first Data Protection Principle as the data were not being obtained fairly because customers ought to have been informed at the time the data were collected and not later. An enforcement notice was served on Innovations which appealed to the Tribunal. The Tribunal agreed with the Registrar and said that the question as to whether data had been fairly obtained related to the time of the obtaining and not a later time. If a purpose for which the data are intended to be used is not obvious at the time of obtaining the data, the data subject must be told of that non-obvious purpose at *that* time. If the data user does not inform the data subject at the time of collection of the data, the data subject's express consent must be sought before nay non-obvious processing can be commenced.

This approach was adopted again by the Tribunal in *British Gas Trading Ltd.* v *Data Protection Registrar,* 24 March 1998. British Gas Trading had inherited a large number of its customers from the previous bodies which made and supplied gas. When it wanted to send marketing material to all its customers, British Gas Trading inserted a note to that effect when it sent out gas bills and statements. The note informed customers that they could opt out of receiving such marketing material by writing in. The Tribunal held that this was not fair processing. a number of factors in the case are important and instructive:

- at least some of the marketing material related to services or products that were not directly related to gas or gas appliances (for example, the 'Goldfish' credit card),
- customers should be able to object without having to perform a positive act like writing in—they should be able to signify consent or otherwise at the time data were collected from them, 'there and then',

- new customers could be informed and given an opportunity to object when completing a contract form, for example by ticking the 'opt-out' box.

Some other submissions by the Registrar that the processing was also unlawful, for example, by being in breach of confidence or contract, were rejected by the Tribunal. This and the *Innovations* case show that, although there was no specific duty to inform individuals of non-obvious uses at the time the data were collected, the duty arose as a direct consequence of the requirement that processing must be fair. However, the duty under the 1998 Act is much more extensive.

Inform on Collection

Part II of Schedule 1 to the Data Protection Act 1998 requires that, where the data are obtained from the data subject, the data controller must ensure, so far as is practicable, that the data subject has or is provided with the 'relevant information' or *has made it readily available to him*. The relevant information to be provided is;

- the identity of the data controller (and representative, if any),
- the purpose or purposes of the processing (but see below on the second Data Protection Principle),
- any further information, having regard to the circumstances in which the data are or are to be processed to enable such processing in respect of the data subject to be fair.

The White Paper, *Data Protection: The Government's Proposals* (Home Office, Cm 3725, 1997) which preceded the Bill suggested that it would be the controller who would decide whether further information was required to be given, though the Act is silent on this point. The second Data Protection Principle requires that data shall be obtained only for one or more specified and lawful purposes and not further processed in an incompatible manner. The interpretation on this allows the purpose to be specified either by notification to informing him, as above. This means that, where the data controller has notified his processing to the Commissioner (which he must do in the case of automatic processing, unless exempt), the data controller will not have to separately provide this information to the data subject. As the purposes of processing are among the registrable particulars, this information will be publicly available where processing is notified. Thus, the data subject can, by consulting the data protection register, find this information out himself.

Unless further information is deemed to be required to ensure fair processing all the data controller will have to do is to identify himself to the data subject, unless a non-obvious use is envisaged or disclosure to a third party is possible. *Innovations* and *British Gas Trading* are likely to remain good law under the 1998 Act. Certainly, if the data are to be used for marketing purposes, this is likely to be a situation where further information must be given. However, it should be noted that the Tribunal in *British Gas Trading* accepted that what is or is not obvious may change over time as consumers become more aware of diversification of business activity carried out by a company or group of companies.

Inform in Other Cases

Other cases will cover the situation where the data have not been obtained directly from the individual concerned. For example, it might be that the data are disclosed by the data controller who obtained the data from the data subject in the first place and now chooses to disclose them to a second data controller. Anther example is where a data controller generates for himself data relating to the data subject.

In cases other than where the data are being obtained directly from the data subject, the data controller must ensure so far as practicable that, *before the 'relevant time' or as soon as practicable thereafter,* the data subject has or is provided with the relevant information or *has it made readily available* to him. The requirement to provide information does not apply where its provision would involve a disproportionate effort or where the recording disclosure is necessary to comply with a legal obligation to which the data controller is subject (other than a contractual obligation) together with such further conditions as may be prescribed by regulations. Although many data controllers will be tempted to claim 'disproportionate effort' it will probably apply in limited circumstances only. It might apply where a large number of individuals would have to be informed and the processing is non-sensitive. It probably will not apply where the proposed use to be made of the data could trigger one of the rights of data subject to processing—for example, where the purpose is direct marketing or involved automated decision taking.

It should be noted that the exception to providing information where a disproportionate effort is involved does not apply to the situation where data are being obtained from the data subject. An example of where the recording or disclosure is required by law is in the field of employment law, especially n the context of official returns and disclosures to the Inland Revenue and Department of Social Security.

The information to be provided is exactly as applies in relation to obtaining data from the data subject. The 'relevant time' is when the controller first processes the data or, where disclosure to a third party within a reasonable period is envisaged:

- if it is in fact disclosed to such a person within that period, the time of disclosure,
- if during that period the data controller becomes or ought to become aware that the data are unlikely to be disclosed to such a person within that period, the time he does become or ought to become so aware, or
- in any other case at the end of that period.

Presumably, the disclosure referred to must be envisaged by both the data controller and the data subject. If it is not envisaged by the data subject, the provision of information in the second and third times would seen fairly pointless.

The need to provide information on first processing cold apply where data have been disclosed to a third party and the third party now processes the data (bearing in mind the very wide definition of 'processing'). As in all cases, the data controller is excused where the data subject already has the information or has it made *readily* available to him. It would seem that, in the latter case, it may be permissible to require the data subject to perform some positive task such as making a request for the information though it must be *readily* available. Where data are disclosed to a third party, it may be that the first data controller is in a position to inform the data subject that this will happen. If he does inform the data subject of the identity (at least) or the third party, then the third party may be excused because the data subject already has the requisite information.

For example, consider two data controllers, Andrew

and Barbara. Andrew obtained data from Clarence and, at the time, provided information as required. If disclosure to a third party within a reasonable period was envisaged, when Andrew discloses the data to Barbara, Andrew must inform Clarence no later than that time that the data have been disclosed. When Barbara first processes the data, she must inform Clarence of her identity (at least), unless to do so would involve a disproportionate effort or where the recording or disclosure is required by law. However, if Andrew previously informed Clarence that the data would be disclosed to Barbara, then Barbara is excused providing this information and any further information which might be required if Andrew previously informed Clarence of it. Figure 15.1 shows the working of these provisions. It assumes that disclosure by Andrew within a reasonable period was envisaged and that the disclosure does in fact take place.

The Secretary of State may by order impose conditions as to the processing of any general identifier (for example, an identity number) should, of course, such an identifier be introduced in the United Kingdom. This may be include further obligations to inform data subjects.

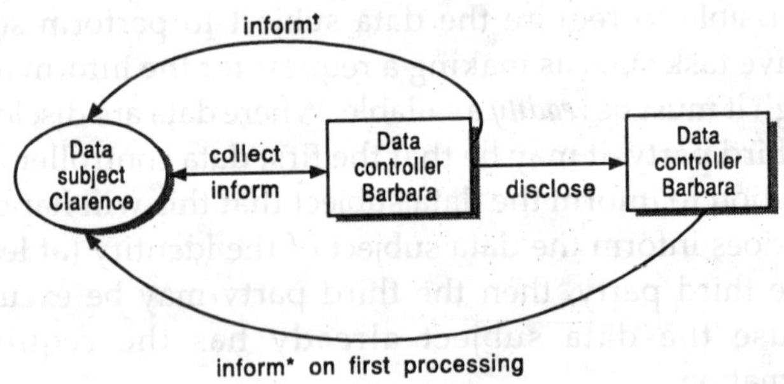

Fig. 15.1 Informing data subjects

Constraints on Processing

The Data Protection Act 1984 imposed relatively few constraints on the processing of personal data providing that the Data Protection Principles were not contravened. As long as the data user had registered under the Act and kept his processing within the scope of his registration, he would be able to process without undue interference. One reason for this was that the Data Protection Registrar would only register a data user if he had supplied sufficient information to enable the Registrar to be satisfied that the proposed processing would be within the Data Protection Principles. At first sight, the new law appears far more restrictive. Apart from the spectre of individuals exercising their new found right to object to processing and prevent it in some cases, processing can only be carried out if it meets one of the conditions for processing or, in the case of sensitive data, two conditions.

The requirement for processing to be allowed only if it meets a particular condition is new and data controllers have to ensure that their processing falls within one or more of the specified conditions. The conditions are central to the controls over processing contained in the Data Protection Directive (Articles 7 and 8). The 1998 Act includes the conditions from the Directive in Schedules 2 and 3 to the Act which are an extension of the first Data Protection Principle, fair and lawful processing, which is expressed as:

1. Personal data shall be processed fairly and lawfully and, in particular, shall not be processed unless—
   (a) at least one of the conditions in Schedule 2 is met, and
   (b) in the case of sensitive personal data, at least one of the conditions in Schedule 3 is also met.

The conditions are examined further below.

Conditions for Processing 'Normal' Data

'Normal' personal data are those not defined as sensitive personal data in section 2 of the Act. The conditions in Schedule 2 are:

1. The data subject has given his consent to the processing.
2. The processing is necessary for the performance of a contract to which the data subject is a party or for taking steps at the data subject's request for entering into a contract.
3. The processing is necessary for compliance with any legal obligation to which the data controller is subject, other than a contractual obligation.
4. The processing is necessary to protect the vital interests of the data subject.
5. The processing is necessary for the administration of justice, for the exercise of functions conferred on any person under any enactment, for the exercise of any function of the Crown, a Minister of the Crown or government department, or for the exercise of any other functions of a public nature exercised in the public interest by any person.
6. (1) The processing is necessary for the purposes of the legitimate interests pursued by the data controller or by the third party or parties to whom the data are disclosed, except where the processing is unwarranted in any particular case by reason of prejudice to the rights and freedoms or legitimate interests of the data subject.

   (2) The Secretary of State may by order specify particular circumstances in which this condition is, or is not, to be taken to be satisfied.

If the data controller cannot fit within any of these conditions, then he may not process the data unless otherwise exempt.

A number of points can be made about these conditions:

- the data subject's consent is not stated to be express or explicit (unlike the case with sensitive data) and it would seem reasonable that it may be implied or result from failing to object, having been given the opportunity, for example, by failing to tick a box on a form;
- the word 'necessary' appears in all the other conditions—this is unlikely to be taken in a strict sense such as it being absolutely essential: although somewhat of a contradiction, it should be taken to mean 'reasonably necessary'—there is authority for this in a registered design case where the word 'dictated' was not taken in a strong sense by the House of Lords: *Amp Inc* v *Utilux Pty Ltd* [1972] RPC 103;
- an example of the vital interests of the data subject could be where his present address is disclosed to an appropriate authority after it has been discovered that he has been in contact with someone with a contagious disease or where he is using a defective and dangerous implement;
- the fifth condition will apply to a great deal of processing in the public sector, including but not restricted to central and local government;
- most commercial organisations will be able to rely on the second or sixth condition (although the data subject's consent may still be required to ensure processing is fair generally): there is, however, a slight difference the language used in the Directive which speaks of the ligitimate

interests to being 'overridden by the interests for fundamental rights and freedoms of the data subject which require protection under Article 1(1)' (being in particular the right to privacy in relation to processing of personal data) —the Data Protection Act 1998 seems slightly more restrictive.

- it is a little difficult to say just what 'legitimate interests' are—one view is that they cover any activity that is lawful while another, perhaps better view, is that they cover activities within the organisation's powers, that is, the organisation is acting *intra vires* (within its powers);
- some flexibility is introduced by empowering the Secretary of State (the Home Secretary in this context) to specify what is or is not within the 'legitimate interests' form of processing—although this power is not mentioned in the Directive it could be important as the requirement for conditions s new to the United Kingdom and the practical application of the sixth condition may be unpredictable.

In most cases data controllers should find that they satisfy at lest one of the above conditions and, in practice, this requirement will not prove restrictive. It is difficult to think of a form of processing that falls outside all the conditions and would yet be deemed to be fair and lawful. Where the personal data are sensitive, the data controller must satisfy one of the conditions in Schedule 2 above as well as one of the conditions in Schedule 3, discussed below.

Conditions for Processing 'Sensitive' Data

'Sensitive' personal data are defined in section 2 of the Data Protection Act 1998 and include data relating to racial or ethnic origin, political opinions, religious or other similar beliefs, trade union membership, physical or mental health or condition, sexual life and data relating to offences (including proceedings, disposal of such proceedings or the sentence of any court).

The conditions contained in Schedule 3 are as follows:

1. The data subject has given his explicit consent to the processing.
2. The processing is necessary for employment law rights or obligations (subject to potential modification by the Secretary of State).
3. The processing is necessary to protect the vital interests of the data subject or another where consent cannot be given by or on behalf of the data subject or the data controller cannot reasonably be expected to obtain the consent of the data subject or the processing is necessary to protect vital interests of another person in a case where consent by or on behalf of the data subject has been unreasonably withheld.
4. The processing is carried out subject to appropriate safeguards by a non-profit-making body or association which exists for political, philosophical, religious or trade-union purposes—processing must be carried out with appropriate safeguards for the rights and freedoms of data subjects and relate only to individuals who are members or have regular contact in connection with the body's or association's purposes and which does not involve disclosure to a third party without the consent of the data subject.
5. The information contained in the data has been deliberately made public by the data subject.

6. The processing is necessary in respect of legal proceedings, legal advice and legal rights.
7. The processing is necessary for the administration of justice, the exercise of functions conferred by or under any enactment, the exercise of any functions of the Crown, a Minister of the Crown or a government department (the Secretary of State may exclude this condition in specified cases or require further conditions to be satisfied).
8. The processing is necessary for medical purposes (includes preventative medicine, medical diagnosis, medical research, provision of care and treatment and management of health care services) and is undertaken by a health professional or a person under a duty of confidentiality equivalent to that owed by a health professional.
9. The processing of sensitive personal data consisting of information as to racial or ethnic origin when it is necessary for the purpose of identifying or keeping under review the existence or absence of equality of opportunity or treatment between persons of different racial or ethnic origins, with a view to enabling such equality to be promoted or maintained, and is carried out with appropriate safeguards for the rights and freedoms of data subjects.
10. The Secretary of State may be order allow sensitive data to be processed in other circumstances.

A 'health professional' is defined in section 69 and includes, *inter alia,* registered practitioners such as doctors, dentists, opticians, pharmaceutical chemists, nurses, midwives or health visitors, chiropractors, clinical phychologists, child psychotherapists or speech therapists, music therapists employed by health service body or a scientist employed as head of department of such a body.

These conditions are fairly extensive and the following points can be made in respect of them:

- where the data subject's consent is relied upon it has to be explicit and it should be informed consent—failing to tick a box on a form will not be good enough;
- what has been said above in relation to the word 'necessary' ought also to apply here;
- vital interests in this context will include situations where an individual is unconscious and disclosure of his blood group is required so that he can be given a life-saving blood transfusion;
- certain types of non-profit-making bodies are included as much of the personal data such bodies will be processing will fall within the definition of sensitive data and it is plainly important for them to process such data belonging to their own members or others having regular contact (note that the condition dos not necessarily relate to charities): disclosure requires the consent of the data subjects and it is likely that express consent should be obtained;
- conditions relating to legal proceedings and justice, legally imposed functions and government functions are as expected but note that the Secretary of State has the power to exclude some of these in particular cases or require further conditions—he is not empowered to add to the list;
- processing for racial or ethnic monitoring is not specifically mentioned in the Directive but it does allow member states to include other

conditions allowing processing where there is substantial public interest subject to satisfactory safeguards;

- there is no sweeping condition allowing processing of personal data relating to to criminal offences such that, for example, commercial organisations which grant credit can process such data—unless exempt (there is a limit exemption for the purposes of crime and taxation but this is unlikely to apply in such cases—this is discussed later in the chapter): such processing generally can only be done under legally conferred functions or for the administration of justice. However, the government has indicated that it will allow processing of data relating to offences and convictions for the purpose of preventing or detecting fraud and other offences by financial institutions and some voluntary organisations, subject to suitable safeguards. This will require an order to be made by the Secretary of State.

Data controllers who intend to process sensitive data must ensure that they fall within one of the conditions above. In some cases, to be specified, the intended processing may fall within the requirement to have a preliminary assessment carried out by the Data Protection Commissioner and, in other cases, where the data controller is unsure, he could consider approaching the Commissioner for guidance or consulting a representative body such as a trade association. It may be that appropriate Codes of Practice will have been published to further assist the data controller in deciding whether he can process the sensitive data in question. Furthermore, the Commissioner may, with the consent of the data controller, individually assess the processing for good practice. This service is likely to be charged for if the Secretary of State so provides.

Data Subject and Their Exercise of Rights to Prevent Processing

Although data subjects are given some new rights under the Data Protection Act 1998 and the rights they enjoyed previously have been enhanced, in the past individuals have not generally exercised their rights to any great extent directly against the data controller. Of course, it is impossible to verify precisely how frequently data subjects made use of their rights (for example, no figures are published on how many data subjects sought to gain access to personal data relating to them); it is reasonable to assume that a much larger proportion of individuals complained to the Data Protection Registrar in preference to bringing a personal action before a civil court against a data controller ('data user' under the old law). Under the 1984 Act, the total number of complaints made to the Data Protection Registrar was 4137 for the year to 1 April 1998. The peak was 4590 for the year to 1 June 1993. The largest numbers of complaints typically relate to consumer credit.

Subject access requests, with some exceptions, do not seem to be made in large volumes (this may be because it was possible to charge the data subject up to a maximum £10 in respect of the request). One exception is in relation to data held by credit reference agencies which, under the old law, was dealt with under section 158 of the Consumer Credit Act 1974. As regards individuals, these requests have been brought within the scope of the Data Protection Act 1998 although the right to have wrong information corrected is still dealt with under the 1974 Act.

In most cases, where a data controller is processing safely within the Data Protection Principles and the processing activities carried on are not particularly sensitive, the data controller should not experience a great deal of activity from data subjects exercising their rights. That being so, the basic rights are stated briefly below but they are described in more detail in the following chapter which focuses on data subject.

The following rights, which existed under the 1984 Act, are enhanced or improved:

- right to subject access (more information should be given now),
- right to compensation available in respect of damage or distress caused by *any* contravention of the new law,
- rights of rectification and erasure (extended to blocking and destruction and somewhat widened in scope).

Of course, the rights are considerably expanded when one takes into account that the new law extends also to certain manual files (relevant filing systems and accessible records).

- rights to be informed, as discussed above,
- a right to prevent processing likely to cause substantial damage or substantial distress,
- a right to prevent processing for purposes of direct marketing, and
- rights in relation to automated decision taking.

Apart from the concerns about the requirement to inform data subjects (although in some cases, this was a requirement under the previous law, as in the *Innovations* case), data controllers expressed some anxiety about the possibility of data subjects objecting to certain forms of processing and being able, in some cases, to require the data controller to stop processing personal data relating to them. The reality is unlikely to be less burdensome. In particular, fair and lawful processing will rarely cause substantial damage or substantial distress; the mailing preference scheme already exists as a way of preventing (or at least reducing the amount of marketing material an individual receives) and the rights in the context of automated decision taking are considerably reduced in a contractual situation or where authorised or provided for by legislation.

Transfers to Third Countries

Of more immediate concern to data controllers are the provisions in the Act which apply where personal data are being transferred to a country outside the European Economic Area (EEA). As mentioned earlier, the rationale behind the Data Protection Directive is that, by providing a level playing field in terms of effective protection for rights and freedoms of individuals, particularly with respect to their right of privacy in relation to processing personal data, there can be no barriers to freedom of movement of personal data throughout the EEA. However, problems may occur where a data controller wishes, as may do, to have his data processed elsewhere and the country to which he wants to transfer the personal data for processing has no specific data protection laws or, if such laws exist, they fail to meet the European standards and safeguards.

The eighth Data Protection Principle requires that personal data must not be transferred to a country or territory outside the EEA unless it ensures an adequate level of protection for the rights and freedoms of data subjects in relation to the processing of personal data. The interpretative provisions in Part II of Schedule 1 state that an adequate level of protection is one which is adequate in all the circumstances of the case, having regard in particular to:

(a) the nature of the data,
(b) the country or territory of origin of the information,
(c) the country or territory of final destination of that information,
(d) the purposes for which and period during which the data are intended to be proceed,
(e) the law in force in the country or territory in question,
(f) the international obligations of that country or territory,
(g) any relevant codes of conduct or other rules which are enforceable in that country or territory (whether generally or by arrangement in particular cases) and
(h) any security measures taken in respect of the data in that country or territory.

Thus, adequacy depends on a number of factors and it will not be possible to say that a particular country does not have an adequate level of protection in all cases. It might be possible to say the opposite, however, where a country embraces a model of data protection law which is, to all intents and purposes, a mirror image of that in Europe. Such a country may be described as a 'white' country.

Even if a particular country or territory does not have an adequate level of protection in terms of the particular transfer envisaged, it may still be possible to make that transfer. The European Community legislators have at least adopted a sense of reality and accepted that there may be good reasons why a data controller might validly wish to transfer data to such a country. The approach taken is to allow the transfer subject to a condition being satisfied; the purpose of the conditions is to try to overcome the danger of inadequate protection. Thus, the eighth Data Protection Principle does not apply to data within Schedule 4 (except by order of the Secretary of State), being where any one of the following conditions is present:

1. The data subject has given consent to transfer.
2. The transfer is necessary for the performance of a contract between the data subject and data controller or for taking steps at the request of the data subject with a view to his entering into such a contract.
3. The transfer is necessary for the conclusion of a contract between the data controller and a third person entered into at the request of the data subject or in his interests, or is necessary for the performance of the contract.
4. The transfer is necessary for reasons of substantial public interest (the Secretary of State may specify circumstances in which a transfer is or is not covered by this).
5. The transfer is necessary with respect to legal proceedings, legal rights or obtaining legal advice.
6. The transfer is necessary to protect the vital interests of the data subject.
7. The transfer is of part of the personal data on a public register and any conditions subject to which the register is open to inspection are complied with by any person to whom the data are or may be disclosed after the transfer.
8. The transfer is made on terms of a kind approved by the Commissioner as ensuring adequate safeguards for the rights and freedoms of data subjects.

9. The transfer has been authorised by the Commissioner as being made in such a manner as to ensure adequate safeguards for the rights and freedoms of data subjects.

In relation to the eighth condition above, the Commissioner may approve kinds of terms which ensure adequate safeguards or authorise transfer as being made so as to ensure adequate safeguards. In any proceedings under the new law, questions as to whether the eighth Principle has been met are to be determined in accordance with any finding made by the European Commission under Article 31(2) of the Directive as to transfers of the kind in question. In the main, safeguards are likely to come from approved contractual terms. Thee are obligations to inform the Commission to the European Communities as to authorisations granted and the Commission may decide certain standard contractual clauses offer sufficient safeguards and member states are required to comply with such decisions. At the time of writing, it appears likely that contractual safeguards will require the recipient in the third country, as appropriate, to abide by the European model of data protection and to be under a contractual obligation to do so.

Security

The seventh Data Protection Principle requires that appropriate technical and organisational measures are taken against unauthorised or unlawful processing of personal data and against accidental loss or destruction of, or damage to, personal data. Security was an important aspect of data protection law under the 1984 Act and is continued under the new law with additional emphasis on the relationship between the data controller and a processor (under the 1984 Act, computer bureaux also had to comply with the security requirements). Factors influencing the level of security include the state of technological development, the cost of implementation, the potential harm of unauthorised processing or accidental loss, destruction or damage and the nature of the data. That being so, a prudent data controller will continually review his security arrangements and monitor technological improvements to security measures available.

Data controllers must take reasonable steps to ensure the reliability of staff having access to personal data. They must choose processors who provide sufficient guarantees as regards technical and organisational measures and take reasonable steps to ensure compliance with those measures. Where a processor is engaged, the processing must be carried out under a contract made or evidenced in writing under which the processor is to act only on the instructions of the data controller and which imposes equivalent security obligations on the processor. Although processors do not have to notify the processing they perform on behalf of others, this mechanism is designed to make sure that they are aware of the importance of security and, in the event of a failure on the part of the processor, he will be liable for breach of contract.

Exemptions

The Data Protection Act 1998, in common with the previous legislation, contains a large number of exemptions from parts of the Act. However, there are significant differences and some of the exemptions under the 1984 Act find no room in the new law. Reference to the section on the transitional provisions illustrates the differences in this respect as specific provision has to be made to cater for these differences.

First, it should be noted that there are some multiple exemptions from the 'subject information provisions' and the 'non-disclosure provisions,' as follows:

- 'subject information provisions' meaning the first Principle, in as much as it requires compliance with Part II, paragraph 2 of Schedule 1 (providing information to the data subject on collection or in other cases) and section 7 (subject access),
- 'non-disclosure provisions' meaning the first Data Protection Principle (but not with respect to the requirement that one of the conditions in Schedule 2 is met and, for sensitive data, one of the conditions in Schedule 3 is also met), the second to the fifth Data Protection Principles, section 10 (the right to prevent processing likely to cause damage or distress) and section 14(1) to (3) (right of rectification, etc. in relation to inaccurate data) to the extent that they are inconsistent with the disclosure in question.

Except as provided for in the exemptions, the subject access provisions are unaffected by any enactment or rule of law prohibiting or restricting the disclosure, or authorising the withholding of information.

The exemptions, some of which are set out in Schedule 7, are numerous. The Secretary of State is given the power to make further exemptions to the subject information provisions and the non-disclosure provisions if he considers further exemption is necessary to safeguard the interests of data subjects or the rights and freedoms of any other individual. This is a basis for exemption in the Directive. Some of the exemptions are out with the scope of the Directive in any case, such as those relating to national security or processing by an individual for a purely personal or household activity: Article 3(2).

It should be noted that a general principle is that exemption from the relevant provisions of the Act is available only in as much as compliance would prejudice the purpose governed by the exemption or if the particular exemption is required for the purpose concerned. For example, exemption is granted from the subject access provisions for the purposes of the prevention or detection of crime. However, if subject access can be granted without prejudicing these purposes (or other exempted purposes), then it must be granted. The exemptions are not generally blanket exemptions and require a value-judgement by the data controller as to whether an exemption is available in a particular circumstance.

All the exemptions are listed in Table 15.2, later, but first a selection of some of the exemptions, which are considered in more depth.

National Security

This exemption is provided under section 28 and applies if it is necessary for the purpose of safeguarding national security. The exemption is very wide-ranging and is from all the principles, the rights of data subjects, notification and enforcement. Furthermore, the offences in section 55 in respect of unlawful obtaining, etc. do not apply if this exemption applies. A certificate signed by a Minister of the Crown who is a member of the Cabinet, the Attorney-General or Lord Advocate is conclusive evidence that the exemption is required. The need for this exemption is plain but the certification arrangements mean that there is little control over the scope and application of this exemption. However, there is provision for an appeal against a certificate to the Date Protection Tribunal. Any appeal will be held before the Chairman and/or deputy chairman as designated by the Lord Chancellor and proceedings will be held *ex parte*, that is, without hearing the person appealing against the certificate.

Crime and Taxation

This applies if the personal data are held for the purpose of the prevention or detection of crime, the apprehension or prosecution of offenders or the assessment or collection of any tax or duty or imposition of a similar nature. Under section 29, the exemption is from the first Data Protection Principle and the subject access provisions. However, the conditions for processing under the first Principle (in Schedules 2 and/or 3) still apply. The exemption applies only n as much as the provision in question would be likely to prejudice any of the purposes covered by the exemption.

The exemption also applies to anyone discharging a statutory function who has obtained the data from a person who held the data for any of the above purposes but here the exemption is from the subject information provisions. An example might be personal at a held by the police which has been given to the Crown Prosecution Service which is considering whether to prosecute the individual concerned. As a judgment has to be made by the data controller as to whether any of the purposes covered would be prejudiced by compliance, a subjective and qualitative element is brought into the practical application of the exemption. This can be criticised as it will be the data controller who decides this, subject only to a challenge by an aggrieved person. Further exemption is granted, from the non-disclosure provisions where the disclosure is for any of the above purposes and where compliance would prejudice any of those matters.

An example of the latter is where a local authority, empowered under section 163 of the Criminal Justice and Public Order Act 1994 and section 111 of the Local Government Act 1972 to use video surveillance in order to promote the prevention of crime, discloses copies of a video to the media in order to facilitate this purpose. In *R. v Brentwood Borough Council, ex parte Peck, The Times,* 18 December 1997, an applicant for judicial review complained when the local authority disclosed a video showing him walking down the High Street, Brentwood, with a knife. He later attempted suicide by slashing his wrists but this was not caught on video. He was not charged by the police. The video was shown on television an some of the applicant's friends and neighbours recognised him. The application was dismissed, Mr. Justice Harrison confirming that the statutory provisions above empowered the local authority to take the actions it had. Furthermore, it had not acted irrationally and had not known of the objection until the video had been broadcast.

Under the 1998 Act, personal data can extend to visual data (this is confirmed by the Directive) and a local authority acting as Brentwood Borough Council did would rely on the crime and taxation exemption. The exemption which applies where disclosure s required by law, discussed later, would not seem to be appropriate as the local authority was empowered to carry out the video surveillance and make the disclosure. It was not required to do so.

Where the data controller is a lawful authority (government department, local authority or other authority administering housing benefit or council tax benefit) and the personal data consist of a classification of the data subject as part of a risk assessment system, exemption from the subject access provisions is granted. This applies only with respect to the purposes of assessment of tax, duty or similar imposition for the prevention or detection or crime, apprehension of offenders or where the offence concerned involves any unlawful claim for payment out of, or any unlawful application of, public funds where the processing is for any of those purpose.

Under the 1984 Act, the Data Protection Registrar had a long-running dispute over the scope of the equivalent exemption with the Halifax Building Society. It all started when an individual complained to the Registrar that he had not received all the information he was entitled to in pursuance of a subject access request. The Society had withheld data which it considered to be 'system security data' on the basis that the crime prevention exemption applied to the data. The Data Protection Registrar issued an enforcement notice and the Society appealed to the Tribunal. After many meetings and discussions and the issue of a preliminary notice in respect of the complainant (with which the Society complied), an agreement was reached between the Halifax Building Society and the Registrar.

The Society had been concerned about the secrecy of its customers' accounts and the need to restrict knowledge to only a few of its own staff. The agreement was to the effect that the Society would not normally give details of transactions on the data subject's account, card number, computer terminal and location of the automated teller machine. However, as part of the agreement (*Agreement in the Enforcement Action against the Halifax Building Society*, 6 January 1992), the Society agreed to inform any person making a subject access request of this fact and that all other information had been made available: for example, details of address, financial circumstances, balance and the Society's views (if appropriate). The data subject would also be informed that the Society would consider requests for other information if there was a genuine need for the data subject to see it. Finally, the Society agreed to inform data subjects that they are entitled to complain to the Data Protection Registrar of not satisfied with the Society's response.

Health, Education and Social Work

Similar to the 1984 Act, section 30 of the Data Protection Act 1998 empowers the Secretary of State to make orders concerning exemptions from subject access. At the time of writing no orders have been made but it is likely that orders similar to those made under the 1984 Act may be made, in addition to an order relating to education. Orders made under the 1984 Act were the Data Protection (Subject Access Modification) (Health) order 1987 and Data Protection (Subject Access Modification) (Social Work) Order 1987. They applied to personal data relating to the physical or mental health of a data subject (health data) or held in connection with social services functions (social data). Similar orders are likely to be made under the 1998 Act.

With respect to health data, the exemption from subject access under the 1984 Act applied if the data were held by a health professional or any other person (so long as the information constituting the data was first recorded by a health professional). The data user could withhold data from the data subject if giving access to the data subject would be likely to cause serious harm to the physical or mental health of the data subject, or lead the data subject to identify another person (other than the health professional involved in the care of the data subject) who has not consented to the disclosure of his or her identity.

The Department of Health made it clear that this exemption should be relied on only in exceptional circumstances. An example might be where a doctor has diagnosed a fatal illness and considers that it would be in the data subject's best interests for him nor to discover this. It was apparent that there was no common law right of subject access in such circumstances to override or supplement that under the Data Protection Act 1984 or complementary legislation such as the Access to Health

Records Act 1990 which gave a right of subject access to information concerning physical or mental health held by health professionals. However, by section 5(1) of the 1990 Act there was exemption from subject access if there was a likelihood of causing serious harm to the physical or mental health of the patient or any other individual—a very similar exemption to that provided under the Data Protection Act 1984.

The basis of such exemptions can be seen in the House of Lords case of *Sidaway* v *Board of Governors of the Bethlem Royal Hospital* [1985] AC 871 which made it clear that a doctor's duty, as with the health authority, was to act at all times in the best interests of the patient and this could, in some circumstances, permit the withholding of information. In *R* v *Mid-Glamorgan Family Health Services, ex parte Martin* (unreported) 29 July 1994, a patient had been refused access to his health records going back to before 1990 on the basis that it would be detrimental for the patient to see those records directly. An offer was made to disclose the records conditionally to a medical expert appointed by the patient but was not accepted. The patient claimed that there was a right of access at common law. However, the Court of Appeal refused to grant access on the 'best interests' principle, denying that there was such a common law right.

The social work exemption under the 1984 Act applied to bodies such as local authorities, the probation service and local education authorities, etc. The body concerned could withhold data if access would be likely to prejudice the carrying out of social work by causing serious harm to the physical or mental health or emotional condition of the data subject or any other person, or to lead the data subject or any other person who is likely to obtain access to the data to identify another individual (other than someone involved professionally in social work) who has not consented to the disclosure of his or her identity. The problems caused by such an exemption could be seen in the case of *Gaskin* v *United Kingdom* (1990) 12 EHRR 36 before the European Court of Human Rights, discussed in the following chapter.

As regards the new provisions allowing exemption from subject access in the case of education, the Secretary of State may make exemption where the data controller is a proprietor or teacher at a school and the personal data consists of information relating to persons who are or have been pupils at the school or in relation to education authorities in Scotland.

Regulatory Activity

This exemption from the subject information provisions covers a wide range of regulatory activities in order to protect the public from dishonesty, malpractice and the like by persons involved with financial services, carrying on any profession or other activity or in relation to charities. It also extends to health and safety at work. A complete list is given in Table 15.2. Under section 31, the function is one conferred by or under any enactment, any function of the Crown or a Minister of the Crown or a government department or any other function of a public nature which is exercised in the public interest. This latter category is potentially very wide ranging.

Further exemption is available from the subject information provisions in respect of statutory functions of the Parliamentary Commissioner for Administration, the Commission for Local Administration, the Health Service Commission and other public bodies. The exemption also applies to certain functions of the Director General of Fair Trading.

In all cases, the exemption is only available where the

application of the subject information provisions would be likely to prejudice the proper discharge of the relevant function. The purpose of the exemption is to prevent, for example, a person under investigation by the Charity Commissioners for the misapplication of the property of a charity discovering that his activities are being investigated. He could find out by carrying out a subject access request or because, under normal circumstances, he is required to be informed of the disclosure of personal data relating to him to the Charity Commissioners.

Journalism, Literature and Art

This is an important and wide-ranging exemption protecting freedom of speech. Under section 32, exemption is from all the Data Protection Principles (except the seventh on security measures), and most of the rights of data subjects including subject access. We have seen in the previous chapter how the Data Protection Commissioner's powers are severely constrained in relation to the purposes of journalism and artistic and literary purposes (the special purposes). Indeed, in a court action in relation to the data subjects' rights or compensation, a claim by the data controller that he is processing only for the special purposes with a view to publication of material not previously published by him at a time 24 hours before he makes that claim, proceedings must be stayed until the Commissioner makes a determination under section 45 as to whether the special purposes do apply or the claim is withdrawn. The same applies if it appears to the court that the special purposes apply.

For the exemption to apply, the processing must be undertaken with a view to publication of any journalistic, literary or artistic material and the data controller must reasonably believe that publication is in the public interest, having regard in particular to the special importance of the public interest in freedom of expression. Furthermore, the data controller must reasonably believe that compliance with the exemption in question is incompatible with the special purposes. In making a determination as to the data controller's belief that publication is in the public interest, regard may be had to his compliance with any relevant code of practice designated by the Secretary of State for this purpose. As noted previously, the Secretary of State can order the Commissioner to prepare and disseminate codes of practice after consultation with trade associations and data subjects or persons representing data subjects.

Research, History and Statistics

In many cases, data processed for statistical or research purposes only will not be within data protection law as the data will be anonymous and, therefore, not personal data within the meaning in section 1(1). However, where the data remain personal data because they contain identifiers or the data controller has or may obtain other data which, together with the research data, allow individuals to be identified, section 33 allows some useful exemptions. These apply where the relevant conditions are present, being that the data are not processed to support measures or decisions with respect to particular individuals and are not processed so as to cause, or be likely to cause, substantial damage or substantial distress to any data subject. These conditions will usually be easily satisfied. If the data are being used to support measures or decisions affecting particular individuals, it may be that other exemptions are relevant—for example, in the case of research data relating to health which are not being processed to identify persons who have been exposed to some virus in the past and are now in need of an urgent inoculation.

The first exemption is simply to the effect that further processing only for research purposes is not to be regarded as incompatible with the purposes for which they were obtained, otherwise this could be a breach of the second Data Protection Principle. The fifth Principle requires that personal data are not kept for longer than in necessary and exemption from that requirement is granted in that data processed only for research purposes can be kept indefinitely. A further exemption is from the subject access provisions but only if the results of any research or any resulting statistics are not made available in a form identifying any data subject.

The exemptions are not lost merely because the data are disclosed to any person for research purposes only, to the data subject or a person acting on his behalf or at the request of, or with the consent of, the data subject or a person acting on his behalf. Nor are the exemptions lost if the person making the disclosure has reasonable grounds for believing any of these apply in the circumstances.

Information Available to the Public

This applies where the data consist of information which the data controller is required to make available to the public, whether by publication or making it available for inspection or otherwise and whether or not a fee is charged. The exemption is from the subject information provisions, the fourth Data Protection Principle (accuracy and kept up to date), the right of rectification within section 14(1) to (3) and the non-disclosure provisions. Clearly where information has to be made available, full application of these provisions would be unnecessary. The type of information that will be within this exemption includes the electoral roll, copies of birth, marriage and death certificates and copies of specifications for patents.

Disclosures Required by Law or in Connection with Legal Proceedings, Etc.

Other exemptions in the main body of the Act are

disclosures required by law or made in connection with legal proceedings or for the purpose of obtaining legal advice or otherwise necessary for the purposes of establishing, exercising or defending legal rights: section 35. A related exemption is in Schedule 7, paragraph 10, being exemption from the subject information provisions on the basis of legal professional privilege. Thus, there can be no barrier to disclosing personal information in connection with legal proceedings. For example, Andrew, who is a self-employed accountant, wishes to sue Brenda (one of his clients) for non-payment of accountancy fees. Andrew has a meeting with his solicitor, Carolyn, and provides her with information about Brenda and the work he did for her. Andrew is a data controller under the Act. Naturally, his notification does not mention such a disclosure but section 35 grants him exemption. As the meeting between Andrew and Carolyn is privileged, neither has to give Brenda any information about it. For example, there is no need to inform Brenda that Carolyn now has personal data relating to Brenda and, of course, any subject access request made by Brenda to Carolyn can be ignored with impunity.

Under the 1984 Act, the question of disclosure of data where the data user was exempt from registration came up for consideration in *Rowley* v *Liverpool City Council* (unreported) 24 October 1989. The judgment amply demonstrates the complexity of that Act (the new Act is no less complex), and Lord Justice Woolf in the Court of Appeal said of the 1984 Act.:

> .... it is right to say straightaway that the act is a complex enactment in which it is difficult to find your way about unless you are very familiar with it indeed.

In that case, the plaintiff brought an action against her

former employer for personal injury and she had made an application for discovery (disclosure to a party in legal proceedings) of information including details of three 'comparative earners.' She wanted details of payments made to three persons employed in a similar capacity to help work out what she would have been paid had she not had to stop working because of her injury. The defendant refused claiming that such disclosure was prohibited by the Data Protection Act 1984.

The defendant was exempt from registration because the data related to payroll and accounts (this exemption disappears under the 1998 Act but is available until 24 October 2001 under the transitional provisions). Section 32(2) of the 1984 Act made it a condition of the exemption that the data are not disclosed except in limited circumstances relating to payroll and accounts. However, section 34(5) of the 1984 Act, in similar though not identical lines to the equivalent provision in the 1998 Act, allowed disclosure if required by law or in the course of legal proceedings and, therefore, the disclosure requested did not contravene the Act. Disclosure was allowed in two ways: first, because it was in the course of legal proceedings in which the defendant was a party and, second, in compliance with an order of the court.

Domestic Purposes

The Data Protection Directive does not apply to processing by a natural person in the course of a purely personal or household activity. Thus, section 36 of the Act exempts from all the Data Protection Principles the rights of data subjects and the requirements as to notification of personal data processed by an individual for that individual's personal, family or household affairs. This also extends to recreational purposes. The Commissioner may still exercise her powers of enforcement in the context of such processing if it is believed that the individual concerned is processing in such a manner as to exceed the scope of this exemption. If this is so, then the exemption will be lost to that extent. In particular, an individual who is otherwise employed but who carries on some private work in his space time may be required to notify.

Schedule 7 Exemptions

For no particular reason, a further set of exemptions is tucked away in a Schedule to the Act. All of these exemptions are listed in Table 15.2, but the following are notable and discussed in more detail.

Confidential References

This exemption is from the subject access provisions only and is given under paragraph 1 of the Schedule. It applies where the reference is given or to be given by the data controller for the purposes of the education, training or employment (actual or prospective) of the data subject or the appointment or prospective appointment of the data subject to any office or the provision or prospective provision by the data subject of any service. The reference must be given or be intended to be given in confidence. There is no distinction between the person by whom the reference is given and the person who receives it. Both will be data controllers for the purpose of this provision *if and only if* the personal data are within the scope of the Act.

To take an example, consider Harold, an employee of the Peak Accountancy Practice who now seeks employment with Flaky Financial Services. Flaky has requested a reference from Peak, which is in the form of letter hand written by Paul, Peak's managing director. This letter is unlikely to be within the meaning of data for the purposes of the Act. It is not automatically processed nor intended so to be and is not a relevant filing system. Both Peak and Flaky can refuse Harold access to it. However, if the letter is produced on a word processor by Paul, it will be within the Act but Peak can refuse Harold access to it providing it is given in confidence. Flaky is under no obligation to grant access, whether it is confidential or not, because Flaky is not processing the data automatically. If the reference is made out on a *pro forma* document, then both Peak and Flaky must provide access (unless it was given in confidence) providing the reference is recorded as part of or with the intention that it should form part of a relevant filing system. This will be so if Peak and Flaky keep a file of references given or received.

Management Forecasts and Negotiations

These two distinct exemptions are discussed together here as they may overlap and often both will apply in the context of business planning and strategy and relationships with employees. Both exemptions are from the subject information provisions. In both cases, the exemption only applies if and to the extent that compliance would be likely to prejudice the activity or negotiations, as appropriate. Both of these exemptions are new and the 1984 Act had no direct equivalent.

The first applies to personal data processed for the purposes of management forecasting or management planing to assist the data controller in the conduct of any business or other activity: paragraph 5, No further guidance is given but this could apply, for example, where a company is carrying out a feasibility study on some new proposed venture. It might involve personal data relating to present and potential employees and other individuals such as investors. The company may wish to gather information on individuals who are candidates for 'head-hunting' to lead the new venture. Alternatively, a company may be considering closing down some of its activities which, if carried out, will affect numerous employees. Fulfilling a subject access request could destroy the secrecy of such forecasting or planing and cause serious prejudice.

Paragraph 7 deals with negotiations with the data subject and records of intentions in respect of such negotiations by the data controller. Under the 1984 Act, statements of intentions in respect of individuals were outside the definition of personal data and, therefore, out with the scope of the Act. This is not so under the Directive and statements of intention are personal data, providing the other requirements are met. It was thought important to grant exemption from the subject information provisions—after all, an intention is not a reality until it is carried out and the data controller may change his mind. The sort of things covered will include an intention to promote an employee or provide some person with a particular service. The exemption is not limited to negotiations between employers and employees and can apply in any context.

Examination Marks and Examination Scripts

The exemption for examination marks is similar to that undr the 1984 Act and gives exemption from the subject access provisions though it can only act to delay subject access. Under paragraph 8 of Schedule 7, the marks or other information must held for the purpose of determining the results of an academic, professional or other examination or enabling such determination or in consequence of the determination of any such results. In the case of an undergraduate, such information might include the marks he obtained in each subject by examination (including assessed coursework) and the details of the degree classification to be awarded to the student. 'Examination' includes a process for determining the knowledge, intelligence, skill or ability of a candidate by reference to his performance in any test, work or other activity. The normal period for responding to a subject access request is 40 days though this may be changed under the 1998 Act. Where the period of 40 days is used below, it is to be taken to be 40 days or such other period as may be prescribed.

Normally, a data controller must comply with a data subject request within 40 days but, in respect of examination, marks, the data controller does not have to respond until either the end of five months after the request has been received or 40 days after the day the results are announced (published or made available or communicated to candidates), whichever is the earlier. If the request is complied with more than 40 days after it was made, the response by the data user must include all the information held at the time of the request *and* subsequently.

The following dates provide an example of the workings of these provisions:

1. Student sits examination — 4 June 1999
2. Marks entered on a computer — 28 June 1999
3. Student makes subject access request — 23 July 1999
4. Result published — 23 July 1999

Normally, the request must be complied with within 40 days from the request at the latest; that is, within 40 days of 2 July, which gives 11 August as being the latest date for compliance. However, in the case of examination marks, the request must be complied with by the earlier of five months after the request (3 December 1999)or 40 days after publication (1 September 1999). Therefore, the data controller must supply the data by 2 September. But, unlike other subject access requests which may take account of amendments, in this case the information supplied must include that held on 3 July (the request date) *and* must also include any subsequent amendments up to the date of reply. Consequently, a data controller holding examination marks must be careful to make sure that he retains copies of the personal data prior to any amendments or deletions so that he can provide all this information. For example, if the student's degree classification is changed, perhaps from a lower second honours degree to an upper honours degree after mistakes have been found in the marking, the response must show this fact indicating the marks before and after correction. This requirement could prove very embarrassing to the data controller.

The exemption that applies to examination scripts is new and is granted in respect of the subject access provisions. The meaning of 'examination' is as above and the exemption relates to personal data consisting of information recorded by candidates during an academic, professional or other examination. As the 1984 Act only applied to automatically processed personal data, there was no real need for such an exemption under Act as most examinations were handwritten, though this is changing rapidly: for example, by the use of multiple-choice tests performed on computers. Of course, the last thing most students want is access to their examination scripts.

Power to Make Further Exemptions

It should be noted that, under section 38, the Secretary of State is empowered to add to the list of exemptions from the subject information provisions and exemptions from the non-disclosure provisions. In both cases the exemption must be necessary for safeguarding the interests of the data subject or the rights and freedoms of any other individual. In the case of the subject information provisions, it must relate to a situation where disclosure is prohibited or restricted by or under any enactment.

An example of an order made under equivalent powers under the 1984 Act was the Data Protection (miscellaneous Subject Access Exemptions) Order 1987. The Order applied to information contained in adoption records and with respect to the special educational needs of children. Also, the Human Fertilisation and Embryology Act 1990 inserted section 35A into the Data Protection Act 1984 and exempted personal data showing that an identifiable individual was or might have been born as a result of treatment regulated under the 1990 Act. An equivalent provision is likely to be made under section 38 of the Data Protection Act 1998. Section 12 of the Charities Act 1933 provided for the making for an Order exempting certain functions of the Charity Commissioner from the subject access provisions. This section was repealed by the 1998 Act.

The exemptions are set out in Table 15.2. In particular, it should be noted that the exemptions under Act relating to payroll and accounts, unincorporated members' clubs, mailing lists and back-up data find no place among the exemptions under the 1998 Act. Not is there any specific exemptions relating to word processing (this was outside the scope of the 1984 Act, providing the data were not used for anything else). The traditional provisions deal with these changes to the exemptions.

Enforcement

The Commissioner's power of enforcement have been described in the previous chapter. It should be note there that a person on whom an enforcement notice has been served may, under section 41(2), at any time after the time for appeal against the notice has expired (expected to be 28 days) apply in writing to the Commissioner asking for the notice to be cancelled or varied on the basis that, because of a change in circumstances, all or part of the notice need not be complied with. This might be relevant where a data

TABLE 15.2

Exemptions Under the Data Protection Act 1998

Description	*Exemption provided from*	*Notes*
National security. s 28	• all the Principles • Parts II, III and V (rights of data subjects, notification, enforcement) • s 55 (offence of unlawful obtaining etc. of personal data - see later)	The exemption must be required for the purpose of safeguarding security but a certificate signed by a Minister of the Crown to that effect is conclusive (as it was under the 1984 Act) - there are provisions for any person affected to appeal to the Tribunal In Schedule 6, para 6 the Tribunal's jurisdiction shall be exercised *ex parte* by the Chairman or a Deputy Chairman - subject to rules made under para 7 for regulating the exercise of the right of appeal
Crime and taxation s 29	• 1st Principle (except to the extent which it requires compliance with conditions in Schedules 2 and 3 - thus the conditions still apply) • s 7(subject access) • all only to the extent to which application of those provisions would be likely to prejudice matters in s 29(1)	Only for purposes of prevention/ detection of crime, apprehension/ prosecution of offenders or assessment/.collection of any tax or duty or any imposition of a similar nature (s 29 (1)) Data processed for purpose of discharging statutory function where information obtained for any purpose mentioned above are exempt from subject information provisions to the same extent Data disclosed for purposes of crime or taxation are exempt from non-disclosure provisions if those provisions would be likely to prejudice those purposes. Where the data controller is a government department, local authority or other department, local authority or other authority administering housing or council tax benefit, data are exempt from

cont...

Description	*Exemption provided from*	*Notes*
		s 7 (subject access) if the exemption is required in the interests of a system of risk assessment for taxation or crime where the offence involves unlawful application for or claim in respect or public funds
Health, education and social work, s 30	• exemptions from subject information provisions will be implemented by SIs	Leaves it to the Secretary of State to make orders - but not to confer exemptions likely to prejudice the carrying out of social work - may cover situation where, for example, a doctor does not want to allow a patient access to his file if it shows the patient is terminally ill and the doctor considers this knowledge would be harmful to the patient
Regulatory activity, s 31	• subject information provisions	if likely to prejudice proper discharge of function covered (to protect public charities persons at work (as appropriate)) functions are: • financial loss resulting from dishonesty, malpractice, unfitness, incompetence of persons concerned in banking, insurance, investment or other financial service or management of bodies corporate • financial loss resulting from the conduct of a bankrupt • dishonesty etc. by professional persons • misconduct or mismanagement in administration of charities • in respect of protecting property of charities • in relation to health and safety at work

Description	*Exemption provided from*	*Notes*
		Exemption is extended to others such as the Parliamentary Commissioner for Administration, Health Service Commissioner Director General of Fair Trading, etc.
Journalism literature and art, s 32	• all the Principles (except 7th -security measures)	An important exemption protecting freedom of speech
	• s 7 (subject access) • s 10 (right to prevent processing likely to cause damage or distress) • s 12 (automated decision taking) • s 12 (automated decision • s 14(1) - (3) (rectification etc.)	Where personal data are processed for the special purposes the exemption applies if: (a) processing is with a view to publication by any person of journalistic, literary or artistic material. (b) the data controller reasonably believes it is in the public interest, having regard to the special importance of freedom of expression, (c) the data controller reasonably believes, in all the circu-mstances, that compliance with the provision is incompatible with the special purposes Codes of practice may be designated by the Secretary of State which will be taken into account in determining reasonableness of public interest belief. Provision for the court to stay certain types of proceedings if data controller makes a claim that special purposes exist and he has not published he material in the preceding 24 hours the stay is subject the the claim being withdrawn or the coming into effect of a determination by the Commissioner under s 45.

cont...

Description	*Exemption provided from*	*Notes*
Research, history, statistics, s 33	• such further processing not incompatible with Principle 2 (purpose for which obtained) • may be kept indefinitely notwithstanding principle 5 • s 7 (subject access) - if processed in accordance with relevant conditions and results not made available in anyform identifying any data subject	Research purposes includes statistical or historical purposes 'Relevant conditions' are: (a) the data are not processed to support measures or decisions with respect to particular individuals, and (b) are not processed in such a way that substantial damage or substantial distress is or is likely to be caused to any data subject Personal data will still be treated as processed for research purposes where disclosure is to any person for research purposes, to the data subject or person acting on his behalf, at the request or with consent of data subject or person acting on his behalf or where person making disclosure has reasonable grounds for believing any of the above disclosures apply
Information available to public by or under any enactment, s 34	• subject information provisions • 4th Principle • 14(1) - (3) (rectification etc.) • non-disclosure provisions	if the data controller is obliged to make the information available to the public whether by publicising it, making it available for inspection or otherwise, whether on payment of a fee or not
Disclosures required by law or in connection with legal proceedings etc., s 35	• non-disclosure provisions	Where disclosure required by or under any enactment, rule of law or by court order or if necessary for legal proceedings, obtaining legal advice or establishing, exercising or defending a legal right

Description	*Exemption provided from*	*Notes*
Domestic purposes, s 35	• all the Principles, • Parts II & III (rights of data subjects and notification)	Processed by an individual only for that individual's personal, family or house hold affairs (including recreational purposes)
Miscellaneous exceptions in Schedule 7		
Confidential references by data controller, para 1	• s 7 (subject access)	Applies to references in respect of education, employment or appointment of data subject to any office (actual or prospective) or the provisions of services by the data subject (actual or prospective)
Armed forces, para 2	• subject information provisions	If likely to prejudice the combat effectiveness of any of the armed forces of the Crown
Judicial appoin-, tments honours, para 3	• subject information provisions	To assess suitability for judicial office or as a QC or conferring honours by the Crown
Crown employment para 4	• subject access provisions (by order of Secretary of State)	Processing to assess any person's suitability for: (a) employment by/under Crown, (b) any office to which appointments are made by a Minister of the Crown or Northern Ireland Department
Management, forecasts para 5	• subject informing provisions	For purposes of management forecasting or planning to assist the data controller in the conduct of any business or other activity where complying would be likely to prejudice that conduct
Corporate finance, para 6	• subject information provisions	Underwriting in respect of issues, advice to undertakings on capital structure, industrial strategy and related matters, advice and services in relation to mergers and acquisitions of undertakings and underwriting such matters

cont...

Description	*Exemption provided from*	*Notes*
		Where compliance could affect the price of an instrument in relation to investment services or if exemption required to safeguard important economic or financial interest of UK. Secretary of State may specify by order circumstances in which exemption is or is not taken to be required or matters to be taken into account in determining whether required for safeguarding important economic or financial interest of UK.
Negotiations, para 7	• subject information provisions (to extent would prejudice negotiations)	Records of intentions in relation to any negotiations with the data subject if likely to prejudice those negotiations)
Examination marks, para 8	• s 7(subject access)	Simply postpones the time for compliance in cases where application made before examination results are announced Time or compliance is 5 months after request or 40 days after results announced, whichever is the earlier If based on the 5-month period, there is a duty to supply details at the time the request was made together with subsequent versions
Examinations scripts, para 9	• s 7 (subject access)	Personal data recorded by candidates during academic,professional or other examination
Legal professional privilege, para 10	• subject information provisions	Information in respect of which legal professional privilege could be maintained in legal proceedings
Self-incrimination, para 11	• s 7 (subject access)	But not in respect of offences under this Act, though such information is not admissible in criminal proceedings

controller, on whom an enforcement notice has been served because the Commissioner is satisfied that there has been or is a contravention of the Data Protection Principles, has modified his processing activity to prevent a particular contravention or has modified his procedures to prevent prevent the reoccurrence of a past contravention. An enforcement notice may also be cancelled or varied on the Commissioner's own initiative.

Appeals against notices and certain decisions and determinations by the Commissioner go to the Data Protection Tribunal. Under section 48, appeals may be lodged in respect of:

- enforcement, information or special information notices,
- a refusal by the Commissioner to cancel or vary an enforcement notice,
- where a notice contains a statement that the notice must be complied with as a matter of urgency within seven days, the Commissioner's decision to include the statement or the effect of the inclusion of the statement as regards any part of the notice, or
- a determination under section 45.

The Tribunal may allow the appeal, substitute another notice if it considers that the notice is not in accordance with the law or, where it involved an exercise of discretion by the Commissioner, if that discretion ought to have been exercised differently, may cancel or vary a notice, make statements ineffective regarding compliance as a matter of urgency in respect of the whole or part of a notice, or cancel a determination of the Commissioner, as appropriate.

The rules of procedure will be made under powers in Schedule 6 to the Act which also deals with the constitution of the Tribunal, *ex parte* proceedings in cases involving certificates in relation to national security and the power to remit to the High Court for contempt. The Tribunal may review any determination of fact on which the notice in question was based. Appeals from decisions of the Tribunal on a point of law go to the High Court in England or Wales (in Scotland, the Court of Session and, in Northern Ireland, the High Court of Justice in Northern Ireland). The volume of enforcement and other notices served under the 1984 Act was relatively small. The Registrar under that Act developed a system of preliminary notices and this continues under the new law as far as enforcement notices are concerned. Under the old law, enforcement notices, de-registration notices and transfer prohibition notices were available but only the enforcement notice has survived the changes, to be supplemented by the information notice and special information notice. Table 15.3 shows how many notices were served under the 1984 Act from the period 1994 to 1998. The years are from 1 April to 31 March. No deregistration notices were served during the period covered in the Table but notices under section 7 of the 1984 Act whereby the Registrar gives reasons for refusing to accept an application to register are listed in the table. These 'notices' are not notices in the normal sense of supervisory notices under the 1984 Act. It can be seen from the Table that relatively few notices were served.

Offences

There are some changes to the data protection offences. In particular, some new offences are brought in to reflect differences in the new law and some of the offences under the 1984 Act relating to processing outwith the scope of the register entry, which were contained in section 5(2) of that Act, have disappeared. In practice, under the old law, the majority of prosecutions were for failing to register.

TABLE 15.3

Supervisory Notices Served by the Data Protection Registrar 1994-8

Form of notice served	*1994/95*	*1995/96*	*1996/97*	*1997/98*
preliminary enforcement notice	4	5	6	19
enforcement notice	2	3	2	5
preliminary transfer prohibition notice	0	1	0	0
transfer prohibition notice	0	0	0	0
preliminary registration refusal notice	9	1	0	0
registration refusal notice	32	31	0	0
Totals	47	41	8	24

Source: The Data Protection Registrar, *The Fourteenth Annual Report*, The Stationery Office, 1998.

The offences in section 55(1) - without the consent of the data controller, obtaining or disclosing personal data or procuring the disclosure to another person and the associated offences relating to selling or offering to sell data obtained in contravention of section 55(4) (5) - are the equivalent to those inserted into the 1984 Act by section 161 of the Criminal Justice and Public Order Act 1994. Section 55 is, however, wider and is not restricted to procuring, selling and offering to sell. The 'procuring' offences only came into force on 3 February 1995 but there have been a number of successful convictions in respect of them. For example, in July 1998, a father and some were found guilty at Horseferry magistrates Court of a number of offences under the 1984 Act. The father operated a private investigation company and his son, who worked for the National Westminster Bank, passed on details of individuals from the bank's database to his father. The son was convicted of two charges of unauthorised disclosure an fined £500 for each. The father's company was charged with being an unregistered data user and with two charges of unlawful procuring of personal data and two charges of unlawful sale of personal data, and was fined a total of £5000. The father was convicted of four charges of consenting or conniving with the offences committed by his company and was fined £500 for each.

The utility of the unlawful obtaining, disclosure, procuring and selling offences is clear. Apart from widening the ambit of them there is also a change to the state of mind required of the accused (known as the *mens rea* to lawyers) as, before it was 'knowing or having reason to believe' whereas now, for the offences in section 55(1), it is 'knowingly recklessly'. A person behaves 'recklessly' if the risk of the relevant act or omission transpiring would obvious to a reasonable man, whether or not the person responsible for the act or omission thought about the possibility of the risk. It is, therefore, an objective test. The seriousness of the risk is not a factor to be taken into account. There are two leading cases on the meaning of recklessness, both decided in the House of Lords on the same day. In the first, *R* v *Caldwell* [1982] AC 341, a case on criminal damage, Lord Diplock described the test of recklessness in terms of a real risk of the relevant harmful consequences which would be apparent to be ordinary prudent individual. The accused would be reckless if he gave some thought about the risk and decided to ignore it or if he failed to give any thought to it at all. However, in *R* v *Lawrence* [1982] AC 510, a case of reckless driving (this offence to longer exists and has been replaced by dangerous driving), Lord Diplock spoke of *serious* harmful consequences.

The fine distinction between these two judgments (that is, the inclusion of the word 'serious' in *Lawrence*) has exercised the mind of many law students ever since. In the case of *Data Protection Registrar* v *Amnesty International (British Section)* (unreported) 8 November 1994, Amnesty

International was charged with offences under section 5(2)(b0 and (d) of the Act after exchanging its mailing lists with another charitable body. The offences were holding data for purposes other than those mentioned in the register entry and disclosing data to a person not described in the register entry (there are no offences directly equivalent to these under the 1998 Act). One of the subscribers to Amnesty International complained after receiving a request for money from the other charity. The exchange of the list was outside the scope of Amnesty's registration. There had been no fee charged for the list and the stipendiary magistrate accepted that Amnesty International honestly believed it was acting in accordance with its registration. The stipendary found that Amnesty International had not been reckless because the disclosure of the list did not cause a serious harmful consequence, relying on Lord Diplock's judgment in *Lawrence,* and dismissed the case. The Data Protection Registrar appealed by way of case stated on a point of law.

The Divisional Court of the Queen's Bench Division allowed the appeal, confirming that, taking the two speeches of Lord Diplock together, it is not a prerequisite of recklessness that serious harm should result. Lord Justice Rose said that in order to prove recklessness for the purposes of section 5(2) of the Data protection Act 1984:

(a) there must be something in the circumstances that would draw the allention of the ordinary prudent individual to the possibility that his act was capable of causing the kind of mischief that section 5(2) is intended to prevent and the risk of that mischief occurring was not so slight that an ordinary prudent individual would feel justified as treating it as negligible, and

(b) before doing the act, the accused either failed to give any thought to the possibility of there being such a risk or having recognised that there was such a risk, he nevertheless went on to do it.

Although the offences involved ar not in the 1998 Act, this case is important authority for the meaning of recklessness for the offences in the 1998 Act, for which recklessness will suffice for the mental element of the offence.

The offences under the 1998 Act are summarised in Table 15.4. The Table contains the section number and a description of the offence, the state of mind required of the accused and whether there are any specific defences. Note that many of the offences are strict liability, that is to say that ignorance of the offence will not excuse.

TABLE 15.4

Offences under the Data Protection Act 1998

Section	*Description*	*State of mind (mens rea)*	*Defences*
21(1)	Processing personal data without having notified where this is required under s 17	Strict liability	None
21(2)	Failing in the duty to notify changes in the registrable particulars or in the measures taken to comply with the security requirements under the seventh principle	Strict liability	Where the person charged can show that he exercised all due diligence to comply with the duty
22(6)	Carrying on assessable processing unless notification has been received from the Commissioner	Strict liability	None
24(4)	In a case where processing has not been notified (because it was not required and the data controller has chosen not to notify), failing to provide relevant particulars to any person on request within 21 days	Strict liability	Where the person charged can show that he exercised all due diligence to comply with the duty

Section	*Description*	*State of mind (mens rea)*	*Defences*
47(1)	Failing to comply with an enforcement, information or special information notice	Strict liability	Where the person charged can show that he exercised all due diligence to comply with the duty
479(2)	In purported compliance with an information notice or special information notice, making a statement which is false in a material respect	Knowing that the statement is false in a material respect or recklessly making such a statement	None
55(1) & (3)	Without the consent of the data controller- (a) obtaining or disclosing personal data or the information contained in personal data, or (b) procuring the disclosure to another person of the Information contained in personal data	Knowledge or recklessness required	Does not apply where the person shows: (a) that the obtaining, disclosing or procuring- (i) was necessary for the purposes of preventing or detecting crime, or (ii) was required or authorised by or under any enactment by any rule of law or by the other of a court,
55(1) & (30 (cont.)			(b) that he acted in the reasonable belief that he had in law the right to obtain or disclose the data or information or, as the case may be, to procure the disclosure of the information to the other person, (c) that he acted in the reasonable belief that he would have had the consent of the data controller if the data controller had known of the obtaining, disclosing or procuring and the circumstances of it, or (d) that in the particular circumstances the obtaining, was disclosing or procuring was justified as being in the public interest

cont...

Section	Description	State of mind (mens rea)	Defences
55(4)	Selling personal data by a person who has obtained the data in contravention of s 55(1)	Strict liability	None
55(5)	Offering to sell personal data if: (a) the person has obtained the data in contravention of s 55(1), or (b) he subsequently obtains the data in contravention of s 55(1) *Note*: offering to sell includes an advertisement indicating that personal data are or may be for sale 55(7) Section 1(2) does not apply for the purposes of this section, and for the purposes of this and the above offence (s 55(4)). 'personal data' includes information extracted from personal data		The defences that apply to the s 55(1) & (3) offences do not apply to this offence
56(5)	Requiring a person to supply a relevant record (enforced subject access0 in connection with: (a) the recruitment of another person as an employee. (b) the continued employment of another person, or (c) any contract for the provision of services to him by another person or Requiring a person to supply a relevant record as condition of providing or offering to provide or offering to provide goods, facilities or services A relevant record is one relating to convictions or cautions or in relation to certain types of benefit	Strict liability	But not where required or authorised by or under any enactment, rules of law or by court order, or where the requirement is justified as being in the public interest

Section	*Description*	*State of mind (mens rea)*	*Defences*
59(3)	The disclosure of information obtained or furnished under the Act which relates to a living individual or business and has not previously been available to the public from other sources by a present or past Data Protection Commissioner, member of the Commissioner's staff or an agent of the Commissioner	Knowledge or recklessness as to the contravention	None
61(1)	Where an offence under this Act has been committed by a body corporate and is proved to have been committed by or with the consent of, connivance of, or to be attributable to any neglect on the part of any director, manager, secretary or similar officer of the body corporate or any person who was purporting to act in any such capacity, he as well as the body corporate shall be guilty of an offence and be liable to be proceeded against and punished accordingly	Consent, connivance orneglect (the latter would seem to be based on an objective test)	None
Schedule 9, para 12	Intentionally obstructing a person in the execution of a warrant issued under this Schedule, or failing without reasonable excuse to give any person executing such a warrant such assistance as he may reasonably require for the execution of the warrant	Intention or not having reasonable excuse as the case may be	None

All the offences, apart from those relating to warrants in Schedule 9, are triable either way: that is, either on indictment in the Crown Court or summarily in a Magistrates' Court. They are punishable on conviction on indictment by a fine or, on summary conviction, by a fine not exceeding the statutory maximum: section 60. Offences in relation to warrants are summary only and punishable on conviction with a fine not exceeding level 5 on the standard scale. There are also provisions for forfeiture, destruction or erasure of documents or other material, subject to persons other than the offender being heard as to why the order should not be made.

Section 61 applies the usual provisions with respect to offences committed by a body corporate where it is proved that the offence was committed with the consent or connivance or was attributable to any neglect on the part of any director, manager, secretary or similar officer or person purporting to act in such a capacity. If this is so, that person as well as the body corporate is liable to prosecution. This also applies where the affairs of the body corporate are managed by its members. They are treated as directors for the purposes of this provision.

In England and Wales, to proceedings for an offence under the Act can be brought except by the Commissioner or by or with the consent of the Director of Public Prosecution: section 60.

Figure 15.2 shows the numbers of prosecutions leading to convictions under the 1984 Act from 1995 to 1998. It will be seen that the majority of prosecutions relate to a failure to register. Offences under section 5(6) and (7) of the 1984 Act, which were inserted by the Criminal Justice and Public Order Act 1994 (the 'procuring and selling' offences), find their equivalent in section 55 of the 1998 Act. During the year 1997/98, there were six convictions each for these offences. Most convictions resulted in fines being imposed. The range of fines in 1997/98 was from £50 to £2500. The maximum fine ever imposed for an offence under thee 1984 Act was £3000, imposed in the year to 1 April, 1997. In 1997/98, five convictions resulted in discharges, either absolute or conditional. In one case a clerk to the justices was prosecuted and he received only an absolute discharge!

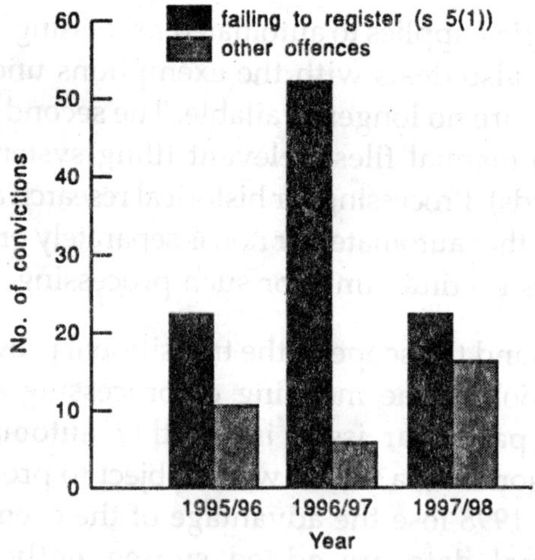

Fig. 15.2 Offences under the Data protection Act 1984

Transitional Provisions

Because the new law marks such as sea change in the regulation of processing of personal data, there is need for comprehensive transitional provisions. Additionally, these make full use of the derogations permitted in the Directive, allowing the application of the law to pre-existing processing to be delayed for up to three years for automatic processing and up to 12 years for manual processing.

Schedule 8 to the Data Protection Act 1998 contains the main transitional provisions. There are two transitional periods as follows:

> 'the first transitional period' means the period beginning with the commencement of this Schedule and ending with 23rd October 2001; and
>
> 'the second transitional period' means the period beginning with 24th October 2001 and ending with 23rd October 2007.

The first period applies to automated processing already underway and also deals with the exemptions under the 1984 Act which are no longer available. The second period relates only to manual files (relevant filing systems and accessible records). Processing for historical research already underway, whether automated or not, is separately provided for and there is no time limit for such processing.

To understand the scope of the transitional provisions, it is vital to look at the meaning of processing already underway. A particular issue is whether automatically processed personal data which were subject to processing on 23 October 1998 lose the advantage of the exemptions if new personal data are added subsequently. Three possibilities exist.

1. The collection of personal data as a whole continuous to be able to take advantage of the transitional provisions.
2. The collection of personal data as a whole is now caught by the new law and the exemption is lost.
3. The new personal data must comply with the new law in all respects but the pre-existing data do not have to .

The Directive is somewhat ambiguous on the point and is couched in terms of 'processing already under way'. However, the data Protection Act 1998 seems clear but, potentially, less generous to data controllers. The exemptions in the act under the transitional provisions are expressed primarily in terms of 'eligible data'. These are defined in the following terms (emphasis added): 'personal data are'. These are defined in the following terms (emphasis added):'personal data are "eligible data" at any time *if, and to the extent that,* they are at any time subject to processing which was already under way immediately before 24th October 1998'. Eligible automated data are eligible data processed or to be processed by automatic means and eligible manual data are simply eligible data which are not eligible automated data. Two points can be made about the definition of eligible data.

1. There is no express requirement that the data are being processed by or on behalf of the data controller. Simply the fact that they are subject to processing by any data controller should suffice. that is, data that exist before 24 October 1998 are eligible data.
2. The phrase 'if, and to the extent that,' implies that data created on o rafter 24 October 1998 are not eligible data and subject immediately to the new law. This suggests that the third alternative interpretation above is the correct one. However, if this is so, the scope of some of the transitional provisions is seriously prejudiced.

Another unresolved issue is what the effect is of commencing some new processing activity in respect of pre-existing personal data. If a strict interpretation is taken of the definition of eligible data, it would appear, at least to that extent, that the personal data will not longer be eligible data.

The two transitional periods will now be examined in greater depth together with other transitional provisions relating to research data and the requirement for a preliminary assessment.

The First Transitional Period

This applies to automated processing and manual processing until 24 October 2001. The provisions differ for automatic data and manual data.

Manual Data

Eligible manual data, other than data forming part of an accessible record, are exempt from the data protection principles and Parts II and III of this Act during the first transitional period. Parts II and III contain the rights of data subjects and th notification requirements respectively. However, if the manual data consist of information relevant to the financial standing of the data subject and the data controller is a credit reference agency, the exemption is limited. It does not extend to the right of access of data subjects (section 7 as modified by section 9) and there is a right to ratification, erasure, blocking or destruction of inaccurate or incomplete data and a right to require the data controller to cease holding exempt manual data in a manner incompatible with the data controller's legitimate interests 9 it is the data controller's legitimate interests that are relevant not those of the data subject). These latter rights are provided by section 12A of the Act which is inserted until 24 October 2007.

Where the data are part of an accessible record, whether eligible data or not, the exemptions are largely subject to the same rights of data subjects as applies to credit reference agencies. Thus, pre-existing and new data contained in accessible records such as health records, educational and certain local authority records have exemption from the Principles (except in so far as the sixth principle in as much as it relates to subject access under sections 7 and 12A), other rights of data subjects (such as the rights to prevent processing) and the notification requirements. The complexity of this can be explained by the fact that the 1998 Act has incorporated some provisions of other legislation allowing access to personal data such as the Consumer Credit Act 1974 (access to credit reference agencies data) and the Access to Personal Files Act 1987, which is repealed in its entirely by the Data Protection Act 1998.

Eligible Automated Data-General Exemption

The new data protection law is significantly different to that under the 1984 Act. As well as applying the possibility in the Directive not to make processing already under way subject to the new law for three years, the transitional provisions have to cope with a number of differences between the new and old law, particularly in respect to a number of exemptions under the 1984 Act that are no longer available.

Paragraph 13 of Schedule 8 to the Act gives general exemption to all eligible automated data and is intended generally to place such data in the same position as applied under the 1984 Act. The exemptions are as set out below (bearing in mind that, nevertheless, the Principles under the 1984 Act still apply to such processing).

- The data controller does not have to provide data subjects with information when data obtained from him and in other cases.
- There is no need for any of the conditions for processing in Schedule 2 to be present nor, in the case of sensitive data, any of those in Schedule 3.
- There is no obligation to impose security obligations on processors in writing or evidenced in writing.
- The new provisions controlling transfers of personal data to third countries not having an adequate level of protection do not apply.
- The requirement to give additional information in response to a data subject request compared to that required under the 1984 Act (such as a description of the data, the purposes of processing, and recipients) does not apply.

- The data controller is exempt from the right of data subjects to prevent processing causing or likely to cause substantial damage or substantial distress, the right to prevent processing for the purpose of direct marketing and the rights of data subjects in respect of automated decision taking.
- The enhanced rights of data subjects to compensation do not apply and are restricted to those under the 1984 Act.

The above exemptions are helpful in showing how the new law differs from the old law in relation to automatic processing.

Eligible Automated Data - Particular Exemptions

Other exemptions for automated processing are needed because some of the exemptions under the 1984 Act disappear. For the purposes of the Data Protection Act 1984, processing had to be by reference to the data subject. An express exception was where processing was performed only for the purpose of preparing the text of documents (the 'word processing' exception). Paragraph 5 of Schedule 8 extends the benefit of the exemption for a further three years for eligible automated data.

An importance exemption under the 1984 Act which disappears and which was relied on by many data users under the 1984 Act was in respect of processing for payroll and accounts. The exemption was not total but was from the registration requirements and the rights of data subjects. This is continued for a further three years until 24 October 2001. Eligible automated data processed for payroll or accounts are exempt from the Data Protection Principles and Parts II and III (data subjects' rights and notification) during the first transitional period. However, the data must not be processed for any other purpose, although the exemption will not be lost by any processing for any other purpose if the data controller can show that he had taken such care to prevent it as in all the circumstances was reasonably required. The burden of proof to show this is so is imposed on the data controller.

Certain disclosures are also permitted, such as to any person by who, the remuneration or pensions are payable; for the purpose of obtaining actuarial advice; or for the purpose of giving information as to the person in any employment office; for use in medical research into the health of, or injuries suffered by, persons engaged in particular occupations or working in particular places or areas. The data subject (or a person acting on his behalf) may also request or consent to the disclosure either generally or in the circumstances in which the disclosure in question is made. The exemption still applies if the person making the disclosure has reasonable grounds for believing that the data subject requested or consented to the disclosure. Further disclosures are permitted which include the purpose of audit or for the purpose only of giving information about the data controller's financial affairs.

The problem is - what if new data, perhaps relating to a new employee, are added to a database or other collection of data which existed prior to 24 October 1998? If the meaning of eligible automated data does not extend to newly added personal data, the exemption is lost. This could be quite serious because the data controller is likely to realise that this is so and, if he does not notify his processing for payroll and accounts, he could commit an offence of strict liability under the 1998 Act. The same applies in relation to unincorporated members' lists and mailing lists which also had an exemption under the 1984 Act. Transitional provisions again attempt to extend this for a further three years. The exemption is, as before, from the Data Protection Principles and Parts II and III of the Act, but again it may not be safe to rely on the exemption where new data are created and added to the pre-existing data. The conditions which applied to unincorporated members' clubs and mailing lists under the 1984 Act, such as the requirement to ask data subjects whether they object to the processing of personal data relating to them, still apply during the transitional period.

A further exemption under the 1984 Act was from the subject access provisions where th data were solely for back-up purposes, for example to replace data on a computer in the event that they were accidentally erased or corrupted in some way. This is continued until 24 October 2001.

The Second Transitional Period

The second period only to processing and is a partial derogation for 12 years, until 24 October 2007, and applies to eligible manual data and accessible records, whether eligible or not. It does not apply to eligible manual data processed only for the purposes of historical research for which there is separate provision. The exemption is from the first Data Protection Principle (except to the extend to which it requires compliance with the requirements to inform data subjects when he data are obtained from the data subject or in other cases), the second, third, fourth and fifth Data Protection Principles, and section 14(1) to (3) which contains the basic rights to rectification, blocking, erasure and destruction. Of course, there is no requirement generally to notify manual processing (except where the processing is assessable). Data subjects will have a right of access to such data and a right to be informed in accordance with the first Principle. Although exemption is granted in respect of some of the rights of rectification under section 14(1) to (3), this is of little consequence as the processing is subject to section 12A instead which grants similar rights in addition to a right in relation to processing not in accordance with the legitimate interests of the data controller.

Even though the new law will not fully affect manual records until 24 October 2007, some data controllers could still find it difficult and expensive to comply fully after that date. This is a particular problem where an organisation has a significant amount of archived data which it wants to retain, for example, for future research purpose or for defending legal claims. During the lead up to the Directive, the Council and Commission made a joint statement to the effect that, in certain circumstances:

> at the end of the 12 years transitional period, controllers must take all reasonable steps relating to the requirements of Article 6, 7 and 8, which do not prove impossible or involve a disproportionate effort in terms of cost.

The manual data exemption does not prevent individuals exercising their right of subject access, their right to prevent processing and their rights to compensation. The security obligations also apply and data controllers need to review this aspect in relation to manual files. For example, are manual files kept in secure locations and is access to them restricted to those having a genuine need to use or access them?

Processing for Historical Research (Partial Derogation)

This exemption is indefinite in time. After 23 October 2001, eligible manual data processed only for the purpose of historical research in compliance with the 'relevant conditions', and relevant automated data which are processed only for the purpose of historical research, in compliance with the relevant conditions, and otherwise than by reference to the data subject, are exempt from the first Data Protection Principle (but no as regards informing data subjects), the second, third, fourth and fifth Data Protection Principles, and the rights of rectification, blocking, erasure and destruction under section 14(1) to (3).

The relevant conditions are those specified in section 33 and are that the data are not processed to support measures or decisions with respect to particular individuals and that they are not processed in such a way that substantial damage or substantial distress is, or is likely to be, caused to any data subject.

Other rights automated data processed only for the purpose of historical research in compliance with the relevant conditions are exempt from the first Data Protection Principle to the which it requires compliance with the conditions in Schedule 2 and 3 (conditions for processing). This more limited exemptions applies where, in spite of the other conditions being present, the data are processed by reference to the data subject.

In respect of these exemptions, personal data are not to be treated as processed otherwise than for the purpose of historical research merely because the data are disclosed:

(a) to any person, for the purpose of historical research, only,

(b) to the data subject or a person acting on his behalf,

(c) at the request, or with the consent, of the data subject or a person acting on his behalf, or

(d) in circumstances in which the person making the disclosure has reasonable grounds for believing that the the disclosure falls within paragraph (a), (b) or (c).

Section 12A does not apply to eligible manual data processed for historical research.

If the relevant conditions are not met, the exemption for eligible automated data is of the more restricted variety and applies only in respect of the first Data Protection Principle but subject to the conditions for processing.

Assessable Processing

Where, by its nature, processing activity is likely to cause substantial damage or substantial distress to data subjects or is likely otherwise to significantly prejudice the rights and freedoms of data subjects, section 22 of the 1998 Act provides that the processing will be subject to a preliminary assessment by the Data Protection Commissioner before processing can proceed. The types of processing affected will be specified by order of the Secretary of State and is likely to be relatively limited covering processing of genetic data, data matching and processing by private investigations. However, by virtue of paragraph 19 of Schedule 8, processing which was already under way immediately before 24 October 1998 is not assessable processing for these purposes. This applies to both the manual and automated data.

16 DATA SUBJECTS' RIGHT

Introduction

This chapter looks at the Data Protection Act 1998 from the perspective of data subjects. We have seen how the Act impacts upon data controllers, and many individuals as well as organisations in the public and private sectors (ranging from central government departments to sole traders) will be classed as data controllers, even if they do not possess a computer. But we are all data subjects. There can be very few, if any, persons in respect of whom someone, somewhere, is not processing personal data relating to them in a manner within the new law. As information processing becomes more powerful, there is a growing need to protect the rights of individuals in that context, because of the threats to privacy and freedom. The 1984 Act contained a number of rights given to data subjects; the new law empowers data individuals to a much greater extent by granting them some new rights whilst strengthening pre-existing rights. Although data controllers may feel some concern about how these new and enhanced rights will be exercised, individuals will welcome the additional control they provide over processing activity, particularly where it is in contravention of the 1998 Act.

In addition to the rights of subject access, rectification and right to compensation for damage and distress caused by inaccurate data or loss, unauthorised destruction or disclosure under the 1984 Act, data subjects have a right to be informed on the obtaining a personal data from them and in other circumstances such as on disclosure to third parties as described in the previous chapter. This alone should increase transparency of processing and enable individuals to know more about who is processing data relating to them and for what purposes. Enforced subject access—for example, where a prospective employer requires a person to carry out a subject access request to show whether that person has any previous convictions or cautions—is made a criminal offence in some cases. Further important new rights granted to data subjects are:

- a right to prevent processing likely to cause substantial damage or substantial distress,
- a right to prevent processing for purposes of direct marketing, and
- rights in relation to automated decision taking.

These new rights have no direct equivalent under the old law. Of course, in some cases, a data subject may have been able to put a stop to a processing activity covered by these new rights by complaining to the Data Protection Registrar (now named Data Protection Commissioner) who, if the activity was in contravention of the Data Protection Principles or within the scope of the criminal offences, may have decided to use her powers of enforcement or bring a prosecution. A good proportion of the criminal prosecutions in the past appear to have come about as a result, initially, of a complaint by an individual. For example, in *Data Protection Registrar* v *Amnesty International (British Section)* (unreported 8 November 1994, Queen's Bench Divisional Court, a subscriber to Amnesty International complained to the Registrar when she receive a mailing from another charity to which Amnesty International had passed on details of its subscribers. This was held to be an offence as Amnesty International's registration under the 1984 Act at the time of the disclosure did not permit such disclosures.

Under the 1998 Act, data subjects may still approach the Data Protection Commissioner. They may ask for an assessment and, in some cases, ask for assistance such as the payment of legal fees. As far as enforcing their rights, data subjects may apply to a court for compensation or to ask the court to order the data controller to do something required, such as comply with a subject access request, or to refrain from doing something — for example, to comply with a notice from a data subject requiring the data controller to cease processing which is causing substantial damage to the data subject or another person. Figure 16.1 shows the relationship between the data subject, the Commissioner and the courts.

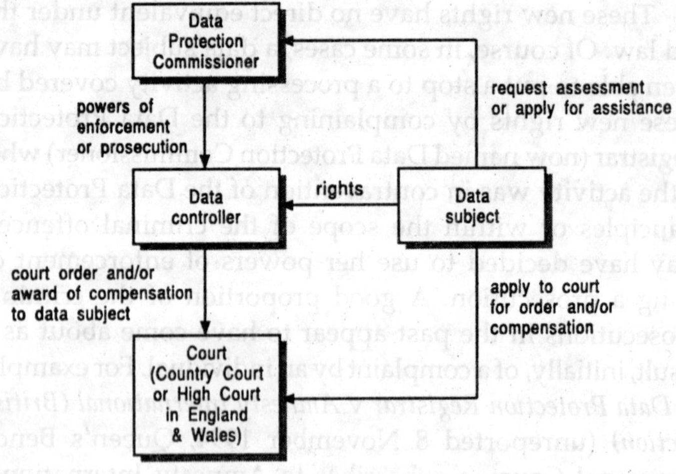

Fig. 16.1 Relationship between the data subject, Commissioner and court in respect of data subjects' rights

Before looking at the new rights provided for by the 1998 Act, the pre-existing rights are described and the changes made to them highlighted. Reference should be made to the previous chapter for a description of the general right to receive information from the data controller as this does not require any act from the data subject to initiate the right to information and is more in the way of a general obligation placed on the data controller.

Right of Access

The data subject's right of access is fundamental to the policing of data protection law by individuals. By seeing what personal data relating to a particular individual a data controller is processing, that person may, with the knowledge of other factors such as the purposes of the processing, take a view on whether the processing is fair and lawful or otherwise within the Data Protection Principles. In particular, individuals are likely to be concerned to satisfy themselves that their personal data are correct and not excessive. This may be important where the granting of credit or obtaining employment or services cold depend on the data and considerable damage can be done if it is incorrect—for example, by falsely indicating that a person has a criminal record, has a county court judgment against him for debt, is an active member of an extreme political group and so on.

A statutory right of access is essential as there is no common law right to access. In *R* v *Mid-Glamorgan Family Health Service, ex parte Martin* (unreported) 29 July 1994, a patient had been refused access to his health records going back to before 1990 on the basis that it would be detrimental for the patient to see those records directly. An offer was made to disclose the records conditionally to a medical expert appointed by the patient but this was not accepted. The patient claimed that there was a right of access at common law. However, the Court of Appeal refused to grant access denying that there was a right of access under common law.

There may be a right of access under the European Convention on Human Rights, in particular as a result of Article 8 which provides that everyone has the right to respect for his private and family life, his home and his correspondence. The Convention will be brought into law in the United Kingdom under the auspices of the Human Rights Act 1998 which is due to come into force in 2000. In *McGinley and Egan* v *United Kingdom* (unreported) 9 June 1998, European Court of Human Rights, two ex-soldiers had witnessed nuclear testing carried out by the United Kingdom in 1957 and 1958 at Christmas Island in the Pacific Ocean. They later suffered health problems which they thought were caused by their exposure to radiation and they lodged claims for war pensions. These were turned down and the government did not disclose documents indicating the radiation levels at the time.

The Court held that access to the documents would have either allayed their fears or allowed them to assess the danger to which they had been exposed and this raised an issue under Article 8. Although Article 8 was primarily a negative undertaking by, for example, protecting a person against arbitrary interference by public authorities, it went beyond that and could give rise to positive obligations (also recognised in *Gaskin* v *United Kingdom*). Those obligations required a balance between the interests of individuals and the general interest of the community. Where a government was engaged in a hazardous activity which might have adverse consequences on the health of those involved, Article 8 required that an accessible and effective procedure was in place to enable such persons to seek all relevant and appropriate information. However, there was no breach of Article 8 in the present case as the ex-soldiers had failed to avail themselves of an appeal under rule 6 of the Pensions Appeals Tribunals (Scotland) Rules 1981 which would have allowed them to apply for an order for disclosure of the relevant documents. The existence of that procedure meant that the United Kingdom had fulfilled its obligations under Article 8.

Article 8 may well be relevant in the future where no procedure exists for an appeal against a refusal to disclose personal data to the individual to whom it relates. It is noteworthy that the European Court of Human Rights interprets Article 8 as imposing a positive obligation to do something, at least in certain circumstances. It must be said, however, at this stage, that its application in the United Kingdom is likely to be somewhat unpredictable at first. One possible area of conflict involving Article 8 may be in connection with the exemptions from subject access provided for in the 1998 Act—for example if a data controller is relying on the exemption from subject access on the basis that the data are being processed for the purposes of national security.

A right of access was available under the 1984 Act but was limited simply to a statement from the data user (now data controller) as to whether he was processing data relating to the applicant and, if so, to access the data. Various rules existed to deal with the applicant and, if so, to access the data. Various rules existed to deal with the situation where access to the data would reveal information relating to another identifiable individual and a similar basic mechanism continues under the 1998 Act but with some significant improvements and other changes.

Section 7 to 9 of the Data Protection Act 1998 deal with data subjects right of access. The information to be given to the data subject is:

whether any data relating to the data subject are being processed by or on behalf of the data controller and, if so, the data controller must give:

- a description of the personal data,
- the purposes for which they are being or are to be processed, and
- the recipients or classes of recipients to whom they are or may be disclosed,
- communication to the data subject in an intelligible form—accompanied with an explanation if necessary, of:
  - — the information constituting the personal data (a copy in permanent form unless this is not possible or would require a disproportionate effort or if the data subject agrees otherwise),
  - — any available information as to the source of the data, and
- where the processing is within the provisions relating to automatic decision taking, a description of the logic involved in that automated decision taking.

Thus, far more information is required than under the 1984 Act, although much of this additional information would be available to a data subject who examined the register entry, except for the description of the logic involved in any automated decision taking. Of course, from the data subject's point of view, it is much easier if the data controller provides all this information directly. As individuals may not realise that they are entitled to more information than was the case previously, the Act allows the Secretary of State to make regulations in particular cases so that a request for any of the above information is to be treated as a request for all the other information required to be given.

To overcome the problem of 'nuisance' subject access requests, made at frequent intervals by the same person, the data controller can refuse to comply with a subsequent identical or similar request by a particular individual unless a reasonable interval has elapsed. In determining what a reasonable interval is, regard should be given to the nature of the data, the purposes of the processing and the frequency with which the data are altered. So, for example, where data are being undated and modified on an ongoing basis, fairly frequent requests may be deemed reasonable. The information to be given must be as it was when the request was received apart from deletions or amendments which would have been made notwithstanding the request. Therefore, if the data are inaccurate and in breach of the fourth Data Protection Principle, the data controller must not deliberately correct the data because a subject access request has been made. However, if the data controller systematically checks the validity of the personal data as part of the management of his processing activity and, as a result of such checking, an inaccuracy is detected and corrected between the time the subject access request is mad and the time when it is complied with, then the data controller need give access to the data as corrected only. As noted in the exemptions in the previous chapter, if the data are evidence that the data controller has committed an offence other than one under the Act, he is excused compliance with the subject access request to the extent that such evidence would be revealed.

Where the processing is by automatic means and has constituted or is likely to constitute the sole basis for any decision significantly affecting him, in evaluating matters relating to the data subject such as his performance at work, creditworthiness, reliability or conduct, the data subject has the right to be informed of the logic involved in that decision taking but not if, or to the extent that, the information constitutes a trade secret. 'Trade secret' is not defined but it would seem sensible to apply the meaning used in the law of breach of confidence, although it is not particularly clearly defined there. Perhaps it would be reasonable to consider a 'trade secret' here to be information the disclosure of which would harm the data controller's legitimate interests, be of benefit to a competitor or expose the data controller to a serious risk of fraud.

The provisions dealing with the situation when compliance with a subject access request would disclose information relating to another identifiable individual have been somewhat modified, partly as a result of a case before the European Court of Human Rights, *Gaskin* v *United Kingdom* (1990) 12 EHRR 36. The applicant for subject access claimed he had been ill-treated while a child in care of the local authority. He sought access to confidential records concerning him and his care from Liverpool City Council, which was required to keep such records. The City Council decided to give Gaskin access provided the persons who contributed to his file consented. Only 19 out of 46 of the contributors gave their consent and the relevant documents were released to him. However, the remainder, where the contributors refused consent or could not be traced, were not disclosed to him. It was held by the European Court of Human Rights that this was a breach of his right to respect for his private and family life under Article 8 of the European Convention on Human Rights. Although the United Kingdom could not be said to have interfered with his private life, there could be circumstances where an inherent positive obligation arose in respect for private life. Whether such an obligation arose in a particular case was a matter of balance and, on the basis of proportionality, required that an independent authority decided whether access should be granted or denied if a contributor to such records withheld consent or did not answer. That had not happened in *Gaskin,* hence the breach of Article 8.

Now, under the 1998 Act, to comply with the request, the data controller must be satisfied that the other person has consented to the disclosure of his personal data to the person making the request. Otherwise, and this is the new provision, access can be given where it is reasonable in all the circumstances to comply without the consent of the other. In determining whether it is reasonable in all the circumstances to comply without the consent of the other, factors that may be taken into account are any duty of confidentiality owed to the other, any steps taken by the data controller to gain the consent of the other, whether the other is capable of giving consent and any express refusal of consent by the other individual.

In other cases such as where it would not be reasonable to comply, lack of consent does not excuse a data controller altogether where he can provide the access to the applicant's data without disclosing the identity of the other individual—for example, by omitting the name or other identifying particulars. This may be done by suppressing the identifying information from a computer printout which is handed to the person making the subject access request or, in the case of manual files caught by the new law, by masking the relevant information when making a photocopy to give to the person making the request.

Further provisions deal with the time in which the data controller has to comply and the need for the data subject to make a written request providing sufficient information and paying the required fee. The basic time period will be 40 days (this may be altered by regulations) and the maximum fee will be set out in regulations. Under the 1984 Act, the maximum fee was £10. For applications to credit reference agencies under section 158 of the Consumer Credit Act 1974 the fee was raised to £2. Different time periods and fees may be prescribed in different cases. As applications under the latter Act will be dealt with under the Data Protection Act 1998, this differential is likely to continue. It will be interesting to see whether a higher maximum fee will be permitted for subject access to manual files as compliance could be potentially more expensive in some cases in respect of such files. Any failure to comply with a subject access request may result in a court ordering compliance.

Credit Reference Agencies

Under section 9 of the Data Protection Act 1998, an application to a credit reference agency is taken to be limited to financial information relating to the data subject unless a contrary intention is expressed. The data controller must include a statement of the data subject's rights under section 159 of the Consumer Credit Act 1974 (a right to have wrong information corrected), to the extent required as prescribed. Section 62 of the Data Protection Act 1998 modifies section 158 of the Consumer Credit Act 1974 and the right under that section to obtain a copy of a file applies only in relation to partnerships. For other individuals the right to a copy of the file is under section 9 of the 1998 Act, although the right of correction of wrong information remains under section 159 of the 1974 Act.

Enforced Subject Access

Enforced subject access has long been perceived as objectionable by the Data Protection Registrar. This occurs where, for example, a potential employee requires a job applicant to provide a copy of his police file showing whether the data subject has been convicted or cautioned in relation to any offences.

The dangers of leaving enforced subject access uncontrolled were clearly seen in *R* v *Chief Constable of 'B', ex parte R* (unreported) 24 November 1997, Queen's Bench Division.

R, who was 29 years old at the time, wanted to travel to a foreign country to teach English to adults and, to do so, he had to apply for a visa. He was required by the Consulate General of the country concerned to provide a certificate of his prosecution and conviction history. Unfortunately, R had a conviction for a minor offence of theft committed when he was 19 years old for which he received a conditional discharge and was ordered to pay compensation. However, the conviction was a 'spent conviction' under the Rehabilitation of Offenders Act 1974, the effect being that by virtue of section 4 of that Act, he was treated in law as a person who had not committed or been charged with or prosecuted for or sentenced for the offence. The purpose is that a person who has 'lived down' the offence and not reoffenced will not be prejudiced by an unwarranted disclosure of the fact of the offence to a third party. The Chief Constable to whom R applied for subject access provided a statement to the effect that R had 'no citeable convictions' but this was not on the standard form issued under the Data Protection Act 1984 and as required by the Consulate General. This form would show R's spent conviction.

The Code of Practice for Data Protection used by the Association of Chief Police Officers generally requires 'reportable' offences to be retained for 20 years, even though they may be spent convictions. However, the Data Protection Act 1984 contained no discretion to exclude some information from being provided under a subject access request and, according to Lord Justice Laws, section 21 of that Act clearly required all the information constituting the personal data to be supplied. Any conflict with the Rehabilitation of Offenders Act 1974 was removed by section 26(4) of the 1984 Act which stated that the subject access provisions apply notwithstanding any enactment or rule of law prohibiting or restricting disclosure or withholding information. The judge expressed sympathy for R whom he described as having lived down his conviction, gaining a series of academic and professional qualifications and generally leading an exemplary and productive life. The judge said it was little comfort to R that enforced subject access under the new law is intended to obviate the problems he had encountered but it came too late for R. Of course, in other situations, enforced subject access can be important such as where a person applies for employment in a position of trust or authority where children or other vulnerable persons are involved.

In a large amendment to the Bill, provisions were added to prevent enforced subject access, in specified cases. Section 56 of the Act sets out the situations where enforced subject access is prohibited, being in relation to:

- the recruitment of another as an employee,
- the continued employment of another person,
- any contract for the provision of services *by another person*, or
- the provision of goods, facilities or services *to any person* (this extends also to the supply of a relevant record by a third party).

The prohibition applies in relation to 'relevant records,' being those showing convictions and cautions where the data controller is a chief officer of police or the Secretary of State. Also included are details of the detention of young persons for long periods of time for grave crimes under section 53 of the Children and Young Persons Act 1933, the Secretary of State's functions under the Prison Act 1952, under the Social Security Contributions and Benefits Act 1992, the Social Security Administration Act 1992, the Jobseekers Act 1995 or in relation to certificates of criminal records under Part V of the Police Act 1997 (with necessary amendments for Scotland and Northern Ireland). Even if the record simply states that the data controller is not processing data relating to a particular matter, this is still to be taken as relating to that matter. For example, if the information provided under the subject access request states that the person concerned has no convictions or cautions, this will still be deemed to be within the prohibition.

Contravention of the enforced subject access provisions is a criminal offence of strict liability. However, this does not apply where the access is authorised or required by law or court order or justified as being in the public interest. However, the latter does not include the ground that it would assist in the prevention or detection of crime—there must be some other public interest involved.

Enforced subject access in relation to health records is also controlled but not by way of imposing criminal liability. Rather, it is a matter of making any such requirement void in contractual terms. Under section 57, any term or condition in a contract is void in as much as it purports to require the supply of, or producing to another person of, a record, copy or part of a record consisting of information contained in any health record as defined in section 68(2), which a record consisting of information relating to the physical or mental health or condition of an individual made by or on behalf of a health professional in connection with the care of the individual. 'Health professional' is widely defined in section 69.

Right to Prevent Processing Likely to Cause Substantial Damage or Substantial Distress

This is a new right as such under the 1998 Act without a direct equivalent under the 1984 Act, although processing which had the potential to cause damage or distress might have been caught by the first Data Protection Principle in particular and dealt with by the Registrar's powers of enforcement. However, processing that could cause damage or distress to an individual might otherwise have been in accordance with the Principles and within the register entry, leaving the individual and the Registrar powerless to act to prevent it. An example might be where sensitive data were lawfully disclosed to a person known to the data subject. Enforced subject access, not unlawful under the 1984 Act, was a good example. This new right is a considerable improvement to the rights of the data subject in that it empowers individuals to require the data controller to stop or not commence processing that has certain consequences for the individual concerned or another. This right is backed by the power of the court to order compliance.

A data subject can require the data controller to cease or not to begin processing for a specified purpose or in a specified manner on the ground that, for specified reasons, it is unwarranted as causing or being likely to cause substantial damage or substantial distress to him or another: section 10(1). However, a limitation is that this right does not apply to processing under conditions 1 to 4 in Schedule 2, being processing where the data subject has given consent, where it is necessary in relation to a contract, where it is necessary for compliance with a legal obligation or where it is to protect the vital interests of the data subject. The Secretary of State may add further exceptions to the right. It can apply to the other conditions for processing 'normal' data (such as processing necessary for the legitimate interests of the data controller or a third party to whom the data are disclosed) and to all the conditions for processing of 'sensitive' data in Schedule 3.

The data subject has to give notice in writing to the data controller, specifying the purpose or manner of processing objected to and the reasons why he or another is likely to be caused substantial damage or substantial distress. Within 21 days, the data controller must give a written notice stating that he has complied with the data subject's notice or intends to do so or stating why he considers the notice unjustified to any extent and the extent, if any, to which he has complied or intends to comply.

If the data controller does not comply with the data subject's notice in whole or in part, the data subject may apply to a court for an order requiring the data controller to comply with the notice. The order will be granted if the court considers the notice justified to any extent and the data controller has failed to comply to that extent. An application to the court might include a claim for compensation under section 13, discussed later.

Right to Prevent Processing for Purposes of Direct Marketing

Direct marketing, otherwise known as 'junk mail' was perceived as a particular problem by the European Commission. It was decided that an individual ought to be able to prevent it in a case where the marketing material is addressed specifically to the individual. Anonymous advertising material that is, material which is not addressed to specific persons, such as advertising inserts in newspapers and magazines or which is simply pushed through leterboxes in a blanket mailing—is not affected by data protection law. For one thing, advertising campaigns of that nature do not require the processing of personal data of the recipients.

The directive gives individuals an absolute right to prevent processing for the purposes of direct marketing and it also requires that member states ensure that individuals are aware of this right. Thus, under section 11 of the Data Protection Act 1998, a data subject has a right, by giving written notice, to require a data controller to cease within a reasonable time in the circumstances or not to begin processing his personal data for the purposes of direct marketing. 'Direct marketing' is defined in the Act as meaning the communication by any means of any advertising or marketing material which is directed at particular individuals. The data controller must give the data subject a written notice within 21 days of receipt of the data subject's notice starting what steps he has taken or will take to comply. Again, the court has the power to order the data controller to comply, following an application by the data subject and if satisfied that the data controller has failed to comply with the data subject's notice.

In the United Kingdom, the presence of the mailing preference system (MOPS) already allows individuals to indicate that they do not wish to receive marketing material. Organisations which send out marketing material are informed from time to time of persons who do not wish to receive such material. Furthermore, if individuals are careful to make sure that they always tick the ubiquitous 'no marketing' box on forms and the like, this should prevent a great deal of marketing material being sent to them. However, neither doing this nor MOPS is foolproof and this additional right may be useful to prevent mailings from a particular data controller. Of course, it does require the data subject to be proactive.

If a data subject does not exercise the right to prevent processing for the purpose of direct marketing nor the right to prevent processing likely to cause substantial damage or substantial distress, this does not affect his other rights under Part II of the Act (the Part dealing with data subjects' rights).

Automated Decision Taking

Another concern in the lead up to the Directive was automated decision taking where the decisions had or could have significant impacts on data subjects. There are obvious dangers where decisions are taken dogmatically on the basis of a number of factors without any discretion that could be used in particular cases. We have already seen the apparent unfairness of decisions to grant credit being influenced on the credit record of the previous occupant of the house or flat presently occupied by the applicant for credit in *Equifax Europe Ltd* v *Data Protection Registrar* (unreported) 28 February 1992, Data Protection Tribunal. In that case, a credit reference agency was using personal data relating to the financial status of individuals by reference to the current or previous address of the data subject together with financial information relating to *any other individual who had been recorded as residing at any time at the same or a similar address.* The use of such third party data was deemed to be unfair by the Data Protection Registrar although, in the event, the Tribunal did not revoke the enforcement notice but substituted its own on much narrower terms: for example, allowing the use of such third party data if there appeared to be a financial relationship or dependence between the applicant and the third party.

A mechanical and predetermined decision-making process can bring unsatisfactory decisions. It could be because a factor which is a good statistical predictor is built into the logic of the decision process. The data subject's postal code is a good example but says nothing about any particular data subject. Another example is where the data subject has a foreign-sounding name. The controls over automated decision taking are aimed at overcoming decisions that are unfair in a particular case. The Directive took a fairly severe approach and permitted such decision taking only in the context of contracts or, subject to safeguards, where national legislation specifically allowed it.

Section 12 of the Data Protection Act 1998 deals with automated decision taking and takes advantage of the Directive permitting it in cases other than contract. The provisions are targeted at decision taking which significantly affects an individual and which is:

> based solely on the processing by automatic means of personal data in respect of which that individual is the data subject for the purposes of evaluating matters relating to him such as, for example, his performance of work, his creditworthiness, his reliability or his conduct (section 12(1).

Note that the definition is not exhaustive. Decisions in the context of contract or specifically permitted under legislation (known as 'exempt decisions') are treated somewhat differently to other forms of automated decision taking. In the latter case, the data subject has the right to prevent automated decisions being taken in respect of him or to require a data controller to reconsider such a decision. In terms of 'exempt decisions,' the data controller must take steps to safeguard the legitimate interests of the data subject.

Exempt Decisions

The precise meaning of 'exempt decisions' is given in section 12(4) to (7), being where:

- the decision is taken in the course of step taken to consider whether to consider whether to enter into a contract with the data subject or with a view to entering into such a contract or in the course of performing such a contract, or is authorised or required by or under any enactment, and
- the effect of the decision is to grant a request of the data subject or steps have been taken to safeguard his legitimate interests (for example, allowing him to make representations).

These may be added to by the Secretary of State. However, the conditions that either the data subject's request is granted or steps have been taken to safeguard the data subject's legitimate interest do not automatically apply to any further types of decision added by the Secretary of State although, of course, any regulations adding to the list of exempt decisions may make specific provisions for safeguards.

As an example of an exempt decision, consider an individual, Herbert, who has applied for hire purchase to buy a used car. The hire-purchase company, Grabbitt and Co. Ltd., use an automated decision system on a computer which is based on a credit scoring formula. If Grabbitt and Co accepts Herbert's application and a hire-purchase contract is duly executed, there is no further requirement under these provisions. (Of course, if Grabbitt and Co. want to disclose personal data relating to Herbert to another company, say for marketing purposes, Herbert should be told this, preferably by having a 'tick box' on the hire-purchase application form). However, if Grabbitt and Co turn down Herbert's application, his legitimate interests must be safeguarded and, as the Act suggests, this will probably be by allowing him to make representations, that is, to respond to the failure to be granted credit. It may be that some years ago Herbert had a court judgment against him for debt and he has been open about this when completing the application form (or Grabbitt and Co have found out from a credit reference agency that he has been in default of a loan). Herbert might now want to say to Grabbitt and Co. that he is a much better credit risk nowadays and that his default was at a time when he lost his job and he has since repaid the amount outstanding in full.

The Act is silent on what, if anything, the data controller should do in response to representations made by a data subject but a reasonable data controller ought seriously to consider any representations made by an individual and, in appropriate circumstances, reconsider the decision, perhaps by personal review rather than by automated decision taking.

Non-Exempt Decisions

As mentioned above, where the decision itself is not an exempt one, data subjects have far greater rights and can even prevent automated decision taking in respect of them where the decisions, based solely on automated decision taking, significantly affect them and are for the purpose of evaluating matters such as performance at work, creditworthiness, reliability or conduct. Probably the greatest proportion of automated decision taking within section 12 of the Data Protection Act 1998 will be in respect of contracts and will be exempt decisions. Other exempt decisions may be specifically authorised by or required by legislation. An example might be an automated system to determine social security payments.

It is not an easy mater to think of examples of automated

decision taking which will be outside the realms of contract. One possible hypothetical candidate is where a doctor in a local NHS Trust hospital uses an automated system to decide on priority for operations where there is a long waiting list. Being an NHS Trust hospital, there is no contract between the patient and the hospital, or for that matter between the patient and the doctor. Indeed, there are probably several other potential area where the public sector confers benefits on individuals out with contract. Some, such as the social security example quoted above, may be specifically provided for by legislation and thus become exempt decisions.

In respect of automated decision taking which is not exempt, under section 12(1) the data subject is given a right to prevent such decisions by serving a written notice on the data controller. There is no mention of any time limit for the notice to take effect nor that it has to be reasonable. It would seem that the intention is for the notice to take immediate effect. As with direct marketing, this right is absolute but does not, of course, apply to exempt decisions.

Where no notice has been served by the data subject, further safeguards are provided. Under section 12(2), the data controller is required to notify the data subject that the decision was taken on the basis of automated decision taking as soon as reasonably practicable. The data subject then has the opportunity to ask the data controller, by written notice, to reconsider the decision or take a new decision by other means within 21 days of receipt of the notice. Within that period, the data controller must serve a written notice on the data subject stating what steps he intends to take to comply with the data subject's notice. These rights of data subjects are backed by court powers to order compliance by the 'responsible person,' being the person taking the decision in respect of the data subject. The use of the term 'responsible person' presumably is used to include the situation were the decision taking is actually carried out on behalf of a data controller by a processor, such as a computer bureau. Any court order does not affect the rights of any person other than the data subject or the responsible person.

A final point is to note that these provisions apply only where the decision is based *solely* on processing by automatic means. The word 'solely' should not be taken in a strong sense. For example, simply having the person operating the automated decision-taking software confirm or ratify the decision in an unquestioning way will not take the decision taking outside the controls on automated decision taking. Simply 'rubber-stamping' the result is not enough to escape the provisions. It would be different, however, if some aspects of the decision were actively reviewed by a human being.

Compensation

Individual are entitled to compensation frm the data controller for damage resulting from a contravention of *any* of the requirements in the Act. Although similar in operation, this is much wider than under the 1984 Act as it extends to any contravention of the Act, whereas before it was available only in respect of inaccurate data, loss of data, unauthorised destruction of data or unauthorised disclosure of or access to the data. Now, under section 13 of the 1998 Act, compensation is available for any contravention causing damage to the data subject. Under the 1984 Act compensation was also available for distress suffered by the data subject but it appeared that this applied only where the data subject had also sustained damage. Under the 1998 Act, compensation for distress is available generally where there is also damage or where the contravention concerns processing for the 'special purposes' (journalism, artistic or literary expression).

Examples of situations where the data subject should be able to claim compensation for damage and/or distress under the 1998 Act are given below:

> Andrew has been turned down for employment because a reference given by a former employer taken from Andrew's personnel file contained a statement that Andrew had been subject to disciplinary action for dishonesty when, in actual fact, Andrew had been cleared of the charge following an appeal within the company's disciplinary procedures. He may now have a claim for compensation for damage and, possibly, depending on the circumstances, for distress.
>
> Brenda is a famous singer who had an illegitimate child some years before she became famous. A local newspaper published details of this last week, including the identity of the child (who was unaware of the identity of Brenda or even that he was adopted), and today the newspaper has sold the story to a national television company which intends to broadcast details in a documentary on single mothers. Brenda (and her son) may have a claim for distress as such processing may not be able to rely on the exemptions for the special purposes. The publication and broadcast would be permissible only if the data controller reasonably believes that it is in the public interest: see section 32. If this is not so, and it may not be so because the information published probably goes beyond what is required in the public interest, the

exemption from fair processing under the first Data Protection Principle will be lost.

Colin is a self-employed management consultant. He recently submitted a quotation to carry out an in-depth management analysis for Fazkin plc, a large manufacturing company. However, the managing director of Fizkin has spoken to the company secretary of Pipkin Trading Ltd who told him that Colin used to be a member of the Communist Party. Colin used to carry out consulting work for Pipkin. Fizkin turns down Colin's question and tells him that the company has discovered from Pipkin that he has a dubious political background. Colin made a data subject access request to Pipkin and the printout from the computer file indeed shows that Colin was a member of the Communist Party when he was a student many years ago. Colin should have a claim for compensation for damage because, although the information is correct, it is probably in breach of the third Data Protection Principle in that the data relating to him held by Pipkin are excessive in relation to the purposes for for processing (keeping information about consultants, their work, payments to them, etc.)

Deborah recently went into hospital to have a toe amputated. Her details were sent to the hospital from her general practitioner and the hospital added further information. Her general practitioner failed to note that, in the last year or so, Brenda has developed an allergy to a certain type of anaesthetic. The information was kept in a structured paper file (a relevant filing system'). Unfortunately the junior doctor entering information into her file made a mistake and this was not spotted by the surgeon. The wrong toe was amputated and, as a result, Brenda is more severely disabled physically than she would have been had the correct toe been amputated in the first place. She has also suffered minor brain damage as a result of being given an anaesthetic to which she is alergic. Brenda should have a claim to compensation for damage and possibly also for distress because the data were in breach of the fourth Data Protection Principle in that that they were inaccurate and not kept up to date (the allergy was not mentioned). Of course, Brenda will also have a claim for damages on account of negligence, apart from data protection law, and it is most likely that this will be her main claim. However, there is nothing in the Data Protection Act to suggest that full compensation cannot be given for the breaches of duty imposed by the Act.

The right to compensation is tempered by the existence of a defence similar to that under the 1984 Act, being where the data controller can prove that he took such care as was in all the circumstances reasonably required to comply with the requirement which has been contravened. Of course, compensation can only be awarded to an individual who goes to court. There are no powers for the Data Protection Commissioner to award compensation. A data subject seeking compensation has to go to either the county court or High Court (in England and Wales). Choice of court will depend, to some extent, on the amount of compensation sought.

Rights in Relation to Inaccurate Data

Fundamentally, the rights of data subjects in respect

of personal data that are inaccurate are similar to those under the 1984 Act. However, there, are some changes and the scope of the right is widened somewhat. There is also the possibility now that any court order may require that third parties to whom the data have been disclosed are informed of the inaccuracy. Another change is that, under the 1984 Act, the rights related to rectification or erasure. Under the 1998 Act, reflecting the fact this Act also covers certain types of manual data, rights relating to blocking and destruction are added. 'Blocking is defined neither in the Act nor in the Directive but it would seem reasonable to assume that it means suppressing the data without erasing them. For example, in a computer database, data may be suppressed from a particular form of processing or a 'flag' may be set indicating that data relating to a particular person are no longer to be processed even though they are not deleted permanently. 'Destruction' clearly is applicable in relation to manual data.

Under section 70(2), data are inaccurate if they are incorrect or misleading as to any matter of fact. This is an identical definition to that under the 1984 Act. There are two forms of control in the 1998 Act, contained in section 14. The first relates to data that are inaccurate. The second relates to serious contraventions of the Act causing damage to the data subject. As with compensation, the data subject must apply to the court for an appropriate order for rectification, blocking, erasure or destruction. However, it should be noted that the Commissioner may also require rectification, blocking, erasure or destruction of inaccurate data as part of an enforcement notice.

Inaccurate Data

Inaccurate data may be ordered by a court, on application by the data subject, to be rectified, blocked, erased or destroyed, if the court is satisfied that they are inaccurate.

PRIVACY IN TELECOMMUNICATIONS

Introduction

The advent of new technology developments in the telecommunications sector, such as the ability to capture information such as a callers telephone number or to see the number from which an incoming call is made before deciding whether the answer, has brought concerns about privacy. Another issue is the growing use of telephones and facsimile machines ('faxes') for marketing purposes. There is nothing more irritating than seeing your fax machine churning out unsolicited advertising material, tying up the machine and using your paper. Other concerns relate to the use and storage of personal data relating to customers of telecommunication service providers, automatic call forwarding and information made available in directories, whether in paper or software foorm. Security and the prevention of unlawful cavesdropping are other privacy issues.

In part, these issues are already addressed in the United Kingdom, for example, by the Interception of Communications Act 1985. Other control is by self-regulation in the public telecommunications sector: for example, where a customer of a service provider can request that his name does not appear in the published directory of subscribers ('ex-directory'). Another possibility is to contact the Telephone Preference Service in the hope of reducing the number of unsolicited marketing calls received ('cold-calling') or, for fax machines, the Fax Preference Service. Once again, however, the stimulus for change and greater protection for individuals' rights to privacy comes about by way of European initiative. Directive 97/66/EC of the European Parliament and of the Council concerning the processing of personal data and the protection of privacy in the telecommunications sector (OJ [1998] L 24/1) was adopted on 15 December 1997 (the 'Telecomms Directive').

In many respects, the Telecomms Directive supplements the Data Protection Directive set in the context of telecommunications. The latter applies to the protection of fundamental rights and freedoms which are not specifically covered by the Telecomms Directive and, generally, to non-public telecommunications networks. Both Directives required compliance by 24 October 1998. It has already been noted that, at the time of writing, the new data protection law should be brought into force imminently. Part of the Telecomms Directive came into force on 1 May 1999 by virtue of the Telecommunications (Data Protection and Privacy) (Direct Marketing) Regulations 1998. A feature of the Regulations is that rights are given to corporate subscribers in addition to individual subscribers. This chapter examines the Telecomms Directive first and then looks at the Regulations.

The Telecomms Directive

The recitals to the Directive indicate that the need for it arises from the introduction of new public digital telecommunications networks and new telecommunications services. The successful cross-border development of such services including video-on-demand and interactive television is, to some extent, claimed to brilliant upon the confidence that users have in respect to their privacy. Integrated Services Digital Networks (ISDN) and digital mobile networks are also highlighted as specific examples. The adoption of appropriate and harmonised legal, regulatory and technical measures is seen as important in the development of new telecommunications services and networks between and across member states. There is a danger that this development could be hindered without some degree of harmonisation. The main provisions of the Directive deal with:

- security and confidentiality
- traffic and billing data
- calling line and connected line information
- unsolicited calls and automatic call forwarding
- directories
- technical features and standardisation.

Scope and Definitions

In line with the Data Protection Directive, the Telecomms Directive provides for the freedom of movement of personal data by requiring a harmonised level of protection of personal data: Article 1(1). It also extends to the free movement of telecommunications equipment. However, unlike the Data Protection Directive, some provisions also extend to legal persons as well as natural persons and the legitimate interests of subscribers who are legal persons, such as corporations, are protected.

The definitions contained in Article 2 supplement those in the Data Protection Directive and are set out below:

(a) 'subscriber' is any natural or legal person, being a party to a contract for the supply of services in relation to publicly available telecommunications services;

(b) 'user' is a natural person using such a service for private or business purposes, without necessarily being a subscriber to that service—thus, an employee of a corporate subscriber is a user if he uses the telecommunications service subscribed to his or her employer;

(c) 'public telecommunications network' is a transmission system which permits the conveyance between defined termination points used in whole or in part for the provision of publicly available telecommunications services—this includes switching systems and other resources and extends to transmission by wire, ratio, optical or other electromagnetic means;

(d) 'telecommunications service' consists wholly or partly in transmitting and routing signals on telecommunications networks but this does not include radio or television broadcasting.

The Telecomms Directive applies to processing personal data in connection with the provision of publicly available telecommunications services (PATS) in public telecommunications networks (PTNs): Article 3. ISDN and public digital mobile networks are singled out as particular examples.

Security and Confidentiality

The provider of a PATS must take appropriate technical and organisational security measures, if necessary, in conjunction with the provider of the PTN: Article 4. Factors to be taken into account are the state of the art, cost of implementation and the risk. Where there is a particular risk of a breach of security, the provider of a PATS must inform subscribers of this risk and any possible remedies including the costs involved.

Confidentiality of communications by means of PTNs must be ensured by national regulations under Article 5.

Listening, tapping, storage or other kinds of interception or surveillance must be prohibited except where authorised by law in order to safeguard national security, defence and public security, or for the prevention, investigation, detection and prosecution of criminal offences, or where covered by the exemptions under the Data Protection Directive. The Interception of Communications Act 1985 already prohibits some foorms of tapping and surveillance to some extent. However, recording of communications in the course of lawful business practice for the purpose of providing evidence of commercial transactions or other business communications which are legally authorised are unaffected. This could apply, for example, where an individual takes out car insurance over the telephone.

Traffic and Billing Data

Providers of PTNs and PATS need to process data relating to calls for the purpose of billing their customers. A considerable amount of information may be collected by the service provider and will include the subscriber's number, the number called, the date, start time, finish time, duration of the call, the call rate and the charge cost. Other information may be involved such as the data volume, the tariff class and data identifying the telephone exchange.

By virtue of Article 6, providers of PTNs and PATS may process personal data for billing and interconnection payments and, with the consent of subscribers, process for marketing their own services. Where the processing is for the purpose of billing and interconnection disputes, it is only allowed until the end of the period during which the bill may lawfully be challenged or payment may be pursued. This should be the limitation period (normally six years) under the Limitation Act 1980. The type of data that can be processed is restricted and is set out in the Annex to the Directive as data containing:

- the number or identification of the subscriber station,
- the address of the subscriber and the type of station,
- the total number of units to be charged for the accounting period,
- the called subscriber number,
- the type, starting time and duration of calls made and/or the data volume transmitted,
- the date of the call/service,
- Other information concerning payments such as advance payment, payments by installments, disconnection and reminders.

The processing must be restricted to persons acting under the authority of the provider of the service or network, as the case may be, handling billing or traffic management, customer enquiries, fraud detection and marketing the provider's own services. Furthermore, the processing must be restricted to that necessary for the purpose of such activities.

Apart from such processing, the general rule is that data relating to subscribers and users processed to establish calls which are stored by the provider must be erased or made anonymous upon termination of the call. However, these restrictions are without prejudice to the possibility of national authorities being informed of billing or traffic data under applicable legislation for settling disputes—in particular, disputes relating to interconnection or billing. In the United Kingdom this would, for example, allow for the disclosure of billing or traffic data to Oftel (the Office of Telecommunications).

Subscribers are given a right to receive non-itemised bills under Article 7. Where itemised bills are sent out, this could conflict with the right of privacy of calling users and called subscribers (outlined below). To reconcile this problem member states must, by national provisions, for example, ensure that 'sufficient alternative modalities for communications or payments are available to such users and subscribers.' The clue to this resides in the recitals to the Directive. One solution suggested is to delete a certain number of digits form the called numbers in itemised bills.

Calling and Connected Line Identification

Article 8, 9 and 10 concern calling line and connected line identification and automatic call forwarding. These Articles apply to subscriber line connected to digital exchanges and, where it is technically possible and does not require a disproportionate economic effort, to subscriber lines connected to analogue exchanges. Any cases exempted on the basis of technical impossibility or because it would require a disproportionate investment must be notified to the Commission by member states.

Article 8 contains various provisions relating to the suppression of calling-line identification (CLI), where this is offered. The provisions are that:

- a calling user must be able, simply and free of charge, to prevent the presentation of CLI on a per-call basis and a calling subscriber must be able to do this on a per-line basis,
- a called subscriber must be able, simply and free of charge, to prevent the presentation of CLI on incoming calls (why a subscriber would want to do this is unclear although it could be relevant where this subscriber is a company and it wants to prevent employees selectively declining to answer calls from, for example, awkward customers),

- where CLI is presented prior to the call being established (that is, prior to connection) a called subscriber must be able by simple means to reject any incoming call for which CLI has been suppressed (an individual called at home late in the evening would probably prefer not to answer a call where CLI has been suppressed),
- a called subscriber must be able, simply and free of charge, to eliminate the presentation of CLI to the calling user (this would prevent the automatic capture of the subscriber's telephone number, say, by a commercial organisation),
- the elimination of the presentation of calling-line identification by a calling user or calling subscriber must also apply to calls to third countries and the other provisions must also apply in respect of calls coming from third countries (that is, from outside the European Community).

Member states are obliged to ensure that providers of PATS publicise the possibility of the ability to suppress CLI and to reject calls in respect of which CLI has been suppressed.

As complete suppression of CLI could hinder the tracing of persons making malicious or threatening calls, providers of PTNs and PATS may override the elimination of presentation of CLI in two cases: Article 9. First, on a temporary basis at the request of a subscriber wishing to trace malicious or nuisance calls. This will allow the storage of the CLI relating to the calling user and the making available of such information. The second case applies to the police and emergency services and like organisations. This will operate on a per-call basis. The overriding of the elimination of presentation of CLI must be by transparent procedures. In other words, the public must know about it or, at least, be able to find out. It appears that CLI relating to a first malicious call will not be stored. It is only in response to a request from the subscriber that the CLI will be stored. Such a request will usually come only after a first malicious call has been made. This is in line with the Protection from Harassment Act 1997 which requires a course of conduct which means there must be more than one occasion or incident. The Directive, as is usual, does not apply to activities outside Community law, which include activities of the state in areas of criminal law.

Unsolicited Calls and Automatic Call Forwarding

Most people find unsolicited calls from organisations trying to sell something intrusive and a nuisance. It can be very irritating to go and answer the telephone while in the middle of cooking a meal, reading a book or performing some other enjoyable activity only to find that it is someone 'cold-calling,' trying to get you to buy double glazing, financial services or whatever. By subscribing to the Telephone Preference System, these cold-calls can be reduced to a minimum, if not eliminated altogether. Another way to reduce them is to be 'ex-directory,' though this defeats the usefulness of telephone directories as a source of information and may prevent a welcome telephone contact.

As far as unsolicited calls are concerned, there are two forms of control provided for in Article 12 of the Directive. In the context of automatic calling machines which operate without human intervention and fax machines, direct marketing may only be pursued by the prior consent of the subscriber. For unsolicited calls for purpose of direct marketing by other means, member states have two choices. They may either require the consent of subscribers or use a system like the Telephone Preference System whereby subscribers make known that they do not wish to receive such calls. The prevention of such calls by subscribers must be free of charge.

The basic rights in respect of unsolicited calls are given to natural persons. However there must also be provisions to give sufficient protection to the legitimate interests of persons other than natural persons (that is, artificial legal persons such as limited companies) with regard to unsolicited calls for purposes of direct marketing. Under Article 10, every subscriber has a right to prevent automatic call forwarding by a third party to his terminal by simple means and without charge.

Directories

Telephone directories may seem innocuous enough but may still contain information that can threaten privacy or even safety. The information may indicate the sex of the subscriber by the appropriate title or may indicate some calling or profession such as where the title is Rev. or Dr. It may indicate that the subscriber possibly lives alone, such as where the title 'Miss' is used. Under Article 11, personal data contained in directories of subscribers, whether in printed to electronic form and which are made available to the public or obtainable through directory enquiry services shall be limited to those necessary to identify a particular subscriber. If they wish, subscribers may consent to the publication of additional data providing such consent is unambiguous; in other words, it should be express and informed consent. Subscribers can request, generally without charge (but see below), that:

- they are omitted from the directory,
- his or her personal data are not used for direct marketing,
- his or her address is omitted in part,
- there is no reference to his or her sex 'where

> this is linguistically applicable' —for example, by requesting that titles such as Mr. or Mrs. are not used.

Member states may allow subscribers wishing to be ex-directory to be charged for this providing the sum does not exceed the actual costs incurred by the operator of the service and such a charge does not act as a disincentive to the exercise of this right. The rights apply to natural persons but member states must also extend the rights in regard to entries to other subscribers such that their legitimate interests are sufficiently protected, within the framework of Community law and applicable national legislation. For example, organisations of a type which may be a target for extremist groups should be able to prevent the publication of their addresses in the directory. An example could be an organisation legitimately performing research into genetic engineering.

Technical Features and Standardisation

If different member states adopt different technical features to comply with the Directive, this will work against the common market by impeding the placing of equipment on the market and the free circulation of telecommunications equipment. The basic rule, expressed in Article 13, is that there shall be no mandatory requirements for specific technical features imposed on terminals and other telecommunications equipment by member states in their implementation of the Directive which would distort the single market. However, where the provisions of the Directive can only be implemented by requiring specific technical features applied to terminals or other telecommunications equipment, member states shall inform the Commission accordingly. Where required, the Commission will ensure the drawing up of common European standards in respect of such technical features in accordance with Council Decision 87/95/EEC on standardisation in the field of information technology and telecommunication (OJ [1987] L36/31).

Other Provisions

Some of the provisions of the Data Protection Directive are extended to the subject matter of the Telecomms Directive. For example, Chapter III of the former Directive (judicial remedies, liabilities and sanctions) apply here also and the Working Party on data protection will also have within its brief the protection of fundamental rights and freedoms (natural persons) and of the legitimate interests (artificial legal persons) in the telecommunications sector.

Although the date for implementation of the Telecomms Directive is not later than 24 October 1998, Article 5 on confidentiality of communications can be delayed until 24 October 2000. A provider of a PATS already processing personal data as at the time the Directive is implemented by national law for the purpose of marketing its own telecommunications services may continue so to do without the consent of the subscribers. However, the subscribers must be informed of such processing and not object within a period of time to be determined by the member state in question. The provisions in Article 11 concerning directories of subscribers do not apply in the case of directories already published by the time the Directive is implemented by national law.

The Direct Marketing Regulations

The Telecommunications (Data Protection and Privacy) Direct Marketing) Regulations 1998 (the 'Regulations') came into force on 1 May 1999 and implement those parts of the Telecomms Directive dealing with direct marketing. Controls are provided in respect of:

- automated calling systems for direct marketing,
- unsolicited fax communications for direct marketing, and
- other unsolicited calls for direct marketing purposes.

The first two apply to corporate subscribers but the last one applies only in respect of individuals, who, in England and Wales, include unincorporated bodies of individuals such as partnerships. Partnerships in Scotland are treated as corporate subscribers.

There are requirements for telecommunications service providers, producers of directories of subscribers and persons providing information to directory producers to notify the Director General of Communications of subscribers who have indicate that they do not wish to receive unsolicited fax communications or other unsolicited calls. The Director General maintains a record of such subscribers as under the Telephone Preference System and the Fax Preference System. Any person suffering damage as a result of any contravention of the requirements of the Regulations is entitled to compensation from the person responsible.

All the controls relate to the use of publicly available telecommunications services for direct marketing purposes, being the communication of any advertising or marketing material on a particular line. A 'line' is the telephone or other line through which the communication is made or, if made wholly or partly other than by line—for example, in the case of a mobile telephone—any reference to a line in the Regulations is to what functionally corresponds to a line. The powers of the Data Protection Registrar are enlarged to enable the use of enforcement notices and entry and inspection under the Data Protection Act 1984. The appeal system under that Act is also available. Presumably, as the main provisions of the Data Protection Act 1998 are brought into force, the Regulations will be amended to relate to the Data Protection Commissioner and the equivalent provisions dealing with enforcement notices and entry and inspection under that Act.

In all cases, it is the person who uses or instigates the use of a publicly available telecommunications system or permits his line to be used for marketing purposes who is controlled and, where applicable, has been notified of the called subscriber's consent to the marketing.

Automatic Calling Systems

An automatic calling system is, under regulation 6, a system which, when activated, makes calls without human intervention. Such systems are strictly controlled and marketing by this method is allowed only where the subscriber, whether an individual subscriber or corporate subscriber, has previously notified the person calling of his consent. Note that it is the person calling who must have been notified so that, where a subscriber has allowed a third party to use his line, it is the third party to whom the called subscriber must have notified his or its consent.

Unsolicited Fax Communications

There is a slight difference in these provisions, contained in regulation 7, depending on whether the called subscriber is an individual subscriber or a corporate subscriber. However, in both cases, an unsolicited fax communication for marketing purposes cannot be made if the record kept by the Director General of Telecommunications indicates that the subscriber does not for the time being wish to receive such communications. Nor may it be sent if the called line is that of a subscribe who has previously notified the person concerned that such communications should not be sent on that line. However, a fax communication is not deemed to be unsolicited if the subscriber has notified

F

G

H

I

❑❑❑